TAKE YOUR EYE OFF THE BALL

PLAYBOOK EDITION

TAKE YOUR EYE OFF THE BALL

HOW TO WATCH FOOTBALL BY KNOWING WHERE TO LOOK

PAT KIRWAN

WITH **DAVID SEIGERMAN**

PLAYBOOK EDITION

TRIUMPH
BOOKS

Copyright © 2010, 2011 by Pat Kirwan and David Seigerman

No part of this publication may be reproduced, stored in a retrieval system, or transmitted in any form by any means, electronic, mechanical, photocopying, or otherwise, without the prior written permission of the publisher, Triumph Books, 542 South Dearborn Street, Suite 750, Chicago, Illinois 60605.

Triumph Books and colophon are registered trademarks of Random House, Inc.

Library of Congress Cataloging-in-Publication Data

Kirwan, Pat.
  Take your eye off the ball, playbook edition : how to watch football by knowing where to look / Pat Kirwan with David Seigerman.
    p. cm.
  ISBN 978-1-60078-617-4
  1. Football-Handbooks, manuals, etc. 2. Football—Rules. I. Seigerman, David. II. Title.
  GV950.6.K58 2011
  796.332—dc23

                                        2011018205

This book is available in quantity at special discounts for your group or organization. For further information, contact:

Triumph Books
542 South Dearborn Street
Suite 750
Chicago, Illinois 60605
(312) 939–3330
Fax (312) 663–3557
www.triumphbooks.com

Printed in U.S.A.
ISBN: 978-1-60078-617-4
Design and illustrations by Paul Petrowsky
Page production by Patricia Frey
Pat Kirwan photo courtesy of Ray O'Connor

=CONTENTS=

=PREFACE=

Many football fans who bought the first edition of *Take Your Eye Off The Ball* told us their books got so much use they were beginning to fall apart. It was the best compliment we could've received.

Readers dog-eared pages, took notes in the margins, and highlighted passages they kept referring to all season. They gave their little paperback books a workout, which is exactly what we'd hoped they would do.

What you're holding in your hands is the Playbook Edition of *Take Your Eye Off The Ball,* and you should feel free to use it as a workbook. We've added extra space in the margins so you'd have more room to make notes. We've added a sturdier cover and a spiral binding, worthy of the reference guide the book was intended to be. We've also added new chapters focusing on special teams and managing injuries, added content to existing chapters (look for the new section on Building Your Own War Room in Chapter 14), and updated and expanded sections throughout the book. There are also new charts and diagrams to help you watch football in a whole new way, as well as space for you to take notes and diagram plays. And, of course, there's the companion DVD, featuring Pat discussing the concepts introduced and explained in the book.

This version exists because you—the football fan—asked for it. We are so grateful for all the great feedback we received on how informative the first edition was. We hope you get the same enjoyment out of this more user-friendly version.

Thank you for all your enthusiastic support. Now, turn the page and get to work.

=FOREWORD=

PETE CARROLL

I had just gotten to the New York Jets when I first met Pat Kirwan. It was around 1990, and he was still coaching at Hofstra University. From our very first conversation, I could tell he had an NFL-level understanding of football, and his perspective was so valuable that we immediately wanted to make him a part of the franchise.

Pat and I hit it off right away, and we wound up spending a lot of time talking about football concepts and philosophies. We didn't always agree on everything, but he had strong opinions that I always respected and an ability to analyze and evaluate players that was accurate and well founded.

When the salary cap was first instituted, I remember Pat and I sat down to read the rules together to determine what it was all about. We wanted to know it backward and forward to gain an advantage over everyone else. Pat's a great competitor. When we were with the Jets, we used to play a lot of basketball together. He was the guy in the paint, Kippy Brown was our versatile player, and they both knew they had to feed me the ball (I only pass during football season). But you can learn a lot about people when you compete together, and Pat was always fun to battle with. Whatever shortcoming that left-hander had, he would will himself to win.

When I moved on to New England and then USC, Pat and I stayed connected, talking football and sharing ideas. He has always been an authority on what's going on in the league, someone whose understanding of players, coaches, situations, and trends has been an invaluable resource for me. That's especially true when it comes to what's important in the makeup of a player. I remember when I was in

New England, Pat mentioned Sean Morey to me during the 1999 NFL Draft. He was a receiver at Brown University who had set a bunch of Ivy League records. But Pat had really studied the kid and found that he was a fine all-around player, a tough guy, and a special competitor. He kept dogging me during the draft, and we finally took Sean in the seventh round. He made the Pats' practice squad, and eventually he became a special teams captain, won a Super Bowl with Pittsburgh, then made the Pro Bowl as a special teams player in 2008. Sean probably never would have gotten drafted if Pat hadn't championed his cause. Pat was able to see the player for who he was and didn't hold his level of competition against him, and I trusted Pat enough to make the pick.

Pat and I have never really ended that football conversation we first started with the Jets. We're like football soul mates, people who just make sense to each other and have developed a level of non-verbal communication that's very special. *Take Your Eye Off the Ball* will give you a sense of what it's like to watch the game of football through the eyes of a true expert.

=FOREWORD=

BILL COWHER

I have spent the last four seasons watching NFL games not from the sideline but from a television studio. As soon as we get off the air, my *NFL Today* colleagues—James Brown, Dan Marino, Shannon Sharpe, Boomer Esiason, and Pat Kirwan—and I head to the green room at CBS Studios in New York to watch every game of the afternoon.

It's great to hear the back and forth with those guys and to get their take on what they're seeing. But as the only coach surrounded by a bunch of former players, there's no question that we just don't see things the same way.

Every time they see a bad play, Dan, Shannon, and Boomer blame it on a bad call by the coach. I then have to remind them that once in a while players do need to execute a play. They're wondering, *What kind of call was that?* and I'm telling them that every play is good by design.

There's a great respect that exists between everybody on the show, and we all do get along very well. But as you can imagine, the conversation can get pretty lively. And while I'm defending coaches around the league, Pat is right there sitting next to me, shaking his head and laughing. He understands the dilemma I'm in with these guys.

Officially, Pat's an "editorial contributor" to the *NFL Today*. But the value of his football knowledge goes way beyond that.

That won't surprise any of you who know him from his show on Sirius NFL Radio or from reading his work on NFL.com. He has a truly unique perspective on the NFL—he's coached in the league, he's worked on the management side of it, and he can talk to both players and owners. He has unbelievable insight into the big picture, into why certain things happen—whether it's on the field or in the front office.

A lot of people know the game of football. It's a complex world we work in, and we all tend to overanalyze it and wind up making it even more complicated than it is. But Pat is able to articulate it all in such a clear way that anyone, any fan, can get it.

I hear him do this with his listeners all the time. They call in with questions about why their team doesn't make a change or do something differently, and Pat makes them think. Rather than encouraging them to have an emotional reaction, he teaches them to see everything that's going on and to look at the entire process.

Pat wants fans to have a better understanding of the game they love. He thinks that the more fans understand the game, the more they can appreciate how complex it is and why things happen the way they do. The more you learn, the more you'll want to know.

And fans can't get enough of the NFL. It's 12 months a year of coverage now. There's the season itself, followed by everything that goes into building a team in the off-season, and fans are intrigued by all of it. Pat is unique in that he can talk with authority about every aspect of today's NFL.

I think a book like this can be so helpful to fans, and I'm flattered to be writing this foreword on behalf of someone for whom I have such great respect.

There are so many things to look at before the ball is snapped that will give you a better understanding of the game…if you know what to look for. This book will go a long way toward helping you understand what happens during the off-season, in the huddle before the snap, during the play itself, and in a team's draft war room. In short, it will teach you about all the complexities that make football America's favorite sport.

=INTRODUCTION=

WHAT YOU'VE BEEN MISSING ALL THESE YEARS

To the untrained eye, football is chaos—a collection of heavily armored men running in various directions and meeting in high-speed collisions all over the field. Every snap unleashes 22 players, each one with a specific assignment. It all happens so fast that most fans follow the game simply by following the ball—from center to quarterback, then on to receiver or running back, and ultimately to the bottom of a pile. They see a handful of players doing their jobs, while everything else appears to be pure bedlam.

In order to watch football from a new vantage point, I'm asking you to break the cardinal rule that every coach teaches every kid the first time he or she takes the field, whether it's a gridiron or a diamond, a basketball court or a tennis court. I want you to take your eye off the ball.

I want you to see the offensive linemen executing blocking assignments that are as intricate as they are intense. I want you to notice the safety sneaking up into the box before the snap, confusing a quarterback who's trying to figure out where the pressure will be coming from. I want you to notice which players are in the game and anticipate what's about to happen. When you take your eye off the ball, you'll be amazed at how much action, athleticism, and gamesmanship you've been missing.

If you're a football fan who loves the action—and based on the NFL's peerless popularity in America, you probably are—imagine how much more compelling the game will be when you begin to appreciate its complexity.

It's not the fans' fault that they miss out on all that action. They've been programmed to watch the game a certain way.

For most fans, their primary source of football is the game broadcast. As intricate, high-tech, and enjoyable as game broadcasts are today, they remain limited in their ability to teach the game to the millions of viewers.

On TV, you simply can't always watch everything going on at once.

And the flow of the game doesn't allow enough time between plays for the analyst to explain all the interconnected pieces that cause a play to succeed or fail. Forty seconds isn't much of a teaching opportunity. Once the play-by-play is finished and reacted to, there isn't a ton of time left for an analyst to analyze before the offense is back at the line of scrimmage and the announcers' focus moves on to the next play.

It's not like baseball, where there's more time for reaction than there is actual action.

Let's face it—when Eli Manning throws an interception, most analysts do not have the time to explain in detail what he misread in the defense's coverage that led to the pick. Too often, analysts have to offer up an ordinary explanation—"That's just Manning's gunslinger mentality"—and an opportunity to teach fans about the game is lost.

The truth is football can't be learned while it's happening. Fortunately, a few outlets like ESPN, the NFL Network, and even the late CNN/ Sports Illustrated—where I first was given the chance to talk and write about blocking and tackling and building rosters and creating game plans and all the other things you'll find in this book—have created programming that allows for some study of strategy and execution. Television delivers a visually compelling experience when it comes to covering a live game, it's just that the in-depth football content often is unexplored.

When football fans are given the chance, they will devour a more detailed examination. Had Manning and the intended receiver read the coverage differently? Did the pressure of a pass rush force Manning to throw the ball a second earlier than he intended or keep him from stepping into his throw? Had he locked onto his target too early, giving the safety an advantage in anticipating where the throw would go? Beyond the occasional Telestrator tutorial, fans get to see the result of a play but rarely get the reason why.

The lack of football savvy can also be attributed to the fantasy football boom. There's no doubt that fantasy football has brought new eyes to the game, and that it's helped turn the NFL into the biggest show in the sports universe. It's a great entry point for millions of fans, and it's a great way for fans to get involved. But fantasy promotes another shallow side of football—statistics. If all a fan is following are the numbers scrolling along the bottom of his TV screen, he's missing the game itself. They see that the Colts' Joseph Addai gained 1 yard; what they didn't notice was the defensive end flashing his helmet to the outside shoulder of the offensive tackle, knowing that running backs are trained to look for such cues and that it would convince Addai to turn back inside where he'd be met by an unblocked defender positioned to make the tackle. Such gamesmanship happens on virtually every play, and yet it's almost all lost on a fan base untrained to look for it. Fantasy football owners are passionate fans; imagine how much more they'd get out of watching a game if they were drawn into the inner workings of real football.

Doing my radio show on Sirius NFL Radio over the years has convinced me that fans are craving insight into the game they love. They call me all the time with thoughtful questions about specific matchups their team will face against an upcoming opponent. The more they learn, the more they want to know about everything from personnel decisions to how to play a three-technique. Football doesn't need to be discussed in either beginner-level terminology (though the last chapter of this book does include a glossary of important terms) or inaccessible coachspeak. This book is designed for the vast majority of fans that fall between these two extremes.

For too long, watching football has been sort of like visiting an unfamiliar city. When you first find yourself in the middle of Paris or Rome or even New York, you recognize a couple of the familiar sights, but it's easy to feel in over your head as your senses get overwhelmed by the swirl of activity and energy. It's not until you start learning the language and recognizing certain neighborhood landmarks that you feel acclimated and comfortable. And then the fun can really begin.

That's why you're reading this book. To learn how to watch a football game and see what's really going on. To indulge your curiosity year-round, throughout the season and into free agency and the draft and then back around to training camp. You understand that nothing happens in a vacuum, and you want to see how it all comes together. The goal is to build more knowledgeable fans, and improved access and appreciation will lead to enhanced enjoyment of the entire football experience.

Baseball has always been considered the thinking man's game. The devout baseball fan finds beauty in the nuances of the game, the subtle little things that casual observers never pick up. If there's a runner on second with one out, and a right-handed hitter with good bat control is at the plate facing a pitcher who's having trouble locating his fastball, should the shortstop or second baseman be the one holding the runner on at second? The slightest shift in positioning could make the difference in whether a groundball gets through the infield and becomes a run-scoring single instead of the second out of the inning.

This book is not about comparing football to baseball (George Carlin covered that territory perfectly years ago). Instead, it's designed to help football fans watch their favorite game with the same attention to detail that baseball fans watch theirs.

Baseball claims to be America's national pastime, but football is its true passion. And if you're ready to finally get fully caught up in the game, just sit back and take your eye off the ball.

CHAPTER 1

GET IN THE GAME

» Uncharted Territory for Fans Looking to Follow the Action

When a baseball fan goes to a ballgame, among the first things he often does is grab a hot dog, a beer, and a program before heading to his seat. Then he flips open the program and fills in the two starting lineups with his little golf pencil.

Already, there's a fundamental difference in the fan experience between baseball and football. The first pitch hasn't even been thrown and the baseball fan has had more of an interactive opportunity than the football fan will enjoy all day. There may be no crying in baseball, but there's no scorecard in football.

Until now.

Before we get to examining strategy and positional nuances and how off-the-field and off-season considerations shape the way games will unfold on NFL Sundays, let's start with an easy first step, a simple way to connect football fans to their game the way baseball fans connect to theirs. If you want to follow football like a coach up in the box, learn to chart a game—football's version of keeping score.

Just like a baseball fan diligently tracks each at-bat and records every 6-4-3 double play, you can compile the same data that coaches use to make decisions in their play-calling and begin to see trends emerge as a game evolves. You can track specific information for each play—the down and distance, the personnel on the field, and the result. And that running play-by-play will show you how the situation dictates

1

the action and gives you a glimpse into how coaches are approaching a particular game, which will enable you to achieve a level of football sophistication that has been off-limits to too many fans through the years.

WHO'S IN, FIRST

Football, like baseball, is all about forecasting. Coaches build their entire game plans around tendencies—what their opponent's track record suggests they might do in a certain situation.

A baseball fan can look at a particular game situation—runners on first and second with one out—and predict what an infielder will do if a groundball is hit to him. Football provides the same opportunity to anticipate the action, and the empowerment of the fan begins with understanding the personnel in the game. It's not enough to know the fundamental concept that there are 11 players on each side of the ball; the composition of that 11-man unit will provide clues for what to expect on any given play.

On offense, there are five linemen and a quarterback on every play—with the exception of the Wildcat or derivations of it, which we'll get to later—leaving five interchangeable offensive pieces. Personnel groups are identified by the number of running backs and tight ends on the field on a given play, in that order. If a team sends out two running backs and one tight end, it's called 21 personnel. If it sends out one back and two tight ends, it's 12 personnel. In both cases, there will be two receivers on the field. The first indicator a defense looks for is the personnel package the offense is sending out. It should be the first thing you're looking for, too.

That's because personnel tips off strategy. If the 22 personnel is on the field—two running backs and two tight ends—it means there's only one receiver out there. Immediately, you can make an educated guess about what play a coach is likely to call—in this case, probably a run. You can make your prediction even before they break the huddle once you've noted who's in the game.

If you're in the stands, as soon as one play finishes, look over to the sideline and try to spot the offensive coordinator. There's probably going to be a group of rotational players standing together beside him—the second tight end, the fullback, and the third and fourth receivers—waiting to see who will get substituted into the game on the next play. It'll be harder to follow on TV, since the time between plays is filled with replays and cutaway shots of fans or players or coaches, but as soon as an offense gets into formation, you can quickly determine what personnel is in the game.

During every game that I watch—and I watch every game every week—I have a pad and a pen in hand to track the personnel used on every play. I keep a very basic chart for both teams, and for every possible personnel grouping—from an empty backfield with five receivers (00 personnel) to a jumbo lineup with two backs and three tight ends (23 personnel)—I mark how many times each team ran or passed the ball.

PERSONNEL	RUN	PASS
00		
01		
02		
10		
11		
12		
13		
20		
21		
22		
23		

As soon as the half ends, I already know the run-pass ratio for both teams according to the personnel that's on the field. Now I can anticipate the halftime adjustments that coaches are discussing in the locker room, because they're utilizing roughly the same data to find an edge for the second half.

TRACK THE FACTORS

Identifying the personnel grouping is a starting point, but there are other factors you need to pay attention to. Down and distance, two factors that always go hand in hand, is perhaps the most significant in terms of influencing what play a coach will call (and what personnel he'll send out on the field). When formulating his game plan, a coach usually will categorize his options by down and distance. For example, his game plan may include four or five plays that worked in practice that can be used on 2nd downs between 3 and 6 yards; four or five plays that have been predetermined for use on 2nd downs between 1 and 2 yards; and four or five more plays for 2nd-and-7 or longer. And each play may be run from a different personnel group and formation.

As you chart the plays a team runs, tendencies reveal themselves and the game plan materializes before your eyes. The chess match is on—and if you can see what's coming all the way up there in Section 315, you better believe the defense does, too. The offensive coordinator knows that the defense is making its decisions based on those demonstrated tendencies, and now he must figure out which play will work best against the defense he expects to face.

You can easily track the action and all the various factors in a simple play-by-play chart. It requires a bit more effort than the running totals you're tallying in the personnel chart you began earlier, but it takes you deeper into the action and gives you a clearer picture of what's really going on out on the field.

Look at this touchdown drive by the New England Patriots from midway through the first quarter of a Sunday night showdown with Indianapolis in 2009 (the game that culminated in Bill Belichick's infamous decision to go for it on 4th-and-2 instead of punting the ball away to Peyton Manning). As they took the field with 8:15 left in the first quarter, the Patriots were trailing 7–0. They'd gone three-and-out on their first possession, running plays out of three different personnel groupings before having to punt. Here's what happened on their next possession:

TEAM	TIME	DOWN & DISTANCE	FIELD POSITION	PERSONNEL	PLAY
Patriots	8:15	1st-10	NE 27	10	Faulk 3-yd run
		2nd-7	NE 30	10	Faulk 6-yd run
		3rd-1	NE 36	12	Brady 3-yd run
		1st-10	NE 39	10	Moss 55-yd from Brady
		1st-G	IND 6	22	Maroney 5-yd run
		2nd-G	IND 1	22	Maroney 1-yd run TD

The Patriots scored a touchdown to tie the game, which obviously made it a successful possession. But there's a lot more information to be evaluated here than just the result.

For instance, New England showed three different personnel groups. The Pats ran the ball out of 10 personnel—one back, no tight end, and four receivers—a package that usually would suggest pass, and they also threw deep to Randy Moss out of the same personnel. A huge part of play-calling is maintaining a level of unpredictability, and the Patriots surrendered few clues to the Colts that could be used against them later in the game.

INFORMATION IS EMPOWERING

There are other factors to watch for as you track the action, field position being an essential one. A fan should recognize that there are really four quadrants of a football field—a team's goal line out to the 25-yard line, from the 25-yard line to midfield, midfield to its opponent's 25-yard line, and from the 25-yard line to its opponent's goal line—and coaches approach their play-calling differently depending on where they are on the field.

Of course, there are two mitigating elements: time remaining and the score. But all that really determines is how much a coach's menu of plays may shrink. For example, a coach is not going to call short-yardage plays out of 22 personnel if he's trailing by a touchdown with less than two minutes remaining.

Keeping score not only affords you an interactive opportunity; it teaches you how a coaching staff watches a game. Your play-by-play account will enable you to assess what's working in certain scenarios, the same kind of evaluation process that coaches go through all game long. Baseball fans develop a sense of what a pitcher will throw in a particular situation, and over time you'll have similar insight into your own team's tendencies.

An ambitious fan doesn't even have to wait until game day to start gathering this information. You can log on to NFL.com or team websites and find the play-by-play of every game played on every weekend. Just a little homework can show you what to expect from the opponent your team will be facing the following week.

Let's say you're a Houston Texans fan and your team was preparing to face Tennessee in Week 11 of the 2009 season. The Titans entered that game on a three-game winning streak, all after Vince Young had been reinstated as the starting quarterback. You might look back at the play-by-plays of the Titans' previous three games and notice that they ran the ball on two out of every three first downs. That kind of information would have told you what to watch for before the Texans took the field for their Monday night matchup. (Sure enough, the Titans ran 21 times in their 30 first-down plays, beating Houston with the same formula that had been working for them in the previous weeks.)

Watching a football game doesn't have to be a reactive experience. Every play doesn't have to be a mystery. A baseball fan can complain when he sees his pitcher throwing a first-pitch fastball to a first-pitch fastball hitter. You, too, have the right—and now the opportunity—to follow the nuances of your favorite sport just as closely.

The information is out there, right before your eyes. You just need to know where to look.

CHAPTER 2

THE 168-HOUR WORK WEEK
» Designing and Installing a Game Plan Is a Round-the-Clock Occupation

The general who wins a battle makes many calculations in his temple ere the battle is fought. The general who loses a battle makes but few calculations beforehand.

—*Sun Tzu*

Everyone has a plan until they get punched in the mouth.

—*Mike Tyson*

Philadelphia Eagles quarterback Michael Vick took the first snap of a *Monday Night Football* game against the Washington Redskins, faked a handoff to LeSean McCoy, and rolled back almost to his own goal line. After a few unpressured seconds, he stepped up to the 4-yard line and launched a ball deep down the middle of the field, where DeSean Jackson caught up to it about 65 yards away. Barely breaking stride, Jackson took it to the end zone. Eighteen seconds into the game, the Eagles led 7–0.

Officially, it was an 88-yard touchdown pass, though it later took on greater significance. It turned out to be a first-punch knockout in a Week 10 win that moved the Eagles into a first-place tie in the NFC East and pushed Vick to the forefront of most MVP speculation. It was the opening statement of a performance unparalleled in the history of NFL quarterbacks.

And while Eagles coach Andy Reid couldn't have hoped for more when he drew it up, that touchdown pass was, in the grand scheme of a football game, just one play. It was only one of the four touchdown passes Vick threw that night, and just one of 118 plays run in that game.

There were 1,833 offensive snaps that occurred during Week 10 of the 2010 NFL season. Elsewhere, Santonio Holmes' touchdown beat the Cleveland Browns in overtime, an incomplete conversion attempt gave the Buffalo Bills their first victory of the season, and Mike Goodson ran up the middle for a nine-yard gain in the second quarter of Carolina's loss at Tampa Bay. Each was just a single entry in the play-by-play world of the NFL.

Roughly 125 plays are run during the course of an NFL game, not counting special teams. And while fans are quick to question the wisdom of almost any play called in a given situation, few have any sense of the time and attention to detail that goes into preparing for every decision a coach will make over the course of a football game.

BIRTH OF A GAME PLAN

A coach's master playbook can contain about 1,000 plays—pretty much anything he would ever consider calling in a game. Every bomb, blitz, and blocking scheme is in there somewhere, along with every gadget play and goal-line scenario. And every call has its roots somewhere in that all-encompassing bible, which every coach is forever adding to and carrying with him from job to job.

The process of paring down that playbook into a single Sunday's game plan begins pretty much as soon as the previous season ends. Coaching staffs spend most of January (if they're out of the playoffs) and February going through some critical self-analysis, evaluating what they did well and what they did poorly during the season that just ended, and starting to decide what they're going to retain or change for the following year.

At the same time, they are preparing for the start of free agency and the upcoming draft. The personnel plan takes shape based on what the coach envisions being able to do in the upcoming season. He'll want to target players and prospects who will fit what he plans to run. You better believe Brad Childress' plan for 2009 changed once the possibility of acquiring Brett Favre first became real. Those early decisions are the building blocks of an eventual game plan.

As a team's personnel changes and its personality evolves through free agency and the draft, the overall game plan is steadily refined. Through organized team activities (OTAs) and minicamps, coaches whittle away at their playbook, identifying the plays that best fit the team they'll have to work with. They try to maximize the strengths they see emerging, eliminate the obvious problem areas, and anticipate the matchups they'll be facing. Coaching staffs meet after practice every day, debating the pros and cons of every play they can imagine using in a game situation. The accumulation of those plays becomes the playbook for the next season, and by June 15, that actual playbook goes to the printer. A coach is now committed to his philosophy for the year.

FROM THE PLAYBOOK TO THE PRACTICE FIELD

Once the playbook is officially down on paper, it then has to be taught.

A coach will develop a summer camp installment schedule, during which he takes everything in that playbook and practices every bit of it with his team. Much of it will have been carried over from the previous season (a real benefit to teams with minimal roster turnover), some of it may have been introduced in the spring, and all of it will be reviewed during the preseason. But every play will be installed during the 55 or so practices—from walkthroughs to double sessions—that make up training camp. What a team does there determines for the most part what it's going to be that season; by this point, it's already too late to dramatically change what a team is going to do.

Heading into the last week of the preseason, it's time to develop the game plan for the first game of the regular season. A coach may look at his opponent and see, for example, that he's going to face a 4-3 defense. The first thing he does is scour the playbook for plays he thinks will work against a 4-3; suddenly, his playbook has been roughly cut in half.

He next considers his own roster. Let's imagine he has two rookies in the starting lineup and three veteran free agents who are still learning his system. As a result, he culls the playbook further, settling down to about 100 plays—only he can't practice 100 plays in the week leading up to a game. There's only enough time for four or five repetitions, including practice and walkthroughs, for each of about 40 plays. That's it. Those 40 plays he's been able to practice are the core of the game plan.

(Some coaches might disagree with that number. Guys coaching a West Coast offense will tell you they have 250 plays in their game plan every week. Technically, that's true, if they count all the various formations out of which they can run the same play. If they run a particular play out of an I formation, with a single back, a split, or maybe even an empty backfield, they might consider that four different plays.)

Next, a coach will sit down with his quarterback and go over the full menu of possible plays. The quarterback provides his input—which plays he's most confident in, which plays he hates running, and which plays he feels his teammates might not be ready to run. That feedback will eliminate perhaps a quarter of the remaining plays. At the end of the day, the team is down to about 30 or 35 plays that make up any given week's game plan. The play-call sheet will sort them by down and distance—five or so first-down plays, seven plays for 2nd downs between 3 and 6 yards, and so on. The 60 to 65 plays a team is likely to run on Sunday will come from that game- and opponent-specific play-call sheet.

The best coaches pare down their game plans more than most fans realize, but not at the risk of making themselves predictable. There is great potential for coaches to become overwhelmed by too much information—the classic case of paralysis by analysis. If he's not careful, a coach will wind up preparing a little for everything he could possibly face rather than learning his opponent's true tendencies and preparing to take away the things that team does best. For the most part, if a coach hasn't seen an opponent do something in its last four games, he's not going to practice against it.

I'm not suggesting a game plan should be simple. It needs to be smart, and it needs to generate matchup advantages against a particular opponent. That is the name of the game in the NFL—matchups.

It's important for a coach to pinpoint the plays he's most likely to use so that he doesn't waste valuable practice time working on something that won't pay off in the upcoming game (plus, players absolutely hate practicing things that they never use). Come game day, it's not what the coach knows that matters, it's what the players know. Or as Marty Schottenheimer used to say, "When you're in trouble, think *players*, not *plays*."

UNDERSTANDING THE WORK WEEK

The tailored game plan now needs to be introduced and installed, which happens during the week of practice. What many fans don't realize is that there's no such thing as a "typical" day of practice in the NFL. Each day has its own focus, and practices are designed to meet different objectives on different days.

Monday

With the exception of opening week, a team spends Mondays reviewing its previous game. Players will come in to watch film and get treatment from the medical staff. Coaches get an initial sense from the doctors about which players are going to be limited and who is going to be unavailable because of injury, all of which affects the shaping of the game plan.

That evening, the advance scout meets with the offensive and defensive staffs, sharing his review of that week's opponent. The advance scout will point out the opponent's tendencies based upon that team's last four games. I was an advance scout for a couple of years both for the Tampa Bay Buccaneers and the New York Jets, and the first thing I was asked to break down in my weekly scouting report was the personnel groups. I'd brief the coaches on tendencies I'd discovered. For example, when our opponent has two backs in the backfield, they run the ball 80 percent of the time; when they're in three-receiver sets, they throw the ball 80 percent of the time. It's that kind of big-picture information that will give the coaches a sense of what their opponent likes to do.

Then the advance scout breaks down the audibles called by the quarterback they're about to face: for example, of the 100 audibles he called over the past four games, 80 of them wound up as pass plays. That tells a coach the opponent is making a run call in the huddle and changing it to a pass at the line of scrimmage once the quarterback sees something in the defense he doesn't like. That piece of information might give your defensive coordinator an idea of how to "sugar"—or disguise—a coverage that may entice the quarterback to changing a play at the line into a pass that the defense is ready for. Or maybe he wants the offense to stay with the run, so he makes sure his two safeties stay up high instead of tipping his hand. Either way, the defense is now better prepared for what's coming.

A good advance scout will provide insight into formation tendencies. Maybe an opponent lines up with its receivers in a bunch. The scouting report will be so specific, it will advise that in a certain down-and-distance situation in a certain personnel grouping in a particular part of the field, the opponent threw 90 percent of the time to the short receiver in the bunch.

These kinds of tips are vital to tailoring a game plan for a specific opponent. Pete Carroll, when he was the head coach of the Jets, would always say to me, "Okay, I'm going to go coach the secondary now. I need to be able to say to them, 'Boys, this is what's going on.'" And so I'd look for the most relevant tips he could give the defensive backs. Maybe I'd find that 90 percent of the time, the quarterback's first read was away from the running back—which means if there was one offset back in the game, the quarterback was looking first to throw to the opposite side of the field from where the back was lined up. The cornerback on the side away from the back can then go into the play knowing he's probably covering the primary receiver, and the safety on that half of the field can cheat over a bit, anticipating the greatest likelihood of where the pass will go.

Just as important as knowing what an opponent is likely to do in a given situation is recognizing what a coach's own team has been doing. His opponent is going to be studying his tendencies too, and he needs to make sure he's not predictable.

On Monday, coaches will review their own tendencies over the three most recent games. A coach may ask, "Are we 50-50 run-pass on first downs?" If he finds they've been running more often when lined up in a two-back set, he might decide to make a change. When the first-down calls are made on Sunday, it will be with an eye toward better balance based on that Monday conclusion.

It's essential that coaches know how to interpret any available information about tendencies. A review of a team's last three games may show that it's been averaging a respectable 4.0 yards per carry on first down. But how did they arrive at that 4.0 yards-per-carry average? Has the back been gaining around 4 yards on every carry, which speaks to a reliable level of consistency? Or did he exploit a weak opponent for 6 yards per carry one week, then drop down to 4 yards per carry the second week and then, finally, to 2 yards per carry against a strong defense in the most recent game?

Coaches need to not only know the information, they need to know how to use it properly.

Tuesday

On Monday night, coaches will start watching "cut-ups"—film of their opponent's games, organized by factors such as personnel groupings, down and distance, and other game situations—and those sessions usually flow into the early hours of Tuesday.

The offensive and defensive staffs meet separately on Tuesday morning, and the assistant coaches will brief the rest of the staff with what "tips"—like a poker player's tells—they picked up from their film study. For example, a coach might say, "When No. 43 is at the line of scrimmage, he's blitzing 90 percent of the time." The offensive coordinator then makes a note to give the quarterback a check for that contingency.

Next, the line coach shares his observations. He's noticed, say, that the nose tackle shades to the tight end side when he's expecting a run to the strong side. Again, the coordinator takes that information and adjusts the game plan accordingly: if the call is 16 Boss to the strong side and the nose leans that way, the quarterback will check to the weak run.

Players are "off" on Tuesday, which means they don't step onto the field or into a meeting. But many come into the complex either for continued treatment or some extra film study.

Q: Who is more responsible for the overall game plan, the head coach or the coordinators?

A: Usually, a head coach came up through the ranks on one side of the ball or the other. Tom Coughlin is an offensive guy. Pete Carroll is a defensive guy. Many times, coaches will build the game plan for the side of the ball they're most passionate about (and most experienced with), and then let their coordinators on the other side build their own game plan. Of course, those coordinators are going to present everything to the head coach before it's installed.

There are some head coaches who construct the game plan and also call the plays. Sean Payton won Super Bowl XLIV that way. In that example, the game plan was built by Sean, and the coordinator was responsible for making sure the players learned it.

Meanwhile, the coaches will be finalizing which 35 or so plays they're planning to run on game day, which will dictate the practice plan for the rest of the week.

Wednesday

The game plan is ready to be installed, and Wednesday's practice focuses on all the plays a coach thinks he might use on first and second downs, plus all the checks that come with those plays. They run through those plays with every personnel group that might be used to run them in the game against a scout unit aligned in the formations they expect to face in those situations.

Aside from the primary plays, the game plan will include a list of audibles that the quarterback can utilize when he gets to the line and sees that the play called in the huddle looks well-defended. The audible sheet is significantly shorter than the regular play sheet. Some quarterbacks—Peyton Manning and Tom Brady, to name two—might have the whole offense available to them at the line of scrimmage, but most coaches have limitations on the number of audibles they'll let their quarterback call. When Bill Parcells had Vinny Testaverde with the Jets, he had no audible system most of the time. He knew Vinny had a strong arm and usually saw a passing answer to any defense he saw at the line (the audible system starts with that premise—to check out of run plays and into passes). So Vinny would either hand the ball to Curtis Martin because Bill told him to or drop back and throw because Bill told him to.

The bottom line is that in the NFL today, with all the different looks a defense can throw at its opponent, teams can't exist without an audible package. And those plays get practiced throughout the week.

After practice, the coaching staff meets to review everything that happened at practice. They'll figure out which plays they hadn't prepared a check for and see what they might not have addressed the first time: Why are we having problems blocking their zone blitz? Why are we not picking up their safety when he's down in the box?

Any adjustments necessary to clean up the first- and second-down packages are determined, and then they turn their attention to preparing plays they might call on third down.

Wednesday is also the day that fantasy football owners need to start paying attention to the injury reports and see who did or didn't practice. If a young player doesn't practice on Wednesday, it could affect how he'll be used on first and second downs. Except in the case of experienced veterans—who know their assignments even if they miss the chance to practice them—coaches prefer to go to battle with the guys they had a chance to work with during the week.

Thursday

By 9:00 AM, players are in meetings, reviewing the previous day's practice with their position coaches. They'll watch film from Wednesday's practice, making corrections first in the classroom and then walking through any changes or fixes on the field.

Then it's time to move on to practicing third-down plays. By the time they break for lunch on Thursday, players will have practiced the plays that are likely to make up 90 percent of their game plan.

For the coaches, the post-practice routine is the same as Wednesday's— they watch the film from practice and assess everything they've done so far. Most coaching staffs ask themselves the same questions: What problems are we encountering? Have we given ourselves enough options on third down, or do we need to add some plays to the mix?

Then, of course, it's time to prepare to install the packages that will be practiced Friday—goal-line and short-yardage situations, as well as the two-minute offense.

Friday

The day begins the same as Thursday, with a 9:00 AM review of the previous day's practice and the incorporation of changes and corrections to the third-down package.

Q: What is the primary responsibility of a position coach?

A: Generally, the coordinator will install the game plan in the team meeting, and then it becomes the position coach's job to teach his seven or eight guys what the plan calls for them to do.

In addition to teaching the game plan, the position coaches help make sideline adjustments during the game. The defensive coordinator may decide, for example, to send the strong side linebacker on a blitz. The position coach for the linebackers might argue that while it's the right plan theoretically, that linebacker missed two blitz calls the previous week and isn't up to that role in the game plan. That kind of input can be invaluable.

Lastly, position coaches need to be experts on their position for the draft. That linebackers coach has an understanding of what the team wants to do, so he'll be asked to identify all the linebackers in a draft class who can do what they'll be asked to do in this system.

One misconception is that position coaches need to have played— and excelled at—the position they're coaching. Matt Patricia is about 5'7", 180 pounds, and has a degree in aeronautical engineering from RPI, and yet he had to coach Jerod Mayo and the rest of the Patriots linebackers. Those guys don't care if he played the position (in fact, he played center and guard in college). They just need their coach to give them tips, like when an opponent opens up its guard-center split, the play is always a draw. That's where a position coach can be most effective.

Then it's back onto the field to install the specialized packages. Friday's practices are shorter than the 90-minute sessions on Wednesdays and Thursdays. Plus, players aren't in pads on Fridays (most teams practice in pads in midweek as long as they can, though by midseason almost everyone on the roster will be nursing one sort of injury or another).

What's being installed on Friday might have some overlap with plays practiced on third-down Thursday, but these might be run with no huddle. Coaches will have a package of six or seven plays for the two-minute drill—even fewer if the quarterback is young, inexperienced, or new to the team. Those plays are likely to be an offshoot of the audible package, and the plays kept in the mix will feature a heavy dose of passes.

I've often argued that two-minute drills are so important they should be practiced every day. Whether a team is on offense or defense, the last two minutes of both halves tend to be the most critical points of a game, but often precious practice time is spent trying to install everything to fit every contingency.

Running out of practice time is something coaches complain about now more than ever. As the game becomes more complex, there's necessarily more to work on—in the same time windows they've always had to work with. That's another reason why the time spent installing and practicing over the summer is so vital. There are things that are put in during the summer that might not get practiced again the entire season. Once something is installed, players are responsible for it. For example, coaches might put in 10 gadget plays over the summer. Then they decide it's time to break out, say, the halfback-option pass for Week 14 of the regular season. If there just isn't enough time to practice it, a coach might pull out the tape of the one or two practice reps that play might have gotten over the summer, and that refresher would have to suffice as the players' preparation.

The other preparation that should be going on all week is the home study each player should be doing. Tim Ryan, my partner on *Movin' the Chains* on Sirius NFL Radio, always says that if he were still playing today, he'd be asking his defensive line coach for a DVD loaded with cut-ups of every run play the opponent has called the entire season, as well as every sack allowed by the guy he'd be lining up against the next game. The opportunity exists for a player to build his own scouting report, and to figure out how to win his own individual matchup. But then, as T-Rock says, not enough players take advantage of the opportunities modern technology provides; they're too concerned with getting home to play *Madden*.

Saturday

Players report by 8:00 AM to review Friday's practice and to walk through any corrections. If there's time, the coach might walk through a special play they've pulled out of mothballs, but it's not an intense practice. It lasts about 45 minutes, players go out in sweats, and there's usually a lot of family around and plenty of other distractions.

If the team is playing a road game the next day, players will shower after practice, then hop on a bus to the airport. If it's a home game, players will go home until they have to report to the team hotel by 8:00 PM.

The team meets again on Saturday night, and this is one of the last opportunities for the head coach either to hammer home any reminders or deliver some inspirational address. Then the focus switches to special teams personnel—something the head coach probably has not been involved in during the week.

With the entire team in the room, the special teams coach will call out a particular unit—the punt coverage team, for example. Every starter on the punt coverage unit stands up, and the special teams captain counts to make sure there are 11 guys standing. Then the coach will have one guy sit down, and that player's replacement must stand up. This exercise is designed to simulate the spontaneous substitutions that happen throughout the course of a game, and you wouldn't believe how many guys screw up this part of the meeting.

Let's say Johnson is the backup to both Jones and Smith on special teams. Jones gets hurt, so Johnson needs to take his spot. That means someone else on the depth chart needs to be ready to take Smith's spot should he get hurt. Johnson sits, Jones stands up. Smith sits… and the next guy in line better know he's now in the game. Coaches spend this time on Saturday night so potential replacements can be sure who they're responsible for replacing. And yet how many times every week do you see a coach have to burn a timeout because he sends out a special teams unit and there are only 10 guys on the field?

From there, the offense and defense break out into separate rooms where they watch some form of video. It could be inspirational (the 10 best plays they've run this season—each of which is included in that week's game plan, of course) or functional, another teaching opportunity to remind players of something they worked on during the week.

Remember—by this point, players have had the chance to talk about a particular play in the classroom, go through one or two physical reps at practice, a review, and perhaps another walkthrough or two. If a player is called on Saturday night to explain what his job is when the nose tackle is shaded to the strong side, he better show that he knows the right answer. There simply isn't any more time to prepare.

THE EVOLVING GAME PLAN ON GAME DAY

Game day is when the plan becomes practical, where a game plan gives way to the strategy of play-calling. And, as you might imagine, game plans change constantly over the course of the game.

Fans may not realize that the first decision of the game is actually the coin toss. Until the 2008 season, the prevailing logic was if a team wins the flip, it should take the ball (unless it had a superior defensive unit). But once the NFL allowed coaches to defer their decision to the second half, an opportunity to strategize was created.

Q: When two familiar rivals meet, do they take into account their head-to-head history or just build their game plans based on their opponent's most recent four games?

A: When a team has undergone a lot of turnover—changing coaches or losing several key players—looking back to past meetings won't provide much of an advantage. Too much has changed for those games to be relevant.

But when two teams are really familiar with each other, they definitely consider their entire history. For example, whenever the Colts are going to take on the Patriots, Peyton Manning will go back and look at everything he personally has faced against Bill Belichick. He wants to be prepared for everything Belichick might do against him—even if it's something that the Patriots haven't done in three or four seasons. Likewise, Bill will want to find a blitz he's never used before against Peyton.

When I was with the Jets, we ran a report that factored in every single game we played against Dan Marino. We saw what we did against him in cold weather, in Miami, at night, and so on. We built our scouting report based on the criteria specific to the next time we were going to face him.

Some coaches will keep a running reel of an opposing coach's tendencies. For example, an assistant coach might be assigned to sit down on Wednesday and review every gadget play run by the opponent. He'll look for any clues that might tell the head coach when one of the gadgets might be coming: maybe it's always on third and short, and always on the opponent's side of the field. He'll notice, perhaps, that a coach only runs each gadget play once per year, and that he'd already run the end around and the flea flicker that season. Any edge that can be found must be found.

Coaches have to ask themselves the following questions: Are we on the road? Do I have an inexperienced quarterback? If so, the coach might want to defer to the second half. The logic is that each team is going to get about six series in the first half. During those series, the defensive game plan for the day will be exposed. A team may be better off gathering as much information as possible in the first half, then making adjustments for the first series of the second half so it's better prepared than it would be on the opening series of the game.

When your team finally takes the field, it will begin to work its plan. Coaches who run the West Coast offense like to script the first 15 plays, the way Bill Walsh used to in the heyday of the San Francisco 49ers. The players know what's coming, they're familiar with the plays and ready for them to be called, and they are going to run those 15 plays come hell or high water.

Their goal is to gather as much information as possible in the first series or two. They send a steady rotation of different personnel into the game because they want to see how a defense is going to line up against each one. Once they've seen 15 different matchups, they'll identify the five or so that appear most advantageous, and they'll feature those plays four or five times each throughout the game. By the end of the first quarter, their game plan for the rest of the day has been refocused and is more specific to the matchups they're seeing.

As the game unfolds, there are coaches up in the booth whose job is tracking the action. I filled that role for four seasons with the Jets in the early 1990s. The booth coach or quality control coach is responsible for evaluating what's working, tracking what opportunities exist, and determining whether the play-calling reflects what the game plan set out to do.

Let's say the game plan aimed at having perfect balance—a 50-50 run-pass ratio—on first down. The booth coach will communicate to the offensive coordinator when the play-calling becomes imbalanced, so no one has to go into the locker room at halftime and tell the head coach they failed to achieve his 50-50 goal. Even if the team is having success running the ball on first down, teams want to stick to the game plan—in this case, so the defense can't start keying on the run on first down and shutting it down.

The booth coach knows the game plan. He knows what the head coach and coordinators intended to do, and he sits up there with the play-call sheet in front of him and checks off how many times they're running each play. The game plan has identified several plays for every down-and-distance situation, and so the booth coach is tracking, for example, which of the seven plays in the 2nd-and-5 box have been called and what the results were.

There is no end to the variables that affect play-calling as the game goes on, and so the game plan must evolve based on what is happening on the field. Let's imagine it's 2nd-and-5 and a coach has seven plays in the corresponding box on the play-call sheet. Among the things he's considering should be the following:

- We've run the ball at this down and distance but haven't thrown it yet. Should we be thinking about our run-pass ratio at this point in the game?
- The first two times we faced that down-and-distance situation, the defense called a blitz. Which of those seven plays might work best against a blitz?
- Our starting tight end got hurt on the last series. Which of those seven plays should we steer away from until he gets back in the game?
- We designed most of our options for this down and distance to avoid their best pass rusher. But now that player has gone to the sideline. Are there plays that should be added to our list of options to take advantage of his absence?
- Is the weather an issue? (Hall of Fame coach Marv Levy used to have contingency plans for those wintry days when Buffalo weather became a mitigating factor. He had a bunch of into-the-wind calls he might need to consider based on the conditions.)
- How much time is left? (Most fans know that teams have a two-minute package for the end of each half, but there is also a

four-minute package. The premise of the two-minute package is to save clock; the object of the four-minute package is to run the clock by staying in bounds.)

Ultimately, coaches are looking to build upon whatever plays are working. If they have success, they can develop variations on that theme and keep a defense off balance.

It's difficult to think sequentially until something is proven to work. Once a quarterback connects on a shallow cross, he'll start to think about what that might set up later in the game. He'll think about throwing that pass until the defense stops it, or plan to run a draw play into the heart of an out-of-position defense that has begun to anticipate that route.

And so goes the chess match, with teams always looking for matchup advantages and challenging their opponent's ability to predict what's coming next. One of the ways a player can figure out what's working is by reviewing those photographs you see them studying when they come off the field. Two pictures are taken on every single play—one just before the snap, and the other when the quarterback hands off or, on a passing play, when he takes his non-throwing hand off the ball (that's a signal that he's made his decision about where he's going with the ball).

The first picture reminds the quarterback—or whichever player is looking at it—of what he thought he saw before the snap. The second picture will confirm whether he read the defense correctly, and whether his decision on where to go with the ball was the right one.

Chances are when you see a quarterback looking unhappy as he's flipping through the photos, he's seeing something other than what he thought he saw during live action.

Those pictures can be great learning opportunities. On every play, the defense is giving up something. Sometimes, those vulnerabilities

Q: Do teams change their terminology when facing former players who might know their system?

A: Coaches spend far less time adjusting to this than the average fan would think. When Minnesota faced Green Bay in 2009, Brett Favre knew everything Aaron Rodgers was calling. If "Blue" was the dummy call back when Favre was with the Packers, all he had to do was listen the first few times Rodgers called out "Blue" to see if it still meant the same thing. If it did, the challenge would be communicating that tip to the players on the field in time for them to adjust. Information that comes in too late can paralyze a defender, forcing him to think instead of react.

What surprises me more, though, is when a new coach comes in and brings with him an entirely new set of terminology. Now he has to teach it to, say, 30 guys on defense rather than learning what they already know and incorporating that into his playbook. Coaches rarely allow players to take the easy road; they almost always force the team to adapt to them. Coaches need to find a logical word association that's easy for players to follow. With the Jets, we used the names of the planets as blitz calls. Mars, for example, meant that the middle linebacker would blitz.

That's why coaches often find it helpful to bring veteran players from all the various units with them when they move to a new team. That way, when they're changing their new team's terminology, they have players in the mix who already speak their language and can translate it for their new teammates.

Q: Do coaches incorporate information about specific officiating crews into their weekly game plans?

A: Absolutely. That's one of the jobs of the quality control coach. He looks at every penalty called during the season and tracks who got flagged, the game situation, and which official made the call. He'll come up with very helpful insight into each official's tendencies. For example, perhaps in the previous two weeks one particular official made 10 holding calls, nine of which went against the left tackle, and eight of those were on running plays.

Prior to Super Bowl XLV, we talked to a bunch of coaches on *Movin' the Chains*, and we discussed Walt Anderson's crew with all of them. Every one of them noted that Chad Brown was going to be the umpire. They all knew him, and they all knew that Chad Brown calls holding. That's something both coaching staffs needed to know and needed to communicate to their players. The players want that information; if a coach isn't giving it to them, he's not doing his job.

There are also ways coaches can work the officials in advance. For example, they might send in a tape to the league office calling attention to an issue they expect to encounter in an upcoming game. Say a team is preparing to play the Texans, and the officiating crew will include the back judge that makes the most pass interference calls in the league. A coach on that team might send the league video of Andre Johnson pushing off against cornerbacks in an effort to highlight something the officiating crew should be looking for. At the very least, it might get them thinking that contact down the field doesn't automatically mean his DB is doing the holding.

When I was with the Jets, we used to send a reel on offensive tackle Howard Ballard every time we played Buffalo. After the season, we once sent a tape with 100 clips of Ballard holding someone. If we got one call to go our way in the right situation, all that work was worth it.

are exposed on the pictures, and teams can capitalize later on when a familiar situation presents itself.

In the old days, I used to shoot all those pictures from up in the booth, and then a runner would take them down to the coaches on the field. The Jets were playing a game in Denver once, and after one trip down to the field, the altitude had completely knocked out our runner. Pete Carroll was calling up to me, looking for the pictures, and our kid was on the bench getting oxygen. I wound up finding a girl in the stands watching the game with her family and wearing a shirt from one of the local high school's cross country teams. I asked her father, "How would she like to make $100 and take home all the NFL equipment she can carry?" I hired her on the spot to run the pictures down to Pete and Bruce Coslet.

HALFTIME ADJUSTMENTS

In the final minutes of the first half, the booth coach typically gets down to the locker room ahead of everyone else. He sets up a quick statistical breakdown on the white board of everything that's gone on so far:

> 1st-and-10: 7 run, 6 pass. Run average: 3.2; Pass average: 11.0 per completion.

> 2nd-and-3-6: 1 run, 6 pass. Run average: 5.5; Pass average: 6.0 per completion.

The goal is to give coaches enough material to use both in determining what adjustments are necessary and lecturing the players about what's working and what isn't. Some coordinators might want to keep it simple—for example, they'll decide that every play that gained 4 yards in the first half will be run again in the second half. If you've been tracking the game the way we talked about in Chapter 1, you should be able to anticipate what the coaches are discussing behind closed doors.

Of course, most coaches aren't going to have emptied the bucket in the first half. There should always be a few plays at various down and distances that a team didn't show. Those will get unveiled in the second half.

Then the coordinators write up new play-call sheets, filling new plays into each box. The key is to not rewrite the entire game plan. A coaching staff may be able to identify three new things to roll out; any more than that and they run the risk of confusing too many players.

The coordinators communicate the adjustments to their coaches and remind them of any checks they need to review. They also flag any plays that might be added that weren't practiced during the week.

All this happens in about four minutes.

Then the players meet with their position coaches, and they get adjustments to their specific assignments. This meeting lasts about two minutes, and then it's time to get back on the field and put all that knowledge to use. The team that had the best game plan going into the game—and the team that makes the best adjustments in the locker room—is usually the one that comes out on top.

CHAPTER 3

THE TOUGHEST JOB IN SPORTS
» What a Quarterback Really Does

He gets the glamour. He gets the girls. He gets the biggest contract, the most commercial endorsements, and all the attention. He's the focus of every fan on every play. There isn't a higher-profile job in sports—or perhaps in any industry outside Hollywood leading man—than NFL quarterback.

There's a pretty good reason why football fans are so fixated on the quarterback.

It's the most important position on the field. In any sport.

The reasons he's so different from everyone else have nothing to do with the physical responsibilities of his difficult job. It's much bigger than arm strength, or the ability to throw a tight spiral or to thread the needle. In fact, it's because of everything that happens *before* the moment the quarterback releases the football. Touchdown passes bring the cheers; the ability to process an amazing amount of information makes the touchdown possible.

PREP TIME

A quarterback's job begins earlier in the week than any other player's. By the time the rest of the team comes in on Wednesday to get the game plan for Sunday's game, the quarterback already knows it backward and forward. On Monday, he probably shared with the coaching staff some of his initial thoughts about what he'd like to do come game day. On Tuesday, he and the coaches had multiple discussions as the plan gets fine-tuned.

By the time Friday's practice is finished, the quarterback will have played an active role—an integral role, in the cases of the true greats— in shaping the game plan. He will have become an expert on the opponent's personnel and tendencies, and he will have an intimate knowledge of everyone's responsibilities in his own offense. No player will have a better sense of what is working and what isn't.

Over the course of the week, players on the offense will have practiced every conceivable down-and-distance situation they could possibly face. Coaches will have watched enough film of the opposing defense to have a sense of their opponent's tendencies in various situations. With those tendencies in mind, the coaches—often with the input of the quarterback—determine four or five plays they feel could work at a given down and distance. On game day, the quarterback and coaches will be in agreement over which plays are going to work on, say, 2nd-and-5.

The game plan takes shape after compiling play-calling options—which include potential audibles—for every down-and-distance situation, with additional contingencies made for the score, the time remaining in the game, the field position, the weather conditions, and various other mitigating factors.

If merely retaining all this information were his only responsibility, the quarterback's would already be the most mentally demanding job of any that exists in sports. But there is no shortage of contingencies and considerations that a quarterback has to pay attention to and be prepared for.

Take injuries, for one. Think back to Week 16 of the 2010 season. Jacksonville was coming off a loss at Indianapolis that damaged not only the Jaguars' playoff hopes but also their star running back. They had not been eliminated, but they were heading into a game against the

Redskins that they had to win, and they were unsure of the status of running back Maurice Jones-Drew.

Quarterback David Garrard went through his typical week of practice, evaluating what plays might work in certain situations. But Jones-Drew—who had never missed a game due to injury in his career—was on the sideline with a knee injury. In his place was second-year backup Rashad Jennings, who had one career start on his résumé.

The Jaguars hoped that Jones-Drew would be able to play. After all, he had missed two days of practice leading up to the Colts game and was able to suit up. But they had to spend practice time getting Jennings ready to replace the versatile two-time Pro Bowl back. Think that complicates matters when a team is fighting for a playoff spot?

A quarterback has to understand how every conceivable factor will affect the offense well before he comes charging out of the tunnel on Sunday.

CALLING THE PLAY

All the tactical preparation gets put to the test on game day. The theoretical comes under fire at full speed.

On the field, the quarterback's real job begins the instant one play ends and the clock starts counting down toward the snap of the next. It begins in the huddle, where the quarterback calls the play sent in by the coaches (few QBs call their own game these days). Usually, he's getting the message through the earpiece in his helmet. When you see him looking to the sideline, he's not getting the call; he's looking to see what personnel is coming onto the field. There's a personnel coach who's responsible for sending the right players into the game, but it's incumbent upon the quarterback to confirm that and also to pay attention to who the specific personnel is. He may realize, *We lost our starting tight end on the last series and he's not ready to come back into the game.* The quarterback then has to ask the backup tight end who has come onto the field, "Do you know what your assignment is?" Sometimes he'll have to coach him up right there if the player is unprepared.

And when it comes to play-calling, the terminology used to actually call the play can be an interesting code for fans to crack. First, the play call provides a formation declaration. Basically, it tells everyone where to line up.

Let's say 21 personnel (two backs, one tight end, and two receivers) comes in and the call is "I Weak Right."

The "I" tells the tailback that he's 6.5 yards behind the quarterback.

"Weak" tells the fullback that he's offset in the B gap on the weak side (the side opposite from the tight end). On this play, the tight end will line up on the "Right."

When only one tight end is on the field, the X receiver will be the split end on the weak side, and the Z receiver lines up as the flanker on the tight end side.

Three words—"I Weak Right"—line up five players.

Then the play call dictates a run or a pass. On a run, the play will communicate which hole is the point of attack. In a traditional numbering system, the holes on the right side are even, and the ones on the left are odd. The numbers increase as you move out toward the sidelines, which means the hole between the center and the left guard is 1, the hole between the left guard and the left tackle is 3, the hole between the center and the right guard is 2, and so on.

In addition, each member of the backfield has his own number: the quarterback is 1, the tailback is 2, and the fullback is 3. A "25 Zone," then, would call for the tailback (2) to attack the 5 hole (outside the left tackle).

ROUTE TREE

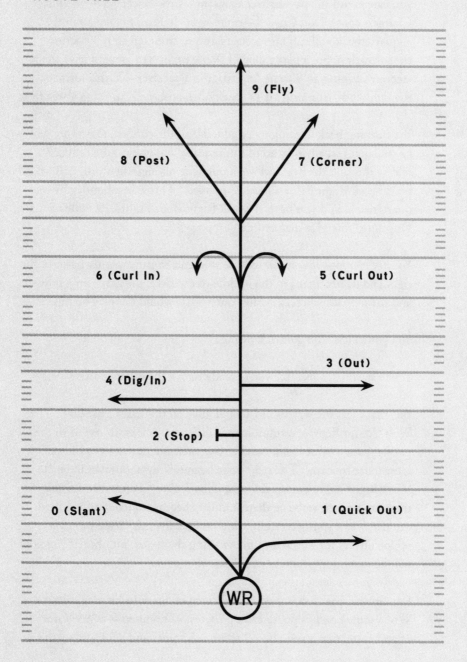

The receivers get their route information from the play call, too. As you can see on the passing tree diagram—first conceived by legendary Chargers coach Don Coryell—every route is also assigned a number. A quarterback will call his receivers' routes from left to right across the formation. So, a play called "I Weak Right 819" would have the X receiver running an 8 route (a post), the Y receiver—in this formation, the tight end—running a 1 (a quick out), and the Z running a 9 (a fly).

If a running back is going to be added into the pattern, that route will be declared verbally instead of numerically. So, to have the fullback release through the line and work opposite his alignment, the call would be "I Weak Right 819 Fullback Opposite." Throw in a bootleg by the quarterback, and you have "I Weak Right Boot Right 819 Fullback Opposite," the play diagrammed on page 36.

You try it now—if you wanted the split end to run a corner pattern, the tight end to run a curl in the middle of the field, the Z to run a post, and the tailback to run a swing route, what would the play be called?

You got it: it's "768 Tailback Swing."

You're starting to feel like you're ready to call the offense, aren't you?

But that's just the way us old-school guys on the East Coast do it. The West Coast offensive terminology is different, at least in regard to the passing game. West Coast coaches like their quarterbacks to call out *every* route by name. The play we've been talking about would be "I Weak Right X Fly Y Stop Z Curl Fullback Free." Personally, I think there's too much verbiage there and the sheer memorization required can paralyze a young quarterback. Too many words create too many opportunities for mistakes. I prefer using the fewest number of words to tell the maximum number of people what to do.

Jon Gruden has always used complicated verbiage in his play calls. While some coaches prefer calling routes off numbers—a "939" out of an I formation would be a 9 route, a 3 route, and a 9 route by the

Q: Is it easier for a team to teach its terminology to a rookie quarterback or a veteran coming over from another system?

A: That depends entirely on the intellect of the quarterback. Boomer Esiason could convert any terminology into something he already knew. He could look at a playbook, see a play called "Purple Eagle," and realize it was identical to a play he knew as "Blue Diamond." A lot of guys can't do that.

That's why the No. 1 trait I look for in a quarterback is intelligence. No player is going to beat a defense with just a country-strong arm and great feet. After that, I look for accuracy. A quarterback first has to know where to go with the ball, and then he has to be accurate getting it there. That was what separated Joe Montana from all the rest. Next comes a quick release. If a quarterback can read the coverage but has a mechanical flaw in his release, guys will have time to jump routes and get back into coverage. Then comes height. That's what saved the 6'6" Joe Flacco during his first few games in Baltimore; there were plenty of times that being able to see over the mess in front of him allowed him to make a play.

If I were building the perfect modern quarterback, I'd take the brain of Drew Brees, the accuracy of Tom Brady, and the release and height of Peyton Manning.

three guys going out into the pattern—Gruden might say, "Shift to I, Z Motion, Strong Curl, Flat Swing."

In my opinion, using terminology like that can be asking for trouble. Remember—ideally a team would like to have the play called, break the huddle, and get to the line with 15 seconds left on the play clock so the

"I WEAK RIGHT BOOT RIGHT 819 FULLBACK OPPOSITE"

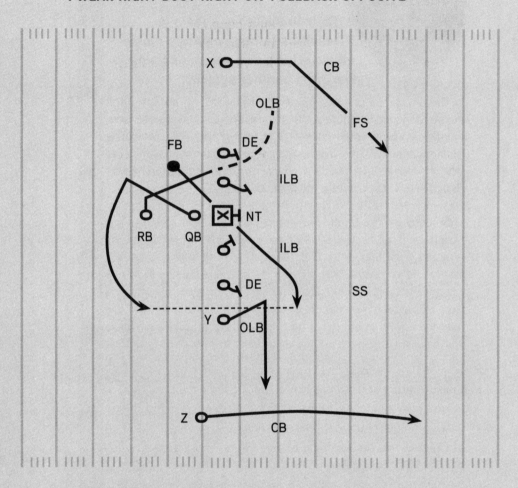

1. In an "I" formation, the running back sets up 6.5 yards behind the quarterback. "Weak" sends the fullback to the B gap on the weak side (the side opposite from the tight end). The tight end goes to the declared side ("Right"). The Z receiver stays on the strong side; the X receiver lines up on the weak side.

2. "Boot Right" tells the linemen which way the quarterback will be moving.

3. "819" directs the receivers from left to right: the X runs an 8 (post pattern), the Y receiver—in this formation, the tight end—runs a 1 (quick out), and the Z runs a 9 (fly route).

4. "Fullback Opposite" tells the fullback to release through the line and then work opposite his alignment.

Q: What can a coach do to make the transition from college to the NFL easier for young quarterbacks?

A: Certain routes can help a young quarterback by reducing the field he has to pay attention to. Teams can line up three receivers in a bunch on one side of the field—say, to the right side where a right-handed quarterback would open up most comfortably. They can line up a back and the tight end on the left side, giving the quarterback enough protection for his blind side. The three receivers then run quick crossing routes, and all the young quarterback has to do is stare at them and see who comes open first.

quarterback has enough time to read the defense, make a decision, and communicate that to everyone else on the offense.

That's one of the reasons Gruden prefers veteran quarterbacks. He needed someone who could handle the language of the offense, never mind the execution of it. Young guys couldn't handle that, and that's a big reason he was never able to develop a young quarterback in Tampa Bay.

PRE-SNAP READ: THE MENTAL PHASE

Let's get back to our quarterback in the huddle. There are times when teams won't actually call a specific play and will instead call one of three "check" principles: a check-with-me run (a run to one side or the other), a check-with-me pass (one of two possible pass plays), or a check-with-me-at-the-line (could be either a run or a pass).

When everyone's lined up and the quarterback has had a chance to survey the defense, he'll call the play that he thinks provides the best matchup against what he's seeing.

Let's say the call is "I Weak Right" with 21 personnel and it's a check-with-me run. The offense gets into formation and the quarterback—sometimes with the help of the center—will find the two safeties on the field. The strong safety is on the tight end side, and the free safety is on the side of the X receiver. The quarterback wants to see which safety is buzzing down into the box to stop the run, so he goes into a fake cadence, threatening to snap the ball at any time, trying to determine which side of the defense will have the extra defender. Once identified, he calls the play to the opposite side. In this case, if the free safety buzzes down, the quarterback would call "Check-24! Check-24!" and the run will go to the B gap on the right side—the 2 back into the 4 hole. If he calls "Check-23! Check-23!" the play is going left.

The bad news is that today's defenses are excellent at disguising their coverages. The defense's first act in pressuring a quarterback is to confuse him, to sugar the coverage—which is to say that the defenders will disguise what they're going to do for as long as they can to keep the quarterback form getting an accurate read. So a quarterback may have to fool around with his cadence in an effort to get the defense to show its hand earlier than it would like.

The quarterback will look for any clue that might reveal what the defense has planned. He needs to identify how many guys will be coming so he'll know whether he has enough blockers to handle them all. The hope is that those long hours of film study provided him tips for little things individual players will do in certain situations.

And, of course, a quarterback is also processing the information he's been obtaining throughout the game. As he surveys the defense, he might be thinking, *Every time we're in I formation, they bring the strong safety down into the box. What opportunities does that create for me? Should I throw every time? Run at the strong safety? Run away from him?*

*   *   *

So our quarterback has come to the line, looking for clues to determine which direction to run the football in his check-with-me-run call; typically, he'll identify which side the safety will be buzzing in from and run the other way. After a few seconds of reading the defense, he recognizes that they're lined up in some form of heavy run defense. He realizes he probably should be throwing the ball against this alignment. Now he has to change the play completely.

Tick. Tick. Tick.

A quarterback doesn't have infinite options in his audible package. A student of the game such as Peyton Manning can line up with the entire offensive playbook in his mind. But it's not just about what Peyton knows; it's about what his *teammates* know. And he has to know which teammates he's working with and what they'll know before he calls a new play. Among other things, audibles are limited by which players are on the field, which is why continuity in personnel is so critical to the success of a football team.

In most cases, the quarterback goes back to his predetermined menu of those four or five plays designated on the play-call sheet as having the highest probability to work at this down and distance against the defense the opponent is most likely to be in. Of course, before picking a new play, the quarterback must also remember what the defense did the last time it was in this situation. Even with the play clock ticking away, he must always be vigilant about keeping the offense balanced, which will keep it from becoming predictable.

On a check-with-me pass, the routes will be determined by the number of steps the quarterback takes in his drop. The QB will read the defense and if he sees a blitzer, he'll call out "30-30-30!" which lets his receivers

Q: All things being equal, what type of defense would a quarterback prefer to face?

A: A "read" quarterback wants to see the blitz. Dan Marino used to beg defenses to blitz him. He saw it coming, he knew where the defense was a man short, and he made them pay.

Younger quarterbacks don't want to see the blitz. They might not recognize it or might get confused by a protection change. Trent Dilfer told me that when he was younger, he couldn't figure out the blitz and he got whacked all the time. When he got older, he knew where his hot receiver was, so he was fine when he recognized the blitz.

know that he'll be taking a three-step drop and that they need to run their three-step routes. If the quarterback calls out "50-50-50!" it would be the five-step drop and the receivers would run their longer routes.

I know what you're thinking: *If I'm at home or up in the stands and I can hear the numbers and know what hole is the point of attack for a run or what route a receiver will be running, wouldn't the defense know it, too?* You're exactly correct, and that's why so many teams use a color system for checks and audibles.

When I was the offensive coordinator at Hofstra University, we used to change the "hot" color every quarter, and most NFL teams still do it that way. We'd use red, white, blue, and black, and depending on what quarter we were in, calling those colors triggered a change of play at the line. It's like the sign a third-base coach flashes to a batter at the plate.

Teams have a hot sheet of audibles, and when the quarterback barks out the hot color at the line, he's changing the play to something on that numbered menu. For example, if it's the third quarter, blue might be the hot color. You might hear something like this: "Red-22. Red-22. Check. Check. White-30. White-30." In that case, nothing is changing. It's all just subterfuge because the quarterback never called the hot color.

But if the players hear, "Red-22. Red-22. Check. Check. Blue-23. Blue-23," the rest of the offense knows an audible is on. The first number might be a dummy signal or it could communicate the snap count. Hearing "Blue-23" tells the offense that the play is changing, that the snap count will be on 2, and the new play will be No. 3 from the audible hot sheet.

If the quarterback changes the play at the line, the protection must also be changed. On half of the teams in the NFL, the center makes the protection calls. Some are better at it than others, of course. The Colts' Jeff Saturday can make a protection change with two seconds to go on the play clock; that maximizes the time Peyton Manning has to evaluate a defense and make a decision.

Not surprisingly, when Saturday was injured at the start of the 2008 season, opponents started blitzing Manning more than they used to. They weren't sure that rookie Jamey Richard would make the right protection calls as reliably as Saturday did; ultimately, it fell to Manning to call the protections.

*   *   *

So the quarterback has changed the play, and the center has changed the protection. To further complicate the matter, the new play has motion in it. The quarterback wants the ball snapped when the receiver in motion gets to a certain point (that motion landmark is different for every play). Different receivers move at different speeds, and the quarterback must know who he has in the game and how that will affect the timing of the motion. When the Giants first lost Plaxico Burress late in the 2008 season, his primary replacement was Domenik Hixon. Aside from the impact that type of change has on the ways routes are run or the timing between quarterback and receiver, it also affects something as subtle as the motion landmark because Hixon may get to the point a shade slower or faster than Burress did.

To set the man in motion, the quarterback continues to call out signals under center. That comes with a new set of potential complications if he's on the road, especially if he's indoors. Crowd noise makes basic communication tricky or downright impossible. Can the quarterback get a call communicated to the center, to the guards, and out to the tackles if his team is backed up near its own goal line in New Orleans' Superdome? If those tackles can't hear a quarterback's cadence, they don't have a strong sense of the snap count. That costs them the slight advantage that knowing the snap count gives them against pass rushers.

In addition, a receiver who can't hear the quarterback has to peek in to see the ball move. That means he's not looking out at the coverage, costing him the chance to evaluate what he's seeing. Or maybe the defensive back is able to get up in the receiver's face and jam him at the line, since the receiver has to concentrate more on the ball. This is one of the most tangible examples of how home-field advantage manifests itself.

Sometimes, quarterbacks have no choice but to keep it simple. Boomer Esiason used the days of the week as his signals. If he yelled out, "Monday! Monday! Monday!" it meant "Get down in your stance. We're snapping the ball on the first sound you hear and running the play I called in the huddle."

By the time the quarterback has taken in all this information and analyzed it, the play clock is about to expire. The quarterback has exhausted his pre-snap checklist and he's ready for the ball to be snapped. That's the easiest part of the process, right?

THE SNAP: THE CONVERSION PHASE

You want fumbles? Keep thinking that getting the ball from the center to the quarterback is a given. Good teams never minimize the importance of the center exchange.

More and more, NFL teams are forced to work on something as basic as the snap because the fundamentals of many young quarterbacks coming out of college are a disaster. They spend so much of their college career in the shotgun that they have almost no experience taking a snap from under center. It's a problem for the centers too, since so many of them have also been predominantly in the gun. It used to never be more than a rehearsal when quarterbacks and centers practiced their exchanges. Now, it's become a skill set that has to be taught at the NFL level.

To this point, everything about a quarterback's job has been mental. Once the ball is snapped, the mental meets the physical.

If a run play is called, the quarterback has to make sure the ball is delivered properly to the back, then also carry out a fake after the handoff. (Brett Favre was always great at that.) Carrying out those fakes after the handoff is critical and can freeze a defender long enough for a back to run through a hole.

If the team is going to pass, the quarterback has to identify what coverage the defense is in as quickly as possible. Eli Manning's development is most evident in this area. Earlier in his career, he struggled to fully recognize coverages and often threw the ball where he shouldn't have. That leads to interceptions. The more reps a player sees over time, the more he can understand what the defense is trying to do to him. Decision-making improves when you know what you're looking at.

Any fan can tell when Eli's seeing the field well—it's when he comes off his first receiver and moves on to his second or third read, hitting Mario Manningham or Kevin Boss or someone who wasn't the primary target.

Drew Brees is the best there is at reading coverage after the snap. In 2008, Brees was sacked about once every 49 pass attempts, despite the fact that the Saints' offensive line was not a particularly strong unit. Quarterbacks who hold on to the ball too long trying to decipher a defense consistently find themselves flat on their backs.

A quarterback dropping back into the pocket also has to know where his launch point is and stick to it. The offensive line only knows one place to protect. They can slide protect, scat protect, or squeeze protect, but they can only protect the spot they think their quarterback is going to throw from. They practice this by putting a dummy in that spot and running protections around that spot. Young or sloppy quarterbacks who don't stay true to that launch point cause breakdowns in protection. If a quarterback was supposed to set up to throw from behind center but instead drifts two feet to his left and winds up behind the guard, there's going to be a protection problem.

Sometimes a quarterback (and his coaches) must accept the reality of a situation and set a launch point far away from an opponent's best pass rusher. For example, a play may call for a half roll to the right because the left tackle can't block Jared Allen. Yes, it's an admission that the offensive tackle isn't good enough to handle his opponent. But it's also a solution because the quarterback is moving away from the midline and now has more time to get the ball off before Allen gets to him. If a quarterback doesn't know his launch point and pulls up at the guard instead of the tackle, he's just given a step and a half back to one of the fiercest pass rushers in the game.

A quarterback also must know where the escape lanes are and where certain protection schemes won't allow him to go. If a team has a true pocket quarterback, the launch point is the midline and he'll want to step up into the pocket. Any escape would be through the A and B gaps in the middle of the line. In the case of a guy like Ben Roethlisberger, he has to remember when the left tackle is working the defensive end to the outside. Ben is good at feeling this, as he showed throughout the Steelers' runs to Super Bowls XLIII and XLV. But his natural instinct is to escape to the outside of the left tackle. If that tackle is working Dwight Freeney upfield, trying to evade pressure that way would be disastrous. Instead, Roethlisberger would have to step up inside first and *then* go outside. Otherwise, he's running right to the spot where the protection is steering the pursuit.

*   *   *

Throughout the pre-snap mental phase, a play clock is constantly reminding the quarterback of how much time he has left. When he's at the line, he's staring at the huge numbers in the end zone. But after the snap, a different clock is running, one that will cost him more than a delay-of-game penalty if he ignores it.

Dan Marino talks all the time about the internal clock that can be a quarterback's most important asset. A player has to have a clock in his head that lets him know how long the play is taking. The great ones have a precision Swiss timepiece that constantly monitors an unfolding play; guys like JaMarcus Russell don't even have a battery in their watch.

That essential internal clock pays off when it comes to delivering the football. There are tiny differences in the way receivers run the same pass pattern, and a quarterback has to remember all of those individual nuances once the receivers head out into their routes.

That clock also tells a quarterback when it's time to move on to the next receiver in his progression. Any disturbance to the route stem— such as the receiver getting jammed at the line and having to modify the depth of his route—can affect the timing of a play. Some teams practice with a buzzer to help quarterbacks develop their sense of timing. Three seconds after the snap, the buzzer will sound, reminding the quarterback that if he hasn't already gotten rid of the ball, he probably just got sacked.

Then again, finding receivers where he expects them to be isn't always a slam dunk for a quarterback. Most teams use option routes, which gives the receiver the opportunity to read how he's being covered and pick the most appropriate route after the play has already started. Of course, that requires the quarterback and receiver be on the same page.

Let's say the Texans call a play in the huddle that includes an option route for Andre Johnson. Based on how he's being covered, Johnson can decide which route to run. If Matt Schaub looks up and sees the cornerback lined up on Johnson's outside shoulder, he might think that dictates a slant route. Or maybe the corner is 7 yards off the line of scrimmage, which might dictate a fade route. Schaub and Johnson have to read the coverage the same way; otherwise, they'll be looking at an incompletion or an interception.

There are some plays that have three or four receivers running option routes. That gives the quarterback multiple contingencies to consider, all while he's dropping back in the face of defensive pressure. There is no end to the things that a quarterback must be able to process if he's going to be able to complete even a single pass.

Q: Other than quarterback, which position is the hardest for a player joining a new team to learn?

A: The middle linebacker is the quarterback of the defense, so he often faces the biggest learning curve. He has to know the fronts, the stunts, and all the blitz calls. He must be in command of the language that the head coach, the defensive coordinator, and his teammates are thinking in and using. If a team brings in a middle backer from a different system, it has to be prepared for him to struggle until he gets the terminology down.

For example, one team may refer to a particular personnel group as 11 (one tight end and one running back). Another team may call it Orange (taking the "o" from "one," as in a single tight end). A third team may call it Ace (again, pointing out there is one tight end in the game). One team may call three-receiver sets "trips," while another calls them "treys." These may seem like small details, but it requires a complete replacement of the language a player had been familiar with.

If the quarterback has made it to this point, all that's left to do is set his feet and throw.

Under ideal conditions (knowing what you know now, how often do you think that happens?) a quarterback wants to step into his throw. That's the technique young quarterbacks are taught. More often than not, however, a quarterback is going to have to deliver the ball from a compromised position.

Marino always tells me the same thing. "If I worked out a quarterback for an NFL team," he says, "he'd have to show me 100 throws off his back foot." Still, too many scouts will downgrade a quarterback prospect for throwing off his back foot. In a collapsing pocket, it's actually an important skill to have.

At last, the quarterback is ready to do what most people consider to be his primary job—throw the football. He brings back the arm that has earned him a lifetime of adulation and begins the throwing motion that is immortalized in posters adorning the bedroom walls of next-generation fans across the country.

CHAPTER 4

GROUND RULES
» Running the Football in Today's NFL

I f someone were to ask Yogi Berra about the state of NFL running backs in the early 21st century, he'd probably say something like, "Guys sure get old young around here."

Brett Favre, Warren Moon, and Vinny Testaverde were productive quarterbacks into their forties. At 40 years old, Bruce Matthews was still a Pro Bowl center. Morten Andersen, the league's all-time leading scorer, had his most accurate season kicking field goals at the age of 47. In running back circles, however, 30 is the new 35.

Thirty might not seem like over the hill, but for running backs it represents a career-ending cliff. Jamal Lewis announced midway through the 2009 season his intention to retire after the season; he didn't even make it to December before lingering effects of a concussion ended his season prematurely. Just like that, after 10 years, more than 2,500 carries, and more than 10,600 yards, Lewis' career was over. At 30.

Lewis is the latest in a long line of feature backs whose starring roles were finished once they turned 30. Edgerrin James. Priest Holmes. Shaun Alexander. Eddie George. And they're the lucky ones who lasted even that long.

Sooner or later, punishment is going to take its toll on productivity. That's why in today's NFL—where, yes, you still have to be able to run the ball in order to compete—there is such a huge emphasis on finding a young running back and playing him early.

The watershed moment was the 2008 season. Matt Forte, Steve Slaton, and Chris Johnson all rushed for more than 1,200 yards as rookies. The top three rushers in the league were a second-year star (Adrian Peterson) and two guys in their first season as starters (Michael Turner and DeAngelo Williams).

Going young at the running back position is not just a trend in the NFL, it's an imperative, for reasons that have as much to do with the bottom line as with what happens between the lines. In the early 2000s, teams were still signing 29-year-old backs to big contracts. Then, within a season or two, they'd be stuck with a guy who couldn't produce anymore.

Running backs once enjoyed three-contract careers. Now, a back is likely to sign his second and final deal at 26. If he makes it through the life of that contract and still has something left in his tank, *maybe* he'll find a minimum deal with performance incentives. It's a tougher market; no longer is anyone willing to carry a declining, big-ticket back on the payroll.

Backs used to get paid based on their track record. In today's NFL, teams pay strictly on the basis of what a player projects to do. And to be honest, that's the smart way of doing things.

The best example of this new mind-set was the difficult decision San Diego faced after the 2007 season. LaDainian Tomlinson had just finished another highly productive season—1,474 yards and 15 touchdowns on the ground, plus 60 catches for 475 yards and another three scores through the air. But Tomlinson was 28 years old and still had four years left on his contract—a deal that was the richest ever given to a running back at the time he signed it.

There was nothing in his play to suggest that Tomlinson might have passed his peak. But the Chargers had Michael Turner on their roster, and they liked his potential so much that they used the franchise tag on him and paid him $2.35 million to be LT's backup. General manager A.J. Smith had a choice to make—stick with Tomlinson, who projected to have another couple of strong seasons ahead of him, or part ways with the popular player and pay Turner as the feature back.

In the end, the Chargers stuck with LT and lost Turner to Atlanta in free agency (Turner rushed for 1,699 yards and 17 touchdowns in his first season with the Falcons). And, predictably, Tomlinson's production fell by 21 percent in 2008. During the 2009 season—as a 30-year-old back—he started missing games due to injuries and managed only 730 yards. The Chargers let him go after the season, and LT landed one of those lower-money deals with the New York Jets. Even though he appeared healthy and revitalized at times during his first season with the Jets, the 31-year-old Tomlinson finished the 2010 season with the fewest carries of his career and clearly was no longer the consistent game-changing force he had been with the Chargers.

A lot of other teams might have gone the other way. Colts GM Bill Polian, for one, has always stayed ahead of the running back curve. He had Marshall Faulk for five seasons in Indianapolis, but after Faulk's best season (1,319 yards in 1998) Polian traded him to the Rams and replaced him with Edgerrin James, the fourth pick in the 1999 NFL Draft. James became the league's Offensive Rookie of the Year and earned four Pro Bowl selections in seven seasons with the Colts, but Polian let him go as a 27-year-old free agent and replaced him with Joseph Addai, a first-round pick, in 2006. In his rookie season, Addai rushed for more than 1,000 yards and Indianapolis won the Super Bowl. And as soon as the injuries started to mount for Addai, Polian spent a first-round draft pick on Donald Brown. Clearly, Polian has a great understanding of when to get out from under an older back, even one who appears to still be at the top of his game.

BUILDING BETTER BACKS

One factor that has made this youth movement possible is that rookie running backs have never been more ready to step into starting roles than they are today, and that's entirely due to the evolution of the college game.

In the old days, scouts watched the running back in an option offense and gained little information about his potential to be an NFL player. They'd see wishbone teams where even receivers would have fewer than 10 catches; finding backs who caught the ball with any regularity was unheard of.

Now, many college teams are playing pro-style offensive football and backs come out of college with experience playing in the types of systems they'll find in the NFL. Chris Johnson, for example, had 125 receptions at East Carolina—only 13 fewer than Darrius Heyward-Bey had at Maryland, and he was a first-round pick as a receiver.

As the spread offense has grown in popularity, many college backs have been lined up as wide receivers and have already learned the matchup game that is so important at the NFL level. You could see that during Matt Forte's first season in Chicago. The Bears would line him up as the X receiver and throw him a back-shoulder fade, and he understood what to do and how to get the defensive back to turn his hips. That's a sophisticated NFL receiver move, and Forte developed it in college. He was the best player on a Tulane team that played from behind every week; he was almost forced to develop receiver skills so his team could find ways to get him the football.

Also, most college teams are running the Alex Gibbs zone blocking scheme that has become so prevalent across the NFL, so scouts can more easily identify the backs ready to step right in and make those runs. And thanks to the Pete Carrolls of the world, more and more college defenses are running NFL blitz packages, so picking up a blitz has also become part of a running back's college education.

As a result, we are getting a much clearer, more comprehensive picture of what a collegiate back will be able to do in the NFL. It doesn't take three years just to get a guy ready to play on third downs the way it used to. Today's backs are showing up with everything they need to be successful sooner rather than later.

And while college coaches don't want to hear this, the NFL would prefer if running backs left school before leaving too much of themselves back on campus. If a 20- or 21-year-old underclassman displays NFL ability, the NFL would prefer he enters the draft before he sustains the wear and tear of getting tackled another 300 times. By the time a back comes out as a 22-year-old senior, he's already surrendered so much physically that it's tough to be encouraged about his NFL longevity.

LIGHTENING THE LOAD

Keeping backs from burning out too quickly is a priority, and the NFL has evolved in a lot of ways to the benefit of running backs. Just look at how many teams run three-receiver sets today. In 2009 and 2010, the Colts played almost entire games out of 11 personnel. When three receivers are on the field, most defenses counter with a nickel defense, and there are usually opportunities to run against the nickel. At the very least, there's one fewer linebacker on the field looking to get a free shot on the ball carrier.

Defenses in general are becoming quick and relatively undersized, emulating the success Tony Dungy had in Tampa Bay and Indianapolis. Speedy defenses geared toward stopping the pass feature defensive ends that are 250 pounds and linebackers that are 225. Those guys are still strong enough to bring down a running back, but they're not going to blow him up the way a heavier player would.

Some coaches, like Miami's Tony Sparano, love the idea of pounding undersized defenses with players like Ronnie Brown and Ricky Williams—a couple of 230-pound backs. He also figured out that the Wildcat offense allowed him to have both big backs on the field at the same time (we'll get deeper into the ways of the Wildcat in Chapter 7). But most guys don't have weapons like the Dolphins do.

Another way NFL coaches are trying to extend the shelf life of their running backs is by turning their backfields into two-headed monsters.

Teams have always used a rotation of backs to share the workload; they're just approaching it differently now than they used to.

Remember the Giants' short-lived "Thunder and Lightning" backfield from 2000 and 2001? Ron Dayne and Tiki Barber were so different stylistically, the Giants figured they could use them to attack defenses in a variety of ways. And while they did get to the Super Bowl in Dayne's rookie season, most people consider Thunder and Lightning more of a washout—at least the way the Giants employed them.

The problem was that Dayne was so one-dimensional that the Giants had to have calls and personnel packages specific to him. As soon as defenses saw Dayne in the backfield, they knew there were only a few things the Giants would be able to do and immediately went into a heavy run formation. As a result, Dayne—the leading rusher in Division I history when he left the University of Wisconsin—proved easy to defend.

The result of the Giants' experiment was an awareness that a team can't get the job done with one big, plodding back for power situations and one scat back for third downs. That old formula doesn't work. Teams can't be that predictable anymore. There has to be some overlap in skills between the two guys sharing time in the backfield in order to keep defenses guessing.

The Steelers won Super Bowl XL with the prototype pairing, even if it happened more by accident than design. In 2005, Jerome Bettis was in the final season of his career. He split carries almost 50-50 with Willie Parker, an undrafted free agent in his second season. Bettis and Parker had different strengths and running styles, but it turned out they could be used interchangeably in the Steelers offense. Defenses couldn't key on one thing based on which player was in the game, and that gave Pittsburgh a huge advantage.

That's not to suggest a team wants two clones in its backfield. An offense still needs versatility, just as long as the guys aren't so dissimilar that their presence on the field becomes predictable. In Atlanta, Michael Turner and Jerious Norwood can both be elusive, but they can also both run between the tackles. When a team has two guys who can run the ball effectively from the same personnel and formations and can be used in the same down-and-distance situations, that team has a tactical advantage.

Being able to distribute the carries also limits the wear and tear a team is exposing its backs to. Gone are the days of the workhorse back and guys getting 25 carries every game. Most top backs around the league average closer to 20 total touches—that's rushing attempts *and* receptions. A diminished workload means fewer hits absorbed, which should lead to healthier backs and extended periods of peak production.

GOT YOUR BACK?

It's not until the running back has the ball that the differences in skill and style really come into play, and defenses always need to know the type of player they're dealing with. A team can call "16 Boss" (an off-tackle run to the right) for any back, but it's going to develop differently if the ball carrier is a front side runner versus a cutback runner.

A front side runner runs downhill, almost invariably in one direction, as if he were on a railroad track headed into the defense. If a play is called to the right side, he's going to run to the right side and try to bust a tackle. A cutback runner has the ability to reverse field against the flow of the play; he's just as likely to change direction into a hole that opens up in the backside of the defense as he is to follow the blockers in front of him. When a defense is facing the Cowboys, 11 personnel presents different challenges depending on whether Marion Barber or Felix Jones is the lone back in the backfield. Barber is a front side runner, so defenses might drop a safety into the front side and get an extra defender in his face. The back side defenders—guys lined up away from the direction of the play—will try to get off their blocks and get upfield faster because they don't have to worry much about Barber reversing direction into a spot they're vacating. Against Jones, teams might sneak up the backside safety, hoping that Jones will cut back right into an unblocked defender.

There aren't many backs who can run both styles effectively, and those who can cause tremendous problems for a defense. When he's healthy, San Francisco's Frank Gore can do everything. On one play, he can run with power right into the A gap (between the center and the guard), keep his pads low and his legs moving, and come out the other side. The very next play, he can stick his foot in the ground and cut back across the face of defenders who were prepared for another power run.

Most teams don't have such a complete back; they're more likely to have one of each, so defenses can take their next cues from the formation.

Let's say the Giants have a back lined up in the I position, right behind the quarterback. First of all, a back in the I formation is not considered a receiving threat. He may go out for a pass, but he's not a big enough concern for the defense to assign a man to cover him. So that focuses the defense's approach.

Then the defense—and you sitting in the stands or watching at home—should make some assumptions depending on which back is in the game. If that back is Brandon Jacobs, defenses will try to close off the A, B, and C gaps to force him to pause in the backfield. The advantage of lining up in the I is that a back will get about three or four steps of momentum and be at full speed when he hits the line. A big back like Jacobs loses his power when he's forced to stop and try to start again, so the defense has a chance to make a play on him. Even an undersized linebacker or a defensive back can tackle a 260-pounder like Jacobs when he's basically standing still. A car stopped in the middle of the street isn't going to hurt you; if it's moving, it's going to kill you.

But if Ahmad Bradshaw is in the I, it's a completely different situation. He's a threat to shift gears, and he needs to set up a defense to create running lanes. He'll take the handoff and try to convince a defense with his first three steps that he's headed right. Because of Bradshaw's speed, the defense has to move fast so that he can't turn the corner. Then, when the defenders are flowing full speed to that side, he cuts back and outflanks them. Defenses need to keep him heading in one direction and force him to become a front side runner. Gap integrity is essential for backside defenders against a cutback runner, because the runner is waiting for someone to overpursue and create a hole for him.

Things change again when the formation lines up the back either offset behind the tackles or in the B gap (between the guard and tackle). From that spot, a defense must consider the back a receiving threat. Again, knowing the skill set of an individual player is as important as recognizing the personnel. Bradshaw lined up offset is a threat to run the draw or swing out of the backfield into the flat, where an outside linebacker or a corner has to cover him. Those Reggie Bush–type hybrid backs create matchup problems for defenses because coaches are always finding ways to get them the ball—screens, swing passes, reverses, you name it. If Jacobs is the offset back, though, he's probably not a threat to catch a pass; he may still run the ball, but he's likely to only be a decoy on a pass play or involved in the protection scheme.

A non-receiving threat like Jacobs, though, can still be useful in passing situations. A big back like him or Baltimore's Le'Ron McClain can be an integral piece of a pass blocking scheme. They're big enough to take on a defensive end in pass protection, whereas Bradshaw isn't. A big back might have to pick up a blitzing backer or defensive back, or he can help chip block the end and then get out into his route.

Of course, chipping the pass rusher is one thing. Knowing which guy you're responsible for blocking alone is another matter entirely.

HAVING THE QUARTERBACK'S BACK

It's not a lack of technique or even an unwillingness to block that sometimes makes it tough for young backs—especially rookies—to get

Q: Do great backs make the system look good or do good systems make great backs?

A: A lot of people like to say it was the zone scheme that enabled the Broncos to have good running backs year after year. But it's never that simple—Clinton Portis went to a different system in Washington and was still a pretty damn good player.

Backs are never going to be effective if there's not a great line in front of them. Dallas only had about three running plays they used to call for Emmitt Smith, but he played behind a great offensive line.

What makes a running game great is having a back who can make the first defender miss. Every defense is designed to have one more man in the box than the offense has blockers. If a back can make the first guy miss, that eliminates the extra defender. That's when big gains happen.

on the field in obvious passing situations. It's understanding where the pressure is coming from and making the adjustments in rhythm with the offensive line.

Let's imagine a shotgun formation with either 11 personnel (one running back, a tight end, and three receivers) or 10 personnel (one running back, no tight end, and four receivers). The five offensive linemen and the back are responsible for pass protection. For the most part, the back and the center work together. If the back is offset, the center typically will block the opposite direction. If the back is offset to the right, the center, left guard, and left tackle will block the left side, while the back, right guard, and right tackle will block the right side.

Now, let's say the defense moves a blitzer into the A gap on the running back's side. If the center steps left like he's supposed to, the blitzer is

RUNNING BACK PASS BLOCKING SCHEMES

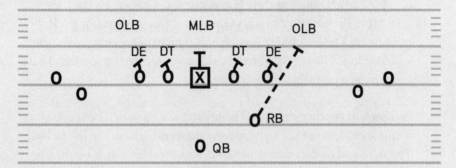

"3-by-3": The center, left guard, and left tackle block defenders on the left; the running back, right guard, and right tackle block defenders on the right.

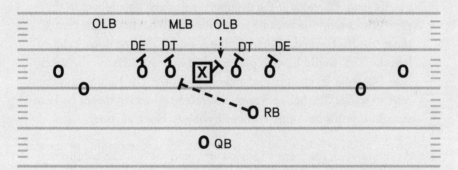

"3-by-3 Opposite": The center and running back switch responsibilities, usually because of a blitz.

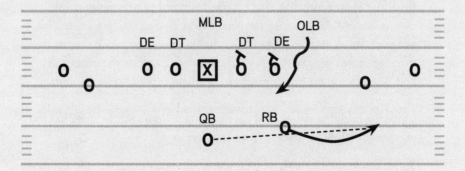

"Scat": The running back is free to release and serves as the hot receiver against a blitz.

going to have a clear path to the quarterback, and the offset back won't be able to move fast enough to get a good shot on him. So the center calls for a switch and takes the blitzer himself. That means the back now has to fill in the space where the center was supposed to go. If the running back doesn't pick up on the blocking scheme change, the team will have four blockers on the right side and only two on the left. That's going to be a problem for the quarterback.

Let's look at another scenario. The offense sets up with 11 personnel, with a back offset to the right and the tight end next to the left tackle. The tight end notices that the outside backer on his side is on the line of scrimmage, so he calls for the blocking protection to slide his way. That means the tackle slides to his left to take the blitzer, the guard slides left to take the tackle's man, and the center slides left to take the guard's man. But what if the defense is also showing a blitzer in the A gap? Who would the back be responsible for blocking? If the center slides, the back gets the blitzer in the A gap. If the line doesn't slide left, the back would have to pick up the blitzing backer on the strong side. But what if the tight end stays in to block? The back would then have to realize that he is a free-release receiver—which means he heads straight into his hot route without having to block anyone.

As you can see, there are multiple combinations that can confuse a running back, especially an inexperienced one. That's why a lot of teams like to have veterans around for those situations. Some Vikings fans can't understand why Adrian Peterson would ever come off the field. But there's only one day a week dedicated to practicing third downs, and AP has a lot on his plate before having to learn protection assignments. A veteran knows when he's supposed to block the front side, when he's got the A gap, when he needs to block the other side, and when he's got a free release. That's where experience really counts.

Once the back has recognized his blocking assignment, he then has to execute the physical phase of pass protection.

Most backs are going to be smaller than the guys they're assigned to block, so the "cut block"—firing at a defender's legs—is usually his best friend. But a cut block only works if the quarterback's taking a three-step drop; if he's in a five- or seven-step drop, the defender has time to get back on his feet and continue toward the quarterback.

When the quarterback takes a deeper drop, the back will try to push the rusher to the outside. He does this by setting up inside, thereby showing the defender a path to the quarterback around his outside shoulder. If he can entice the outside rush, the back can use his feet to run the rusher farther outside the pocket, which either will send him out of the play or allow the quarterback to step up and avoid the pressure. If the back doesn't show a legitimate outside path to the quarterback, the defender is going to bull rush him and drive him right back into the pocket.

There are plenty of times when the back is actually as much the target of a pass rusher as the quarterback. Brian Westbrook and I have talked about this many times. As soon as teams see him on the field on any passing down, they blitz him. They send a linebacker whose only job is to bull rush Westbrook in an effort to wear him down. If the defender winds up forcing the quarterback into a hurried throw or getting the sack, that's a bonus. The primary objective of that blitzer is to beat up the back. That's not the kind of wear and tear you can measure by carries or touches. Guys like Westbrook, who are great receiving threats, want to block a blitzer with their inside shoulder, count to two, then release and get open for a screen pass. He can't do that when the defender is blitzing straight down into his facemask, intent on beating him up and keeping him from getting out into the pattern.

A HOLE NEW PERSPECTIVE

While backs are a huge part of the passing game, the primary job of a running back is running the football, and there are several things to look for if you're trying to figure out why a run worked or failed.

The first is the point of attack. The back knows where the ball is intended to cross the line of scrimmage, and he wants to cross the line with his shoulders squared. If, for example, the play is an off-tackle run to the right, the point of attack is the C gap, outside the right shoulder of the right tackle.

While he's still in his stance before the snap, the back will begin reading the defense. He needs to scan the entire formation, from left to right and back across. Sometimes, a back will stare at the point of attack and accidentally tip off the "Mike," or middle linebacker. Like a poker player, every back has to be sure the defense isn't reading his eyes.

As the ball is snapped, the back takes his first step—his "read" step, during which he gets his first indication of whether the point of attack is open or if a defender has surfaced in that gap. A key read for the back is the helmet of the blocker leading him into the hole.

You can see it at home, too—just watch the helmet of the lead blocker when he engages the defender. If his helmet is outside the defender, the gap is open and the back will continue to the outside of his blocker in this off-tackle run. If the lead blocker's helmet is inside the defender, the back is going to have to cut back into the B gap (between the guard and the tackle).

So the next time you see a run get stuffed at the line of scrimmage, you can figure out what went wrong. You might hear the announcer say something like, "Wow, they just can't block these guys," but that's not necessarily the case. If the tackle is driving the defensive end outside (the tackle's helmet would be inside the man he's blocking) and the back continues to the outside, he's running right into the defender. That's the back's fault. On the other hand, if the back read his key correctly and cuts back to the B gap only to find the defensive end has driven the tackle right back into him, then the failure can be blamed on bad blocking.

Sometimes a savvy defender will be locked up by a blocker but is still able to flash his helmet to the outside, fooling the runner and forcing him back inside. In the middle of all that mayhem on the line of scrimmage, even the tiniest bit of gamesmanship can affect a play. That said, when a run fails it's usually either because the back misread the blocking at the point of attack or the blocking got beat.

At least that's how it works with zone blocking teams. In an angle blocking offense, the back has no responsibility to read his blocking. His job is solely to get to the point of attack. We'll talk more about the different blocking schemes in Chapter 6; for now, just be aware that as the popularity of G-Power (a play in which the rusher runs behind a pulling guard) makes a resurgence in the NFL, a back is going to the point of attack, and it's everybody else's job to get their men blocked. If the hole isn't opened and the back runs into darkness, you shouldn't view that as his fault.

It's also important for you to watch how certain running plays are used to set up other calls later on in the game. If a team is running a bunch of inside zone plays, it could be to eventually set up the "dip" play. A dip is when a back takes his first step inside, squares his shoulders, and really sells an inside run. He then dips back outside, and that sudden C.O.D.—change of direction—catches the defense off guard. The back's not making that cut because he saw the point of attack was closed; he was making the cut by design. The dip play can work for a front side back like Marion Barber—because the defense will be expecting him to stay on his railroad track inside—and it can work for a cutback guy like Chris Johnson, who's fast enough to get outside on anybody.

The other outside run—the toss—is also effective at setting up plays for later in the game. The toss itself has been negated in today's game because defenses are built for speed, and the toss works best against a big, stout defense that may overpower a team at the line of scrimmage but doesn't run well. It today's game, the toss normally only gains a few yards. But it's real value is setting up a fast-flow read by the defense. Once an offense has the defense thinking about the toss, the quarterback can fake the toss, bootleg the opposite way, and hit the tight end crossing away from the defensive pursuit.

TAKING A HIT

No matter what running play we're talking about, there's one common denominator—the running back is probably going to find contact. Backs get tackled more than anyone else on the field, so a lot of teams like to find guys who enjoy the position's inherent violence. Teams know those guys are going to have short careers, but they're going to be very effective when they're out there.

Walter Payton was the king of violent backs. He knew when he had nowhere left to go that it was time to explode into the tackler, and he looked forward to it.

Guys like that are basically linebackers with the football. They have great acceleration, powerful hips, get their pads low, and at the moment of impact, they're the tackler; they just happen to have the ball.

Marion Barber is the top of the class in today's game, and Tim Hightower is right behind him. As explosive as he is, Adrian Peterson is getting known as a violent back, and that's where some of his fumble problems come from.

In fact, most fumbles aren't caused by the defender making contact—it's the defender coming from behind that's the problem. The first guy to get to the ball carrier is the tackler; the second is going for the strip.

A running back needs to protect the ball by covering the point of the ball and tucking it up into his armpit. His arms move when he runs, and if the ball is away from his armpit, it's exposed. Good defenses practice stripping or punching away the football every single day.

Another important skill for a back is knowing when a play is over. I'm not talking about being a quitter and just going down or running out of bounds just to avoid contact; guys who do that won't play long in this league. But a back who knows there is nowhere left to go needs to bring the ball from high in his armpit to tight across his chest, get his second hand on the ball, then drop his shoulder and go down protecting the ball.

CHAPTER 5

THERE'S ALWAYS A CATCH

» *Receivers Need to Be More Than Just Good Hands People*

Throwing the football in today's NFL isn't the change-of-pace alternative to the running game that it was to offenses a generation ago. In the modern game, it *is* the offense.

In 1978, 26 of the league's 28 teams attempted more runs than passes. And that was with guys like Dan Fouts, Roger Staubach, Terry Bradshaw, Bob Griese, and Fran Tarkenton—all Hall of Famers— playing quarterback. In 2010, only *four* of the 32 NFL teams ran the ball more than they threw it—and not one team in the NFC.

No longer does the run set up the pass; today, the pass just sets up more passing. More and more head coaches are being hired from the offensive side of the ball because of their knowledge of the passing game, and most play-calling comes from the world of pass-minded coordinators— all of which benefits no position more than receiver.

The wide receiver spot has arguably surpassed quarterback as the NFL's star-making position (just ask the receivers). Some of the biggest names in the game—Terrell Owens, Randy Moss, Larry Fitzgerald, and Chad Ochocinco among them—are receivers, as well as some of the game's biggest personalities. Wideouts are notorious for being divas, with super-sized skills and egos to match.

The guys starring at receiver today didn't play football in the 1960s and 1970s. Back then, you found those athletes grabbing rebounds and running the floor in the NBA and the ABA. Then the NFL changed its rules to severely limit the defense's ability to cover receivers down the field, which opened up the passing game and opened the eyes of some amazing athletes to the opportunities available on the football field.

More passing created the need for more pass catchers. The 21 personnel group (two running backs, one tight end, and two receivers) that was once the primary offensive alignment in the NFL has been replaced by the 11 personnel group (one back, one tight end, and three receivers).

What many fans don't appreciate is the different roles receivers play in the passing game. It's no one's job to just go out and get open. Each receiver position has distinct responsibilities, and different types of player are best suited for the unique demands of each spot.

THE ABCs OF THE XYZs

Let's start with the No. 1 receiver.

I would argue that most teams don't actually have a No. 1 receiver—a weapon that dictates coverage and a guy who defenses will roll coverage to. We're talking about guys such as Fitzgerald, Andre Johnson, Reggie Wayne, and Calvin Johnson. There certainly aren't 32 of them in the NFL, so not every team has one of those guys.

So let's not refer to receivers in terms of first, second, and third options; instead, we'll refer to them the way they are delineated in the offense— as X, Z, and slot receivers. (The Y, by the way, is the tight end.)

The X receiver position is where you'll find guys like Moss, Fitzgerald, and the Johnsons. These guys are the filet mignon of receivers, the true stars of the position. They are tall—usually at least 6'3"—strong, fast, and have great leaping ability. During the Arizona Cardinals' stunning run to Super Bowl XLIII, Bill Cowher joked with me that it didn't matter whether Fitzgerald was double-covered all over the field; he was *always* open four feet above his head.

The Z receiver is usually a little shorter but often is a more physical guy who is going to line up on the same side as the tight end. He needs to be a good blocker because running plays will come to his side— the strong side—more often than they'll go in the direction of the X receiver, and he'll often be asked to take on the strong safety that's lined up on his side.

The Z also will often be sent in motion, and he'll be part of a lot of two-man patterns, either with the tight end or out of the slot next to the X. That means he'll be asked to change his routes based on the route of the other receiver. For example, if the tight end runs a corner pattern, the Z will run a curl. If the tight end runs a quick out, the Z runs a dig behind it. Most of the time, he'll run shallow crossing patterns, catch a quick pass, and then use his requisite running back skills in the open field.

The Z will still have some vertical routes, so he does need the speed to run a 25-yard out, the deep post, or a go route. But his toughness and elusiveness are his more valuable skills, which also make him a threat to run the reverse more effectively than a receiver better suited for the X spot.

Clearly, each position is different, and so is the mentality of the men doing that job. You hear a lot less talk from Z receivers. They know they're complementary pieces, and that they're going to do more of the dirty work than the divas will be asked to do. They understand that their effectiveness is a direct result of the threat the X poses to a defense. On a team with a top-shelf X receiver, the Z is going to flourish because all the coverage rolls away from him. Reggie Wayne enjoyed such benefits in his early years with the Colts as all the coverage rolled to Marvin Harrison. Anquan Boldin took advantage of the holes left as defenses concerned themselves with Larry Fitzgerald when both were with the Cardinals. T.J. Houshmandzadeh caught more than 90 passes in three straight years with the Bengals as coverages rolled their attention to the X man formerly known as Chad Johnson.

It's the slot receiver position, though, that has grown the most in recent years. A decade ago, a team's third receiver was a backup. Everyone was in 21 personnel, and that third receiver rarely got on the field. Now, everyone essentially has dropped the fullback and brought in the slot receiver to be a third weapon. It's become such an important position that it forces a defensive substitution whenever that third guy comes into the game. There's a defender on the opposite sideline waiting for a guy like Wes Welker to come onto the field. Welker comes in, in comes the nickel back, and out goes the "Will," or weak side linebacker. The slot receiver's mere presence changes the game.

Usually, the slot receiver is an option- or pivot-route guy, and he's often under 6'0" (Welker is 5'9"; Wayne Chrebet, a prototype slot guy, was 5'10"). There are times when teams will use taller receivers in the slot. For example, Jerry Porter and Joe Jurevicius were used in the slot to create size mismatches against nickel corners, who tend to be similar in size and skill set to most slot receivers. But for the most part, the slot receiver is a tough, smart, smaller guy with in-and-out quickness.

The slot guy usually plays on the weak side where he can take advantage of the attention being paid to the X. The Patriots of 2007–09 were a perfect example of a team with a top-tier tandem at the X and the slot. Moss would release vertically, carrying the corner down the field until he's passed off to the safety. Welker, meanwhile, would react to the coverage, run a 10-yard out underneath, and take the free yards the defense was giving up. If the defense moves a linebacker outside to help with the X or rolls the nickel toward him, the slot guy jumps inside. His routes are reactions to the opportunities being presented, and a smart slot receiver really can be open on every play. That's why a guy like Welker catches more than 100 passes every year.

The slot guy is also the hot receiver, which is the quarterback's emergency outlet on a blitz. With 11 personnel in the game, an offense has at most seven blockers. Teams blitzing away from the tight end are going to send the slot nickel corner. As soon as he's clear of the blitzer, the slot receiver turns and immediately looks for the ball.

Q: Which is more important for a receiver: great speed or great hands?

A: A receiver has to be able to catch the football, first and foremost.

Sure, vertical speed presents a problem for the defense. They will never ignore it. Vertical threats like Bernard Berrian and Lee Evans make everyone better by being decoys on deep routes, thereby opening coverage underneath.

But as the late Chip Myers used to tell me, there's a point of diminishing returns with speed and receivers. Guys with straight-ahead speed can't necessarily get in and out of their breaks at that speed. If I'm a defensive back covering him down the field, he's going to pull away from me. But when he breaks down to make the cut on the 20-yard out route, he slows down. I can catch up and close on him, essentially negating his speed advantage.

If an offense has an accurate quarterback, it can run shallow crossing routes all day that don't require world-class speed. After all, Jerry Rice—the greatest receiver of all time—wasn't a 6'4" receiver with a 4.0 time in the 40. He was 6'2" and ran a 4.5, but he ran perfect routes and had great hands.

READING COVERAGE

So much is made of a quarterback's ability to read defensive coverage, but it's equally important for a receiver to do the same. What good is it if a quarterback recognizes where the opportunities to attack a defense exist if the guy he's throwing to doesn't see things the same way?

It used to be that receivers simply ran the routes they were assigned. The great Dallas teams of the early 1990s would call "408"—which dictated a 4 route for the X receiver (Michael Irvin), a 0 route for the Y receiver (tight end Jay Novacek), and an 8 route for the Z receiver (Alvin Harper). So Irvin ran the 15-yard in, Novacek ran the shallow cross, Harper ran the post, and Troy Aikman went through his progression, trying to identify which route had the best chance of beating the coverage he recognized the defense was in. The next play would be "804"—Irvin ran the post, Novacek ran the shallow cross, and Harper ran the in. Bottom line, the players ran the play as it was drawn up and called in the huddle.

While that type of approach eliminates a lot of confusion for the players, the downside is that opportunities to take advantage of the vulnerabilities presented at the last second were being missed. As a result, offenses evolved to a point where receivers have options for the routes they can run. The principle remains the same—a 408 today still calls for the X receiver to run the 4 route, and so on. But it also gives him options based on the coverage he and the quarterback identify at the line of scrimmage. He could run the 15-yard in, a stop, a quick slant, or a takeoff route, depending on what he determined was the best option to beat a particular coverage—and *every* coverage has vulnerabilities.

There are three basic coverages every defense will utilize; each is designed to take away certain routes, and each leaves the defense vulnerable to other routes.

"Off and soft" means a cornerback is going to be dropping back, possibly into a Cover 3 Zone (three defensive backs each covering one-third of the field deep), which creates opportunities for routes to open underneath the coverage.

"Off and inside" is a soft man-to-man coverage. This will take away quick inside routes, like the slant that Jerry Rice ran all the way to Canton, but is vulnerable to quick outs—which are tougher for the quarterback to complete.

PASSING GAME VS. "OFF AND SOFT" COVERAGE

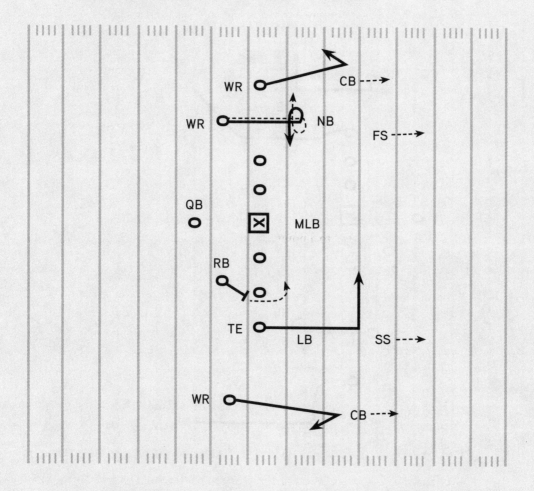

When cornerbacks are backpedaling on the snap, receivers will convert deep routes into out routes. The tight end will split the safeties and attempt to draw the middle linebacker toward him. The slot receiver can run a pivot route; the running back is free to release if there is no blitz.

PASSING GAME VS. "OFF AND INSIDE" COVERAGE

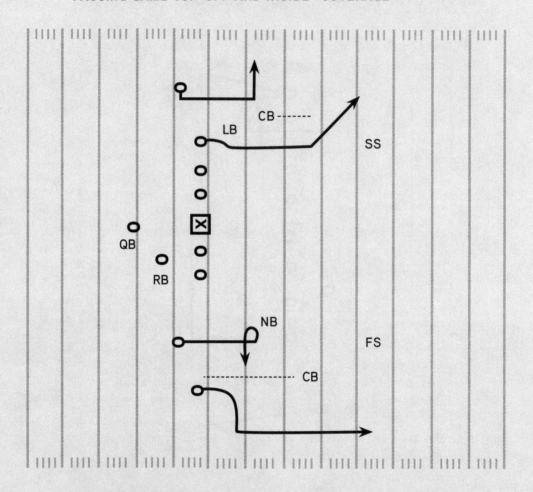

Dan Marino was famous for throwing the out route against this coverage. He claims not enough quarterbacks throw it these days; I remind him that not many QBs have his arm.

"Press" is the classic man-to-man defense (or as close to it as NFL rules about making contact with a receiver will allow these days). The cornerback is going to line up inside, force the receiver to release outside, and then turn and run with his man with inside position. A derivation of press coverage is "press bail," which means the cornerback lines up as though he's going to press, but before the snap, he shuffles out.

Before the snap, the receiver looks for clues in the alignment of the corner. Don't forget—the cornerback is trying not to tip his hand, so he may be baiting the receiver and the quarterback into thinking he's playing one coverage when he's really in another. Gamesmanship goes both ways on every play of an NFL game.

It's on the post-snap read that a receiver gets the true indicator of what the defensive back is going to do. If the cornerback lines up 7 or 8 yards off the line of scrimmage and is aligned with the receiver's outside shoulder, it might look like "off and soft" to the receiver. But the receiver can't be sure until after the snap, when he'll see the cornerback backpedal and reveal his deep coverage principles. The receiver then immediately must decide whether he's going to run a post, a deep curl, or something in front of the deep coverage. That decision will also depend on another factor—the drop his quarterback will be taking, something the receiver must always be aware of.

If the play has called for a three-step drop, the receiver knows he must choose a short pattern, such as the slant, fade, or stop. If the quarterback is in a seven-step drop, the slant won't work since the receiver will be across the field before the quarterback is ready to throw.

Keep this in mind as you're watching from the stands or your sofa—the number of steps a quarterback drops is usually half the number of steps a receiver will take before the ball is delivered. If a quarterback is in a seven-step drop, the receiver has 14 steps to work with. He could drive downfield 14 steps and run a skinny post or a stop-and-go. He could drive for nine steps, run the next three to the post, and then the last two back into a curl. If his quarterback is dropping three steps and he reads "off and soft," the receiver might run a stop route at six steps, where he's guaranteed about 10 yards of separation and will have only one man to beat in open space after catching the ball.

So many factors dictate what route a receiver will choose to run, but the key remains the post-snap read. A cornerback might lay nine yards off the receiver before the snap, indicating "off and soft" coverage, but if he doesn't start backpedaling on the snap of the ball, he's sitting on the underneath route he's hoping to bait the receiver into running. If the receiver doesn't pick up that first post-snap cue, he'll run the stop route and get hammered as soon as the ball is delivered. (The correct decision in that situation would be to take the route downfield, blowing past the cornerback sitting on the underneath route.) There are endless examples of talented receivers with poor post-snap awareness; Eli Manning took a lot of unnecessary sacks during the 2007 regular season, eating the ball on three-step drops because Plaxico Burress made wrong decisions on his option routes.

The X receiver is the one who has to worry about press coverage; cornerbacks can't commit to pressing the Z or slot receivers because those guys line up off the line of scrimmage. Pressing an X is designed to keep the biggest, strongest receiver from releasing cleanly off the line, disrupting the timing he and the quarterback depend on for receiver and ball to arrive at the same place at the same time. A lot of rookie receivers arrive at their first NFL camp thinking they're going to be the next great X man, and then find they can't get off the line and into their route against press coverage from a good NFL corner.

In the red zone, the X will see almost exclusively press coverage. Randy Moss wouldn't have it any other way; he'll run a fade against a pressing cornerback, unconcerned about forfeiting inside position. Moss wins that battle every time with his eyes. A cornerback is trained to read a receiver's reactions; when the eyes get wide or a receiver starts moving his hands into position to catch the pass, the corner puts his hands in to knock it away. For all of his freakish athletic abilities, Moss' greatest asset on the fade is his poker face. His eyes give nothing away, and he doesn't bring up his hands until the ball is virtually on top of him.

Q: What's the biggest adjustment college receivers face when they get to the NFL?

A: Usually, it's the release. Some great college receivers can't even get off the line of scrimmage in the NFL. They never faced big, strong cornerbacks, guys who are 6'0", 200 pounds, and can bench 400 pounds. Some great college receivers never even have a chance to think about reading coverages (another huge adjustment) because they're too busy trying to get out of their stance.

The corner has no clue when the ball is on its way and therefore is defenseless to stop it.

So as you're watching the game, pay attention to the cornerback's alignment on the X receiver. That will help you predict what route that receiver might choose to run. Then watch the quarterback drop back. The number of steps he takes will also narrow down the route possibilities. When an incompletion occurs because the quarterback throws to one spot and the receiver is in another, you probably have enough evidence to determine which player made the wrong decision.

CATCHING ON

As you can see, the receiver position is far more complex than most fans realize. Different receivers have different responsibilities and opportunities, and the job requires more strategy than the old sandlot standby, "Go long."

But there is one aspect of the receiver position that hasn't changed since the forward pass was introduced in 1906. The most important skill every receiver must possess is the ability to catch the football.

Q: How important is a receiver's ability to block?

A: Even in an era when the running game has been deemphasized, teams are still running the ball about 25 times per game. So receivers often can play a big part in springing a big run.

First, they have to identify who to block, something they can't do until the snap. Guards and tackles know who they have to block on a power run call, but receivers have to determine whether they have the cornerback, safety, or someone else.

Then they have to sustain the block, and receivers are responsible for the longest blocks in the game. A guard blocks the defender in front of him, and when the back clears the line a second later, his work is largely done. A receiver may have to stay with his man all the way down the field.

Most of all, receivers need to have the right attitude about blocking. Too many of the divas in the NFL don't even like when a run play is called. Sometimes, a pass play is called in the huddle and the receiver splits out, all bubbly about getting the ball. Then at the line, the quarterback checks to a run...and the receiver actually gets angry about it. A big part of blocking is a willingness to do it.

Like everything else on the football field, it sounds a whole lot easier than it is.

There are certain mechanics that are fundamental to catching a football: extending, catching, tucking, and turning.

In readying for the ball, a receiver needs to extend not only his arms but also his fingers into catching position. On rainy days, you'll notice that receivers don't extend as much; they use their body as a third point of contact for the ball, which helps them maximize control in slick conditions. When the ball makes contact with the hands (always the hands, by the way), a receiver needs to bring it into his body and secure possession. He then needs to tuck it into position the same way a running back does. Once it's protected, he can turn up the field and try to gain those valuable yards after the catch. How often do you hear an announcer say, "He was running with the ball before he had possession"? If the receiver turns to run before he's secured possession, that's likely to wind up as an incompletion; if he turns to run before he's tucked it away, that's a fumble waiting to happen.

Extend, catch, tuck, and turn—sounds simple, doesn't it? Well, the best hands in the world belong to receivers in the NFL, and still balls are dropped every Sunday under all conditions. Once you understand what goes into a catch, you can look at the replay of a drop and see which part of the process went wrong.

Take Braylon Edwards during the 2008 season. A year after making his first Pro Bowl and setting team records for receiving yards and touchdown catches for the Browns, Edwards led the league in drops—16 of them, or basically one per game.

Most of the reaction toward Edwards among those passionate Cleveland fans no doubt was subjective: "He lost his confidence." "He was better in college." "He's not comfortable with the Browns quarterback situation." (The phrasing emanating from the Dawg Pound was probably a bit more adult-oriented.)

A dispassionate and objective eye, though, could watch the replays and determine what phase of the process Edwards failed in. Did he not extend his arms, which allowed the defensive back to knock the ball away? Were his fingers not extended properly to welcome the ball? Was he just sloppy in the tuck, and bobbled the ball away before he could secure it?

If you were a Browns fan, of course you got upset over the drops. But now instead of being the one who starts yelling "This guy can't catch!" you'll be the one who knows exactly why the pass was dropped.

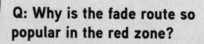

Q: Why is the fade route so popular in the red zone?

A: It's the only route that defenses can commit only one defender to covering. They might get a second guy over there late, but for the most part, a quarterback sees a one-on-one matchup, ideally with a big receiver.

Once an offense can establish the fade route, a lot of other options open up because of it. Say the quarterback throws the fade route to the Z receiver on the tight end side of the field. If the safety commits to the fade, you have the tight end run a seam route on the very next play. The quarterback drops and watches the safety; if he stays at home and covers the tight end, the QB throws the fade. If the safety cheats to the outside, he throws the seam route.

CHAPTER 6

LAYING IT ON THE LINE
» Why the Offensive Line Makes It All Happen

I f you were to walk into a room and see an NFL offensive lineman standing in front of you, he'd be impossible to miss. But somehow, if you put five of them together on a football field, they can go virtually unnoticed. We're talking about 1,600 pounds worth of human beings—nearly a ton of football player—right there in the middle of all the action. And yet too many football fans never pay attention to what's going on along the offensive line.

Cincinnati's offensive line coach Paul Alexander likens his linemen to the Secret Service. "We're in the security, protection, and insurance business," he says, knowing that it requires a special degree of unselfishness to take a bullet for your teammate on every single play.

Offensive lines succeed when a running back has a big day or the quarterback's jersey stays clean, but they get little credit in the public eye. When they do get noticed, it's usually for something like allowing three sacks…even though one came when the quarterback was chased down on a bootleg, another came on a safety blitz, and the third came when the linebacker collapsed the pocket by steamrolling the running back. Even when Hollywood makes a movie about an actual offensive lineman like *The Blind Side*, it focuses on the drama of his life off the field rather than his job on it.

But then most football fans don't really understand line play, and it's too intricate for an announcer to explain effectively within the confines of a TV broadcast. Plus, there are no stats that truly illuminate an individual lineman's performance (in that way, they're the only players impossible to include in fantasy football).

Let's start by introducing you to the individuals playing each position, since there are differences in the type of skills and responsibilities at each spot along the line.

THE LINEUP

A team pays its left tackle big money for one reason: the ability to pass block by himself. That is the top priority for the man protecting the blind side of the quarterback. If he can run block, that's a bonus. But he is going to go up against the other team's best pass rusher, and most of the time he needs to take on that guy all by himself.

The left guard needs to be a combination of agility and power. He'll need to be your best puller so he can establish the point of attack on a G-Power run. When Alan Faneca was with the Steelers, they ran 80 percent of their running plays behind him. But a guard will also need to be a power blocker on passing downs. Against a 4-3 defense, he'll match up against a defensive tackle; a 3-4 defense could slide the defensive end closer to the nose guard, where he becomes the guard's responsibility. Watch the Vikings' Steve Hutchinson and you'll see what would happen if a coach designed the ideal guard.

The center is the brains of the offensive line, usually the one responsible for calling out protection schemes at the line of scrimmage. But he also has to possess the strength to take on a nose tackle without getting bull rushed back into his quarterback, as well as the agility to get out on a linebacker if need be. Ideally, the center will be able to make the protection calls and handle at least one of those physical demands, depending on the team's situation. A team in the NFC South in 2010 faced exclusively 4-3 defenses within its division, so it would want a center who could get out on a backer. But a team like Buffalo only saw 3-4 defenses playing in the AFC East, so the Bills would want a guy

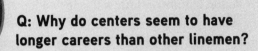

Q: Why do centers seem to have longer careers than other linemen?

A: Experience is very important for centers. They are the quarterbacks of the offensive line, making all the protection calls and adjustments. A line coach puts a huge premium on finding a veteran who can do that, and he'll push that player onto the field until the guy can't walk anymore.

It also helps that they play primarily in close quarters. Centers don't pull very often, so they don't have to run like other players do. That cuts down on the wear and tear.

The Colts never want Jeff Saturday on the sideline for even a play. When a team finds a great center, it will play him forever.

who could handle a steady diet of Vince Wilfork, Sione Pouha, and 355-pound Paul Soliai. If you ran the Bengals, what would you look for in a center who had six games' worth of Casey Hampton, Ahtyba Rubin, Kelly Gregg, and their 330-pound bodies six inches from his head?

The two guard positions share more in common than the tackles do. But the right guard doesn't need as much quickness as the left guard, since he's not likely to pull as much. That's because on most teams, the tight end will be lined up on the right side, and teams tend to direct their power runs to that strong side.

Like the right guard, the right tackle has to be a powerful run blocker first and foremost. Yes, his team would like him to be able to pass block as well, but an offense can help him in pass situations with either the tight end or a running back. If a team can't establish the point of attack in the running game, it's going to be faced with long third downs and low-percentage pass situations all game long.

In Chapter 8, you will be introduced to a measurement called the Explosion Number, which will help you identify which prospects in the defensive front seven have the necessary athleticism to win battles at the line of scrimmage. There are particular traits we look for at the individual offensive line positions, too.

For tackles, teams look first at arm length. If you're a tackle, you need to be able to get your hands on the defender before he gets his on you. Of all the things the Vikings liked about playing Phil Loadholt at right tackle as a rookie, his 36.5-inch arms—the longest of any lineman in the 2009 draft—were right up there.

Arm length is important for interior linemen, too. But for guards and centers, teams are more interested in seeing a guy's time in the short shuttle—a drill that tests for agility and lateral movement. It's easy to see why the Bills thought Andy Levitre would have the pulling skills to play left guard when they drafted him in 2009; he ran the short shuttle in 4.52 seconds, considerably faster than most other guards in the draft.

The draft is usually a pretty good indicator of how teams prioritize their needs along the offensive line. Left tackles come off the board first. Right tackles are next, followed by left guards, centers, and then right guards. In fact, it's probably safe to say that the third tackle on a team's roster is more important than the right guard. That third tackle has to be a legitimate swing guy, with the requisite skills to play either tackle position. He needs to be able to play out of both a right-handed stance and a left-handed stance, and he may even wind up as a tight end in short-yardage packages. And because he's not going to start often, most teams look for veterans to be their swing tackle since they can come in and play with limited reps at practice.

I can envision the day when a new role is created for linemen: the situational tackle. The offensive line is the only position (aside from quarterback) that doesn't use situational substitutions. Why not take a veteran with the skills and savvy to still play the position—but perhaps not the stamina to handle 65 snaps anymore—and allow him to be your pass-blocking specialist? Think of what that might mean to a guy such as Walter Jones, Seattle's nine-time Pro Bowl tackle. By the end of the 2009 season, the Seahawks realized the inevitable was approaching— Jones was coming off an injury and his great career was nearing its end. But what if they could have made Jones a designated pass-blocker? He would play only in passing situations, maybe 30 plays per game or so, and Sean Locklear would play the run downs. Teams sub in pass rushers all the time, so why not sub in a guy to block him?

ZONE BLOCKING VS. ANGLE BLOCKING

There are two running schemes that you'll see teams use on Sunday— zone blocking and angle blocking—and the quickest way to figure out which one your team is running is to look at the guards. If the guard is pulling, your team is angle blocking. If he doesn't pull, your team is zone blocking.

Most teams today use a blend of both, but let's look at what distinguishes one scheme from the other.

Zone Blocking

Zone blocking was popularized in the modern era by Alex Gibbs, who implemented the scheme when he was the offensive line coach in Denver in the mid-1990s. Instead of having each lineman identify who he was going to block before the snap, Gibbs applied a sense of choreography to the entire line and instructed each player to move together in the direction that the ball would be run. Instead of blocking the defender who happened to line up in front of him before the snap, a lineman would block whoever showed up in the zone he moved toward.

Gibbs' scheme was a reaction to all the defensive movement that goes on before the ball is snapped. The offensive linemen were identifying who they were responsible for, the ball was snapped, and then the defender wouldn't be there. So Gibbs had his line drop together one way or the other and take a post-snap read step. They'd let the defense do its running around, then they'd attack whoever happened to be in front of them.

INSIDE ZONE BLOCKING

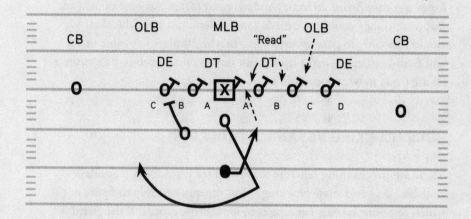

The linemen take a step to their right and block the defender in their gap.

OUTSIDE ZONE BLOCKING

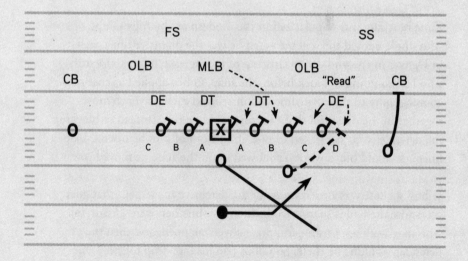

The linemen and tight end take a drop step with their right foot and block whichever defender appears in their gap.

The zone scheme solved the problem of having to run against eight defenders in the box. Gibbs figured out which of the defenders was the farthest away from the running back—and thereby had the least potential impact on the play—and decided not to block that man.

The scheme required quick and smaller linemen, players who often weighed less than 300 pounds, but its record speaks for itself: in the nine seasons from 1995 to 2003, Denver was a top-five rushing team seven times. It almost didn't matter who was carrying the ball for the Broncos; Gibbs' system helped four backs in five years each gain more than 1,100 yards (Terrell Davis, Olandis Gary, Mike Anderson, and Clinton Portis).

Before Gibbs moved to Atlanta in 2004, the Falcons had a middle-of-the-road rushing attack. He spent three seasons there (one as the line coach, two as a consultant), and Atlanta led the NFL in rushing all three.

It was a revolutionary system for many reasons, not the least of which was that Gibbs was the first line coach to take total control of the running game. He wouldn't let anyone else coach the back; his philosophy was to find a disciplined back who would run exactly where he was told to go. Gibbs told the Broncos he didn't need backs drafted in the first round (Davis, Denver's all-time leading rusher, was a sixth-round pick); he just wanted guys who would do what he told them to do.

Defenses have caught up over the years, and now they're at the point where they know more about stopping a zone scheme than offenses do about running one. Defenses began to take advantage of lines built to play the zone scheme on passing downs, because the linemen often weren't big enough to pass block effectively. Today, even big linemen know how to zone block, but defenses still have it pretty well figured out. Even Gibbs started to diversify and adopt some angle blocking principles in his two seasons with the Houston Texans before joining the Seattle Seahawks in 2010.

Angle Blocking

If the zone scheme is content to let the defense throw the first punch and then counterpunch, angle blocking is all about throwing that first punch. Angle blocking linemen don't take a read step; instead, they get to do what they like to do best—go "big on big" against the guy in front of them. It's a power scheme that also removes the need for the running back to read the defense at the point of attack. The linemen lead him to the gap they want him to run through with a pulling lineman, usually the guard.

When the Jets signed free agent Alan Faneca in 2008, it was with an eye toward building an angle blocking scheme. In his second season in New York, Faneca was a key cog in the NFL's No. 1 rushing offense.

When you see a team run G-Power (one of the most common runs in an angle blocking scheme), here's basically what happens: the center blocks the first defender to his left, essentially replacing the left guard who is going to pull. The right guard then takes the first guy to his left, replacing the center, and the right tackle takes the first guy to his left, replacing the guard. Everyone is blocking "down," or away from the point of attack.

The left guard is pulling and, in coordination with the fullback, heads to the point of attack, where the ball is supposed to cross the line of scrimmage. The fullback is closer to that spot, so he is responsible for reading the defensive end. If the end does as he is coached to do and steps with the right tackle toward the inside, the fullback will block the end's outside leg and the pulling guard will lead a power sweep around the corner. If the end stays outside, the fullback fills the spot where the right tackle was and blocks the linebacker, and a guard like Alan Faneca comes by to blow out the end.

The running back can also play a role in helping to set up his blocks. If a team is running G-Power Right, the back can take one quick jab step with his left foot when he gets the ball. Any defender reading the back would step that way, giving the offensive lineman a perfect opportunity to get an angle on him once he turns to follow the back, who is now

ANGLE BLOCK (SWEEP)

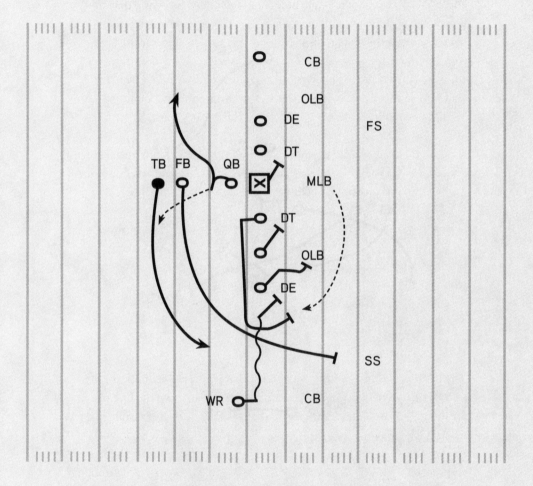

In an angle blocking scheme, the offensive linemen block down to the inside. On this play, the right tackle blocks down on the DT, the tight end blocks down on the OLB, the receiver in motion blocks down on the DE, and the right guard pulls and picks up the MLB.

"G-POWER"

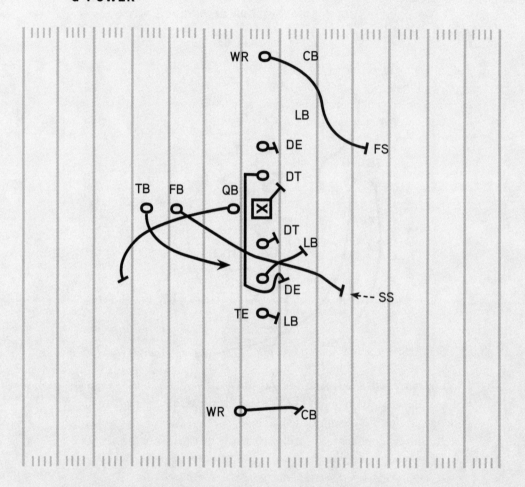

The center, right guard, and right tackle angle block, which allows the left guard to pull and lead the running back. Alan Faneca has made a lot of money over the years running this play to perfection.

Q: Do offensive linemen have to be smarter than defensive linemen?

A: Generally speaking, defensive linemen either read and react or attack. Offensive linemen, on the other hand, have to diagnose what the defense is showing, make the proper protection calls, and then execute those changes. Those adjustments are a vital difference in the job descriptions of opposing linemen.

I'm not a big believer in the Wonderlic test, but offensive linemen traditionally score higher on it than any other position player...by far. And it helps that offensive linemen tend to stay in school all four years; of the 56 underclassmen eligible for the 2011 NFL Draft, only two were offensive linemen—and Tyron Smith came out early because he projected to be a surefire first-round pick.

headed to his right. That little hesitation step can give the guard time to get in front of the back, since it doesn't do any good if the running back beats that guard to the point of attack.

Again, many teams are using both schemes, the way the great Buffalo Bills teams used to do under Marv Levy. They preferred to run a zone scheme against 3-4 defenses and an angle blocking scheme against a 4-3 front. And while some teams still prefer one scheme over the other, they are finding ways to use both and retain some unpredictability in their ever-evolving chess match with the defense.

WHAT TO LOOK FOR

No matter which blocking scheme your team prefers, there's a lot you can pick up on by watching the offensive line.

The first thing you should look for is the stance of the linemen. If the tackle is down in a three-point stance, you can anticipate a running play (unless the down and distance suggests otherwise). If they're standing up in a two-point stance, you can predict with a high degree of certainty it's going to be a pass or a draw.

If you can't tell while the players are lined up, watch the height of the linemen's helmets after the snap. If the helmets are raising upward, it's probably a pass—or a draw, which depends on selling the threat of a pass.

If you're in the stands and you're relatively close to the field, you can tell what's coming by just keeping your ears open. Pass blocking doesn't have the same sound of pads and helmets crashing together. If it's relatively quiet, it's a pass.

If you want to see where most individual blocks succeed or fail, keep an eye on which player takes the third step in the sequence. Usually, the offensive lineman is going to take the first step. Defenders are usually going to be faster than an offensive lineman, but any speed advantage is negated because the offensive line knows the snap count and the defender doesn't (as previously mentioned, this advantage is minimized somewhat in road games in front of loud crowds).

As the lineman takes his read step, the defender takes his first step. To be successful, the blocker *has* to take the next step; if the defender is quick enough to take that third step in the sequence, he'll be the first to get his hands in position on his opponent's body. Now, he's in a good position to bull rush the blocker. It's critical that the offensive lineman takes that third step and initiates contact with width in his base if he's going to make a successful block. (When two players come together, one of them is going to have a wider base than the other. Whoever it is will have the best chance of holding his ground and winning that one-on-one battle.)

Also, try to watch the center before the snap and see what he's looking at. Remember, he's the one making the protection calls in all likelihood, so try to envision what he's seeing. He's looking to see how many defenders are in the box and have to be accounted for, and you can count right along with him.

The center is also keeping an eye on the other team's best pass rusher. If you're playing the Chicago Bears and they're moving Julius Peppers from side to side, the center is trying to locate him. That way, if the game plan called for the line to slide protection toward Peppers, the center can slide the line right or left, accordingly.

When you see the center and the quarterback pointing at the defense, they're trying to locate the middle linebacker. Identifying the Mike is how the linemen decide who's going to be responsible for the guys they think are coming. Of course, the actual middle linebacker might not even be in the game; sometimes, the Mike and Will linebackers switch places to disguise what they're doing. What the center and quarterback are actually doing is declaring who they consider to be the Mike on that particular play, and everyone's blocking assignment is dictated from there. The running back, for instance, is responsible for the defender who is lined up outside whoever has been designated the middle linebacker.

When you see the center pointing at the defense like that, it's usually safe to expect a pass play. Then again, more and more centers and quarterbacks go through the exercise of declaring the Mike and then running the ball anyway, trying to take advantage of a defense anticipating a pass. Ben Roethlisberger loves to use this technique, which is especially useful on second-down situations.

You can also tell what kind of day a guard or a tackle is having by watching how long he can keep his shoulders square to the line of scrimmage. If you're seeing a lineman being turned by a defender or bailing on the snap of the ball, it's a pretty good indication that the guy he's trying to block may be too much for him to handle. That should signal to the offense that it's a good time to run a "draw block" or "trap block" against that defender. On a draw block, the guard allows his man to go upfield past the ball carrier. On a trap block, the guard who is being dominated starts a play looking like he's going to block his defender but instead slides over toward another defender or acts like he's been beat. The other guard then comes from the opposite side and replaces the first guard, thereby surprising and "trapping" the defender. Believe me, it's a great way to slow down aggressive defensive tackles.

If you really want to watch the game from the inside out, buy a ticket for a seat in the end zone, where you get the best perspective on the action in the trenches. You can't get a good sense of it from the traditional TV angle, but from the end zone you can study the "splits" along the line— the space between the tackles and guards, the guards and the center, and the tackle and the tight end. Those players should be about three feet from each other, but teams will adjust their splits to create matchup advantages, to make adjustments, or to expose a defense's vulnerability.

When you notice that there's a universal tightening of the splits along the entire line, it's a signal that they're trying to prevent a penetrating defensive front. They're narrowing the gaps to make it tougher for the defenders to fit through them. If you see a consistent widening of the splits, the line is preparing for a two-gap defense, giving each lineman extra space he is individually responsible for.

Q: What can an offense do to boost the running game if it doesn't have a true feature back on the roster?

A: The team has to commit to running the football. The 2009 Bengals are a great example. In previous seasons, they were first and foremost about Carson Palmer and their passing attack. But in 2009, they committed to running the football, became a tremendous running team, and won the AFC North.

Of course, a lot of coaches will say they are committed to running the ball, but I would test their commitment by asking two simple questions:
1. Are you willing to run the ball on second down after running on first and gaining zero yards?
2. Will you run the ball when you're down seven points?

If the answer to those two questions is yes, then that team is truly committed to the run.

Even if it's only a matter of six inches between each player, it's significant. If the guard splits six extra inches from the center, and the tackle splits six extra inches from the guard, the edge rusher has to line up one foot wider—which might be just enough to keep him from reaching the quarterback.

Often, you'll see inconsistent spacing; for example, the guard and the center may be the standard three feet apart, but the split between the guard and the tackle is only two feet. That's a pretty good indication that there's a run coming, and that the guard and tackle will be involved in some sort of combination block together.

Watch the split between the tight end and the tackle, and the impact it has on the defense if the tight end starts to flex farther and farther out. The tight end may start the game in a three-foot split and have the "Sam," or strong side linebacker, on his outside shoulder. The next play, he's at four feet, and eventually he's out to five feet, where he's head-on with the linebacker. It's a subtle adjustment that can set up the opportunity for the tight end to hook the Sam on a toss to the strong side.

When the tight end is split out as a wide receiver, turn your eyes to that Sam backer, because that's exactly what the quarterback is doing. If the Sam goes wide with the tight end, it sets up the possibility for a run to that side (some of the best running teams use a "flex" tight end). If he splits the difference halfway between the tight end and the tackle, you know the defense is in a zone. If the Sam comes all the way back inside and into the box, there's a pass opportunity for the tight end against the safety.

They may be subtle, but every little battle waged among the biggest guys on the field will affect the big picture. Reason enough to deserve more of your attention.

CHAPTER 7

YOU SAY YOU WANT AN EVOLUTION?
» *How Innovations Like the Wildcat Catch On*

When it comes to debuts, it's tough to beat the way the Wildcat offense burst on to the NFL scene.

It was September 21, 2008. The Miami Dolphins were taking on the New England Patriots in Foxborough, Massachusetts. The Patriots were on a 21-game winning streak—at the time, the longest regular-season streak in NFL history.

On six occasions, Miami coach Tony Sparano took quarterback Chad Pennington and split him out wide as a receiver and had running back Ronnie Brown taking the snap from center out of the shotgun. On *four* of those six plays, the Dolphins scored touchdowns—three on runs by Brown, and one on a pass from Brown. Sparano had his first win as a head coach, and that victory wound up breaking a tie with New England at the end of the season that gave Miami the AFC East title.

First impressions don't come any bigger in the NFL. No one noticed when the Carolina Panthers ran 12 plays out of a Wildcat formation on Christmas Eve two seasons earlier. But when Miami—and offensive coordinator Dan Henning, who had been the Panthers' offensive coordinator that night in 2006—unveiled it against Bill Belichick, everyone in the NFL paid attention.

Within a year, 22 teams had experimented with some sort of Wildcat formation. It was never a gimmick—though I heard a lot of analysts refer to it that way—and it's not a trick play. The Wildcat was a legitimate package from the start because of the matchup problems it created for a defense. For the Dolphins, it allowed Sparano to get his two best offensive weapons—Brown and Ricky Williams—on the field at the same time.

But before we get into that, you have to understand how trends evolve in the NFL. Like everything else, it begins with finding favorable matchups.

A PERPETUAL CHESS MATCH

Back in the 1960s, most NFL teams ran the ball on first and second down, hoping to get into 3rd-and-4 (as my friend and longtime offensive line coach Bob Wylie likes to say, coaches all want to live in a world of 3rd-and-4). In that down-and-distance situation, they could run or pass and, more importantly, keep the defense guessing.

Then along came the AFL with its mad-bomber quarterbacks and all bets were off. A lot of young coaches who couldn't get jobs in the NFL wound up in the AFL and they didn't have to go by the old rules. They weren't afraid to throw, throw, and throw again, no matter what the down and distance.

After the merger, it was the defenses that had to evolve, as coaches scrambled to come up with ideas for defending first- and second-down passes. Dick LeBeau, one of the NFL's great defensive coordinators, was a Pro Bowl cornerback in those days, and he saw the future of offensive strategy. When he became a coach, he created new ways to pressure the quarterback—including the zone blitz, which we'll get to in Chapter 9. LeBeau realized that he had to defend the pass and stop the run all with one call, so he decided to blitz on early downs. If a team was in an I formation and had a great blocking tight end, LeBeau would blitz from the strong side—if the team called a run, it would be right into the blitz; if it went with a play-action pass, someone would be coming 800 miles per hour at the quarterback. Behind the blitz, LeBeau played bump-and-run coverage, just like he himself played in the 1960s, under a three-deep zone. The result: if the blitz didn't get to the quarterback, any completion would go for just a short gain.

Enter Bill Walsh. He gladly took those short gains, only he set up his receivers to run after the catch. The legendary Raymond Berry told me that back in his era, he and Johnny Unitas would run out routes against the blitz. Walsh's pivotal innovation was having his receivers run slants against blitzing defenses instead. That way, when one of Walsh's receivers caught the ball, he'd be running into the middle of the defense, not out of bounds.

Jerry Rice carved out a Hall of Fame career running that slant for Walsh's 49ers. San Francisco would send Rice on a slant from one side of the field, then have another receiver (Freddie Solomon or John Taylor) and tight end Brent Jones run shallow crossing routes—one at 5 yards, one at 11 yards—from the other side. It didn't matter where the blitz came from; Joe Montana would simply throw the other way and someone would be open.

That's a simplified example of how things change in the NFL, but it's a pretty good representation of how the chess match progresses. The defense finds a way to solve what the offense is doing, then the offense responds and the pendulum swings back. As the passing game (aided by rules restricting man-to-man defense) grew more sophisticated in the 2000s, defenses reacted by getting smaller and faster.

Which set the stage perfectly for the power running of the Wildcat.

BACK TO THE FUTURE

Sure, it's innovative, but in reality the Wildcat is a classic conservative offense. It's really a derivative of the old single wing formation, which is about as old as football itself. Is it any surprise, then, that Bill Parcells is the guy who brought the Wildcat to the NFL? When he came to Miami to rebuild the Dolphins, Parcells brought in Sparano, Dan Henning, and David Lee, who was the offensive coordinator at the University of Arkansas when Darren McFadden and Felix Jones ran the Wildcat with terrific results in 2007.

Parcells recognized the matchup problem the Wildcat would create for a defense. That's because the entire package is built on a simple premise—NFL teams do not defend the quarterback.

Yes, they consider his arm and his mobility and his decision-making to be dangerous weapons, but defenses don't assign a specific player to the quarterback. Every once in awhile, they'll assign a spy to a quarterback who's a particularly dangerous running threat (Michael Vick being the perfect example). But for the most part, the quarterback is the rallying point for the defense. Everyone's trying to beat his man to get to the quarterback.

Also, the Wildcat doesn't use different personnel than other offensive packages, so there's nothing to tip off the defense that it's coming. It's not until the offense breaks the huddle and the quarterback goes out to the wide receiver spot that the defense realizes it has a problem. Now it has to assign someone to cover the quarterback because he's suddenly not the quarterback anymore.

The entire foundation of the defense has now been turned upside down. Every defense is built on simple math—they all want to have one more defender than the other team has blockers. No defensive coordinator thinks he can stop the run consistently by having his guys beat their blocks. Instead, they build schemes around the principle of the extra defender—putting eight in the box against the run, for example.

Imagine that 21 personnel (two backs and a tight end) comes onto the field and the defense is preparing to bring the strong safety into the box as the extra defender against what it anticipates might be a run. Except now the quarterback is split out and the safety who was going to come into the box has to go out to cover him. The free safety can't come down to play the run either—if he does, both corners will be left to play single coverage on both receivers, with no possibility for help coming over the top. And so the offense can now run one of its regular plays, except without the handoff from the quarterback and with one fewer defender it needs to block.

Think about how this affects the linebackers. Whenever possible, an offense wants to run the ball to the side opposite where the safety is buzzing into. The linebacker's job is to "leverage" the lead blocker—to take on the blocker with his inside shoulder and force the running back inside. When a back sees the helmet of his lead blocker inside the linebacker at the point of attack, he's trained to cut inside, which is where either the safety or another linebacker will be waiting, unblocked, to make the tackle.

But against the Wildcat, there *is* no free defender. The backer has no opportunity to leverage the lead blocker. The other backer is being blocked, and the safety is off covering the quarterback. Now the linebacker has to beat the blocker to make the play.

Jon Gruden calls that the No. 1 problem caused by the Wildcat, and it's the reason the Wildcat is not going away until someone figures out how to stop it consistently.

WILDCAT OPTIONS

The type of plays that teams call out of the Wildcat formation depends on the skills of the player taking the snap. Ronnie Brown has one set of skills, and Cleveland's receiver/return specialist Joshua Cribbs—who was a high school quarterback—has another. Regardless of who is taking the snap, the one thing you're not likely to see is a run toward the side of the field where the quarterback is lined up; teams don't want to put him at risk by asking him to block.

As a result, the two plays you'll most often see are the dive option and the power lead. In the dive option, the back in the shotgun receives the snap and sticks the ball in the belly of the second back. He then reads the defensive end on that side. If the end closes, he pulls the ball out and takes off to the outside. If the end steps outside, he completes the handoff and the second back becomes the ball carrier. Keeping the ball from getting outside is one of the keys to defending the Wildcat.

The power lead is the play the Dolphins love. They snap the ball to Ronnie Brown or Ricky Williams, while whoever doesn't take the snap gets in front and leads the ball carrier to the point of attack. It's just as if the quarterback had handed off to one of them, but now there's one less defender in the box.

The next problem for the defense presents itself when the player taking the snap is also a threat to throw the ball. Sure, Brown has showed he can pass, and receivers like Antwaan Randle-El and Brad Smith are converted college quarterbacks. But in the 2009 NFL Draft, the Dolphins showed they were already thinking about diversifying the Wildcat when they drafted Pat White. A highly productive quarterback in West Virginia's spread offense, White was too small to survive in the NFL as a full-time quarterback. But Miami thought he might be perfect for the Wildcat.

The ideal scenario would have seen White and Pennington on the field at the same time running the Dolphins' regular offense. I figured Parcells and Sparano would teach White to play receiver so that his entrance into the game wouldn't trigger an automatic Wildcat alert for the defense. Unfortunately, Pennington got hurt and White became the team's backup quarterback, so instead of preparing him to play receiver, White had to spend all of his practice time getting ready to play quarterback. That experiment failed, and White was released after just one season with the Dolphins. Still, it demonstrated that people were thinking of ways to diversify the Wildcat.

Having a guy who can throw is the next natural step for the Wildcat package, and if the Wildcat is going to be dependable in the red zone—especially inside the 10-yard line—teams are going to have to identify and acquire that type of player. The guy taking the snap doesn't have to be a great passer to complete a pass on a shortened field. As long as he

THE WILDCAT DIVE OPTION

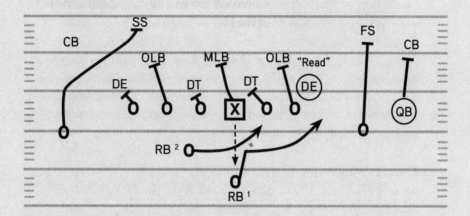

In the Wildcat, moving the quarterback to a receiver position forces the defense to account for him with a specific player, something it does not have to do when the quarterback is under center. Now the offense can block everyone and read the defensive end: if he steps toward the running back, the back pulls the ball and runs outside; if he steps outside, the back hands off the ball to the other back, who runs inside.

THE WILDCAT POWER LEAD

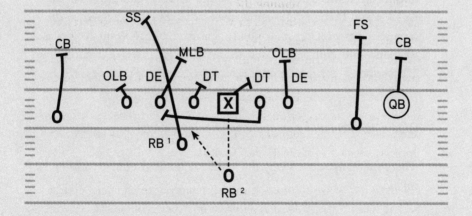

In a normal power lead, there is a free defender once the ball is handed off to the running back. In the Wildcat, the offense has enough blockers to account for every defender.

Q: What killed the run-and-shoot offense?

A: It died because it couldn't protect the quarterback. With the exception of Warren Moon, quarterbacks in the run-and-shoot were getting broken in half. Those teams rarely carried a tight end, so they became soft on the edges and pass rushers teed off on the quarterback.

It also indirectly caused problems on special teams. In order to carry that extra receiver on the roster, teams cut either a tight end or a fullback. The second and third tight ends and the fullback are real factors on special teams. Once a team replaces them with three 5'9", 160-pound receivers, it can no longer stop anyone's return units.

doesn't have to worry about getting the ball downfield with accuracy, a short pass inside the 10 should be a Wildcat back's best chance to complete a pass.

Ultimately, teams will have to run multiple plays out of the Wildcat. As soon as it becomes one-dimensional, the advantage gained by the offense is offset by its predictability. The more the Wildcat evolves as a weapon—and Philadelphia showed a ton of variations of it during the 2009 season—the more things it forces a defense to prepare for.

COPY CATS

There are many reasons why the Wildcat has caught on, even in its infancy.

First, it's hard to argue with its effectiveness. In 2009, the Wildcat produced a touchdown once every 20 times it was used. It resulted in a first down once every four times it was used, and it gained an average of 4.6 yards per play.

No team used it more than the Dolphins—10 percent of their plays in 2009 were out of the Wildcat. Those 100 plays resulted in nine touchdowns, 29 first downs, and averaged 4.8 yards per play. When coaches around the league see numbers like that, they're going to find a way to work that into their own playbooks.

The Wildcat is also an effective way to maximize the utility of the two-headed backfields most teams are employing today, as we discussed in Chapter 4. The Wildcat gave the Dolphins a way to get their two best players on the field together without either Brown or Williams having to be a fullback.

The benefit of having two backs like that together on the field has another implication that not enough people talk about. Think about the security it provides a young, ineffective, or even a banged-up quarterback. If a quarterback is struggling, you can run a few plays with the Wildcat and give him a breather—without taking him out of the game or tipping your hand that you're doing it for that reason.

After Pennington got hurt in 2009, Chad Henne became the Dolphins' starter. If Henne was struggling to read all the different defensive coverages a team was throwing at him, Miami could run a few plays out of the Wildcat and give their young quarterback time to regroup. Imagine you're coaching the Giants and Eli Manning gets the wind knocked out of him in the middle of a drive. Why not have a Wildcat package with both Brandon Jacobs and Ahmad Bradshaw to buy Eli some time without taking him off the field?

Similarly, Oakland could have taken some of the heat off JaMarcus Russell by running the Wildcat with its deep stable of backs (especially Darren McFadden, who became a Heisman Trophy candidate running out of that package in college). When Jake Delhomme was having his interception issues with the Panthers, Carolina could have used DeAngelo Williams and Jonathan Stewart as a potent Wildcat attack.

The Jets, Lions, and Bucs all had rookie quarterbacks in 2009; the Wildcat could've helped those guys handle any bumps in the road.

If you're a fan of a team whose quarterback is struggling, no matter what the reason may be, you may wonder why your coach isn't using the Wildcat.

Of course, not every team is going to have a Wildcat package. When you have a great quarterback whose arm is a threat on every play, you're not going to take that threat off the field for any reason. So you shouldn't expect to see New England or Indianapolis bothering with the Wildcat. You probably wouldn't see it in New Orleans, even though the Saints' running backs would be ideal in the Wildcat. Why give the defense a reprieve from worrying about Drew Brees' arm on even a single play?

Q: What will be the next big offensive innovation that catches on?

A: The spread offense is already prominent in the NFL, and I think it's going to continue to grow in popularity. In 2009, about 5 percent of all offensive plays featured empty formations with no one in the backfield. That could grow to 20 percent or more in the coming years.

The key will be whether teams can find backs who can be used in the spread offense as a receiver (in the mold of a Reggie Bush) but can also stay on the field as a legitimate run threat. Once an offense has a player like that, defenses can't go to their dime package; if they do, the offense will run the football. If they stay in nickel or their base defense, their opponent will spread out the offense—stretching the field with a vertical threat tight end, for example—and the defense has lost the matchup game.

WHAT'S NEXT FOR THE WILDCAT?

As more and more teams utilize the Wildcat, a lot of people wonder whether we will ever see a team run it as their base offense. I've talked about this a lot with Bill Cowher, and he doesn't think a team can survive with the Wildcat as its core offense. I agree with him.

Cowher believes a defense can disrupt the Wildcat by blitzing it. He's not talking about just blitzing the back who's taking the snap—he's talking about attacking the mesh point where the two backs come together for either the handoff or a fake handoff. And if a team calls a pass play out of the Wildcat, the blitz could unnerve the guy taking the snap because he's not a regular quarterback. A defense needs to dare him to throw the ball. Maybe he'll get away with one or two completions against the blitz, but he won't beat it consistently.

Because the pass isn't a sustainable threat out of the Wildcat, it's not a formation that's conducive to playing from behind. Can a team run it when it's down in the fourth quarter? When it needs to move the ball quickly and conserve clock? Can a team run it on 3rd-and-12 at any point in the game? Probably not.

Certainly, the Wildcat can be more than an occasional changeup with the right players running it. If Tim Tebow doesn't develop into an every-down quarterback the way the Broncos hoped when they took him in the first round of the 2010 NFL Draft, he could find a niche as an ideal Wildcat back. He plays like a linebacker, and at 6'3" and 245 pounds, he could be especially effective running the power lead.

If the NFL ever expands its schedule, I can see situations where injuries to quarterbacks might force a team to run the Wildcat for an entire game or two. It also presents an interesting consideration for choosing a team's third quarterback.

The ideal quarterback rotation for most teams would be a 28-year-old starter entering the prime of his career, a veteran backup, and then a third quarterback being groomed for the future. If the starter has five years left on his deal, the team may not want to invest in preparing a quarterback for the future. So why not make that third quarterback the Wildcat guy? It would justify activating him, because he'd be used on roughly 10 percent of a team's snaps, or roughly six plays per game.

Imagine if the Colts had a Wildcat package at the end of the 2009 season. (Again, no team with Peyton Manning wants to take him off the field, but there's nothing wrong with being prepared for the unknown.) Instead of struggling to decide whether they should play Manning against the Jets or Bills in the final two games during their quest for a 16–0 season, they could have inserted a Wildcat back—Michael Hart, for example—to take the pressure off rookie quarterback Curtis Painter, who saw the bulk of the playing time.

Ultimately, I don't believe a team can win in the NFL without a real quarterback, a guy who's going to make decisions while he's dropping back, stick his foot in the ground, and deliver the ball with accuracy. Even scrambling quarterbacks in traditional offenses haven't been able to win a Super Bowl (Steve Young being the lone exception).

In the NFL, the pass rushers are so good that eventually they will get to whoever is taking the snap. So if an offense has some guy back there who's only half a quarterback, he won't be able to hold up.

The Wildcat has its place, but it will always be a far better counterpunch than punch.

» THE NEXT BIG THING

Even as the Wildcat was finding its way into offensive arsenals across the league, a new innovation emerged during the 2009 season that challenged the way defensive fundamentals are taught.

The Pump Fake Draw is the hybrid offspring of the draw play and the play-action pass, two plays which have been around forever. The quarterback takes the snap and then his three-step drop as the offensive line stands up, which gives an initial pass read to the defense. Then the QB sets and takes his non-throwing hand off the ball (defensive backs and linebackers are taught to break in whatever direction the quarterback is facing when they see his hand come off the ball).

But on the Pump Fake Draw, the quarterback doesn't throw the ball. Instead, he sells a violent pump fake and then hands off to the back on a draw against a defense out of position. Not only have the Mike backer and the safeties moved in the wrong direction, but the defensive line has been affected, too. Because the quarterback took a three-step drop, the linemen believed they were not close enough to getting the sack when they saw that non-throwing hand come off the ball. At that point, they've been coached to stop and get their hands up to knock down a pass attempt. The only problem is the offensive linemen know the run is coming and they can decleat any guy unfortunate enough to jump up in the air.

Every team is going to be running this play—though it's going to be harder for some quarterbacks than others. To sell the pump fake, it helps to have big hands. Brett Favre was great at using the pump—his receiver would run the slant, Brett pumped, the defender bit, the guy took off deep, and Favre hit him in stride. Bill Cowher will tell you that the pump fake might be Ben Roethlisberger's best weapon. But if a quarterback has small hands, he can't pull off the pump fake as well. He has to keep two hands on the ball, and safeties don't fall for that.

As long as a quarterback has the hand size and strength to sell the deception, the Pump Fake Draw is going to become a staple across the league.

CHAPTER 8

WHY 7 DOESN'T EQUAL 7
» The Principal Differences between 3-4 and 4-3 Fronts

The most critical decision Mike Tomlin made along the road that would eventually lead the Pittsburgh Steelers to another Super Bowl championship was his first one.

Tomlin was hired to be Pittsburgh's head coach in January 2007 after serving as the defensive coordinator in Minnesota. Under Tomlin, the Vikings had the NFL's best run defense in 2006.

Earlier in the decade, Tomlin was the defensive backs coach in Tampa Bay. The Bucs had the league's top-rated defense in both 2002 and 2005, the high point being a victory in Super Bowl XXXVII when they intercepted five passes and returned three of them for touchdowns.

And so a man who cut his coaching teeth in the heyday of the Tampa 2 defense and its 4-3 front moved to another team and built another dominant defense, also with a 4-3 front. Still, when he was hired to replace Bill Cowher in Pittsburgh, he concluded that switching away from the 3-4 front that the Steelers had played under Cowher for more than a decade wouldn't work. The roster he inherited was built for a 3-4 system, and converting to the 4-3 he was more familiar with—and probably preferred—would've destroyed what the Steelers had built and might have set the defense back at least a couple of seasons.

Tomlin's decision to stay in a 3-4 was one a lot of coaches wouldn't have been able to make, primarily because of their egos. But it was the right call, as the Steelers' sixth Lombardi Trophy confirmed.

A lot of fans wonder, *What's the real difference? 3+4 and 4+3 both equal 7, right?*

Well, not exactly.

In fact, the identities of the two defensive fronts are entirely different—from the philosophy driving them to the personnel needed to play each system.

JOB DESCRIPTIONS: 3-4

Not long ago, there were only a handful of teams in the NFL operating out of a 3-4 front (three down linemen and four linebackers). But just as Bill Walsh's West Coast offense spread across the league in the wake of San Francisco's success, the 3-4 is becoming increasingly popular as coaches watched Bill Parcells (its prime architect), the Patriots, and the Steelers stock their trophy cases.

By the start of the 2010 season, 15 teams were operating a 3-4 scheme. There were more 3-4 defenses in the AFC (10) than 4-3 defenses (six).

With more players standing up in a two-point stance, 3-4 defenses can adapt to the exotic offenses they're seeing more and more of, and they're better equipped to handle a quarterback in the shotgun with an empty backfield. Since only three defenders are playing with their hand on the ground, a 3-4 team can send pressure from anywhere. As Tim Ryan, my partner on *Movin' the Chains*, says, "The offense doesn't know who's coming or where they're coming from." It confuses offensive linemen trying to identify their protection responsibilities.

The difference between the two systems starts right up front. The job of the defensive line in a 3-4 is not to penetrate into the backfield; it's to occupy as much of the offensive line as possible, freeing the linebackers to make plays. Each lineman is responsible for two gaps—the nose tackle has to handle the A gaps between the center and the guard on both sides, and the defensive ends have to handle the B (between guard and tackle) and C (outside the tackle) gaps. To do that, a team needs big, tall, strong defensive linemen with long arms. The ideal example is the 2001–08 Patriots, who built their defensive line with first-round draft picks who all stood 6'2"or taller. The front three need to get their hands on the offensive linemen and lock their arms out so the blockers can't get on them. They have to be strong enough so that they can't be pushed off the ball, and they have to be tall enough to see over the offensive line and locate the ball carrier in the backfield.

It starts with finding a nose tackle who will command a double-team; a 3-4 defense works best when it forces one of the guards to help the center on every play. The prototype nose tackle would be between 6'2" and 6'4" and somewhere in the neighborhood of 350 pounds. Guys like Shaun Rogers (6'4", 350), Jamal Williams (6'3", 348) and Vince Wilfork (6'2", 325) are perfect examples.

The quintessential 3-4 defensive end is a guy like Richard Seymour— 6'6", 310 pounds, and blessed with long arms. Again, he's not penetrating, so he needs to be able to see the ball carrier over the tall tackle he's lined up against. Arizona had two textbook 3-4 ends while winning consecutive NFC West titles in 2008 and 2009—Darnell Dockett (6'4", 285) and Calais Campbell (6'8", 290).

The ends in a 3-4 are not the pass rushers you find in a 4-3. They need to sacrifice themselves for the sake of the scheme, and that type of mentality is something teams need to identify in a player before plugging him into their system. A 3-4 defensive end lines up over the tackle, and his job is more about keeping the blockers from getting onto the linebackers than it is getting into the backfield and creating havoc. Some guys don't have the capacity to be that selfless, and they could become problems if asked to play a supporting role. [Exhibit A: Albert Haynesworth in Washington.] They know that in today's NFL, ends get paid for sacks. In a 4-3 defense, the ends get the sacks. In a 3-4, the outside backers get the sacks, the credit, and the cash.

BASE 3-4 ALIGNMENT

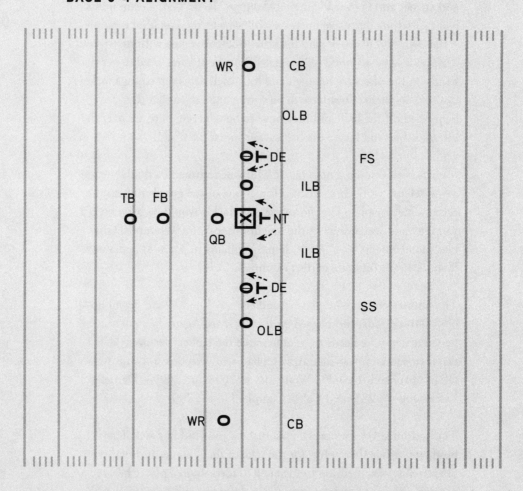

In a 3-4, the nose tackle and defensive ends line up directly across from the center and offensive tackles. If the nose tackle requires a double team, the inside linebackers will be free to make tackles.

The outside backers are the true glamour position in the 3-4 defense. They are the premier pass rushers in the mold of Lawrence Taylor—who revolutionized the position during his Hall of Fame career—Rickey Jackson, Andre Tippett, and Kevin Greene. Guys like Shawne Merriman, DeMarcus Ware, and Pittsburgh's pair—LaMarr Woodley and James Harrison—are today's prototypical 3-4 linebackers, guys with the speed to bring pressure off the edge, the strength to take on tackles, and the athleticism to drop into pass coverage.

While the Patriots built their line with draft picks, they found their outside linebackers on the free-agent market—guys like Rosevelt Colvin, Mike Vrabel, and Adalius Thomas, all of whom were standout defensive ends in college. Since very few college teams play a 3-4 scheme, NFL coaches are always looking for undersized college ends with pass-rushing skills but not necessarily the big, bulky body of a traditional lineman. During individual workouts, they'll test a prospect's agility, have him drop into the flat, throw balls at him to judge his hands, and make sure he's athletic enough to open his hips. If they have the requisite athleticism, many great rush ends in college will find their NFL home is at outside linebacker in a 3-4.

A 3-4 defense obviously needs two inside linebackers—preferably of different types. One has to be able to play over the strong side guard. The strong inside backer ideally should be a 6'3", 250-pound thumper who can step up and engage a guard with power (think the Jets' David Harris, who is 6'2", 245). The weak inside linebacker—the guy who lines up on the same side as the split end—can be a bit smaller because the guard on the weak side isn't going to get out to him as much, allowing him more free space to run and hit (Baltimore's Ray Lewis).

JOB DESCRIPTIONS: 4-3

Unlike the 3-4, the 4-3 front comes with little mystery. Unless a defense is in a Fire Zone blitz situation (which we'll talk about in the next chapter), the offense knows who's coming—the four down linemen are going to bring the heat. When they are able to get pressure on the backfield—tying up five offensive linemen with a four-man line—it's a tremendous advantage for the defense, which now has seven guys in coverage against, at most, five receivers.

You want to know what NFL teams are looking for when building a defensive line for a 4-3? Look no further than the 2009 Minnesota Vikings: Kevin Williams (6'5", 311) and Pat Williams (6'3", 317) at tackle, Jared Allen (6'6", 270) and Ray Edwards (6'5", 268) at end. Those are four guys with the size and quickness to get into the backfield and disrupt an offense.

Unlike the nose tackle in a 3-4, the two tackles in a 4-3 are penetrators. One lines up on a guard, the other shaded on the center. They use their speedy first step to get into the one gap they've been assigned, to get under the pads of the center or guard who's blocking them, and to penetrate. No one did it better than Warren Sapp back in his prime, though Chris Hovan also thrived at Sapp's spot in Tampa Bay's 4-3 front.

Smaller interior linemen aren't as much of a risk in a 4-3 scheme as they are in a 3-4. When the Jets drafted Dewayne Robertson (6'1", 308) with the fourth overall pick in 2003, they were playing a 4-3 defense under Herm Edwards. When Eric Mangini came in and immediately converted the team to the 3-4, Robertson was lost. As a nose tackle, he was too short to see the play coming at him. When ball carriers came through the A gap, he couldn't get off the block to make the play, primarily because his arms weren't long enough to maintain separation. Plus, he didn't warrant a double-team, which is the cardinal sin for a nose tackle. Eventually, Robertson was traded to Denver, where he contributed to the Broncos' 4-3 scheme…until they switched to a 3-4 after the 2008 season. Robertson subsequently was released.

The ends in a 4-3, of course, are the pass rushers and line up on the outside shoulders of the tackles. They tend to be a little lighter and considerably faster than their counterparts in the 3-4, since they need to be able to apply pressure with both speed and power. Whether it's

Jared Allen, Mario Williams (6'6", 295), Dwight Freeney (6'1", 268), or Julius Peppers (6'7", 283), these rush ends are the big-ticket items on a defense. They put up the big numbers but also cost the big dollars, which is why so many general managers are coming to the conclusion that it may be less expensive to stock a roster with 3-4 players.

The linebacking corps in the 4-3 features three distinct positions: the Mike (middle), Will (weak side), and Sam (strong side) backers. Looking at the Mike gives you an interesting snapshot of how different the two schemes are. Compare the inside triangles in each system: in a 4-3, you see a smaller, quicker linebacker lined up behind a pair of leaner, quicker tackles; in the 3-4, you have a big, stout nose tackle playing in front of a pair of big inside backers.

The 4-3 Mike backer tends to be small and quick, since he's going to drop into coverage more often, particularly to the deep middle in a Cover 2. In the 4-3, the Mike will have two tackles in front of him, occupying two or three blockers, so he's free to run to the ball. Zach Thomas (5'11", 242) was a great example during his days with the Dolphins. Guys like Carolina's speedy Jon Beason (6'0", 237) and Washington's London Fletcher (5'10", 245) are other prototypes.

The Will backer is also a shorter, faster guy who can go sideline to sideline to make plays. A team can hide him behind one of the defensive tackles and virtually guarantee that an opponent won't get a blocker on him, so they can afford an undersized player at this position. Coy Wire was a safety in Buffalo; he became a Will linebacker when he moved to Atlanta. There's no place for a 225-pound tackling machine in a 3-4 front; that type of player is unique to the 4-3 system.

The Sam backer is a bit of a hybrid player. Lining up on the strong side, he's usually the tallest, strongest linebacker, so he probably can fit just as well as an outside backer in a 3-4. He has to be stout enough to take on the tight end (or even the right tackle) when offenses run their power plays at him, but he also must be agile enough to cover the tight end when the safety is inserted into the box to provide run support. Picture

BASE 4-3 ALIGNMENT

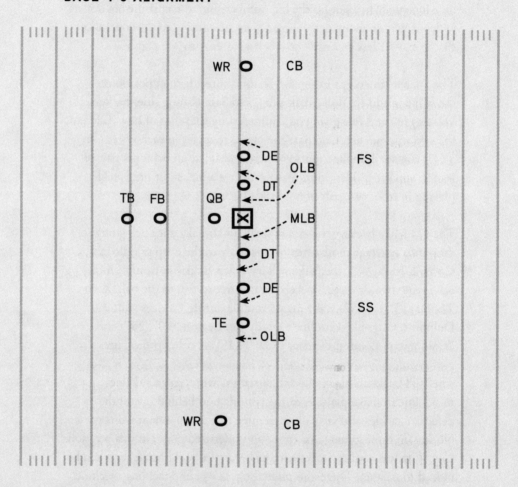

In a 4-3, every player is responsible for one gap. Defenders often switch gaps in an effort to confuse the offense.

Junior Seau during his 12 Pro Bowl seasons in San Diego and you have the textbook Sam backer. At 6'3" and 260, Houston's Brian Cushing is another excellent example.

FINDING THE RIGHT PIECES

I was down in Mobile, Alabama, watching the practice leading up to the 2009 Senior Bowl, and one of the guys who stood out was B.J. Raji, the defensive tackle from Boston College. I noticed right away he had an incredible first step, could burst into his one gap of responsibility, and would get into the backfield.

I spoke to him before the draft about whether he preferred one scheme over the other. I asked him if there was one play left in a game, would he rather play two-gap against the center or be turned loose to penetrate? His answer—"It's not even close. I want to use my quickness to get off the ball and penetrate."—told me that he'd be an ideal candidate for a 4-3 team shopping for a tackle.

Raji, of course, was drafted by Green Bay, which envisioned him as a cornerstone for its conversion from a 4-3 to a 3-4. They saw him as a nose tackle, even though he was on the short side of ideal (6'2") and his best asset—his quickness—wouldn't be utilized.

The transition worked better for the Packers than anyone could have hoped. In one season, they became the NFL's best defense against the run and second-best defense overall. The next year, they won the Super Bowl. Raji struggled as a rookie while splitting time between nose tackle and defensive end, but he started all 16 games in his second season and had developed into a key piece of Green Bay's championship defense.

Not every guy can fit any system. Raji was quick enough to play in a 4-3, but he also weighs 337 pounds—perfect for an NFL nose. Glenn Dorsey, for example, was drafted fifth overall by the Chiefs to play tackle in their 4-3 defense. But when they switched to a 3-4 front,

Dorsey (6'1", 297) was too small to play nose tackle and was moved to defensive end.

More often, you find players who are suited for one system better than the other. That is why two coaches can stand next to each other at the NFL combine, evaluating the same player at the same time, and come away with vastly different conclusions.

Heading into the 2010 NFL Draft, everyone was excited about the potential of Nebraska's All-American defensive tackle Ndamukong Suh. At 6'4", he projected to be versatile enough to play in either system. But at barely 300 pounds, he was built more like Tommie Harris than Kris Jenkins, and seemed more like a 4-3 tackle than a 3-4 nose. The Lions took Suh with the second pick, plugged him into their 4-3 front, and he became the 2010 NFL Rookie of the Year. Had he gone two picks later to Washington, who knows how he would have fared in the Redskins' new 3-4.

No matter which system a team is looking to stock, there are a couple of reliable indicators it can use to project a prospect's potential impact in an NFL defensive front.

Explosion Number

As you're reading mock drafts online and following reports out of the combine and individual pro days, you will find yourself buried under an avalanche of numbers—a player's measurables. You'll find official data for his height, weight, bench press, short-shuttle drill, 40-yard dash, and a variety of other categories. Taken individually, none of these numbers has much value. But if you plug them into the right formula, you get a better picture of what an athlete can do.

I created a formula to measure the explosion quotient for players in the defensive front seven and offensive linemen:

BENCH PRESS (number of reps at 225 lbs) + VERTICAL LEAP + STANDING BROAD JUMP = EXPLOSION NUMBER

On the snap of the ball, the front seven and the offensive line are going to engage physically. It's a series of adjacent bar fights, and we need to be able to project who has the athleticism to win these all-important battles in the trenches. This formula shows me how explosive a player is, and indicates whether he will be able to push and slide and get into position to make plays.

A prospect with an Explosion Number of 70 or higher has my attention. A guy with that capacity for explosiveness is going to win his share of bar-room brawls at the line of scrimmage, so I'm comfortable that he has the athleticism to play in the NFL.

Let's take a look at the Explosion Numbers for the 11 defensive linemen and linebackers selected in the first round of the 2009 NFL Draft:

Player	Position	Team	Bench Press	Vertical Leap	Standing Broad Jump	Explosion Number
Tyson Jackson	DE	KC	20	28-6	8-6	57.0
Aaron Curry	LB	SEA	25	37-0	10-4	72.3
B.J. Raji	DT	GB	33	32-0	8-7	73.6
Aaron Maybin	DE	BUF	22	38-0	10-4	70.3
Brian Orakpo	DE	WAS	31	39-6	10-10	81.3
Brian Cushing	LB	HOU	30	35-0	10-0	75.0
Larry English	LB	SD	24	36-0	8-11	68.9
Robert Ayers	DE	DEN	18	29-6	8-6	56.0
Peria Jerry	DT	ATL	28	31-0	9-6	68.6
Clay Matthews	LB	GB	23	35-5	10-1	68.5
Evander Hood	DE	PIT	34	33-0	9-0	76.0

As you can see, most of these guys had Explosion Numbers deserving of the first round. Tyson Jackson, the third overall pick, had a lower number than you'd like to see, which should raise a yellow flag. Jackson went to a 3-4 defense, where explosiveness isn't as important for a defensive end as it is in a 4-3. Still, the Chiefs would have liked more than one sack from Jackson in his first two seasons.

Robert Ayers also had a low number. He was named the Best Defensive Player at the Senior Bowl after a three-sack performance, but we've been fooled before by Senior Bowl performances (Blair Thomas leaps immediately to mind). There are things to like, but this might have scared me off taking him in the first round. As it turned out, the Broncos moved him to outside linebacker—a pass rusher in their 3-4 front. And he managed only 1.5 sacks in his first two seasons.

It's an even more helpful formula as you look into the deeper rounds for potential sleepers. The Texans took Connor Barwin in the second round, and he spent his rookie season backing up Mario Williams at defensive end. Some teams might have been dubious about Barwin, a converted tight end who played just one college season at defensive end. But Barwin's Explosion Number (72.3) made someone in Houston take notice. Anyone with a 40-inch vertical leap is an explosive human being.

Production Ratio

Of course, explosion is only part of the equation. I also want to see a player make plays. For that, I created a simple formula to see how many plays behind the line of scrimmage a prospect averaged per game:

SACKS + TACKLES FOR LOSS/NUMBER OF GAMES
PLAYED = PRODUCTION RATIO

Here's a look at those same 11 first-round picks from 2009:

Player	Sacks	TFL	Games	Ratio
Tyson Jackson	18.5	27	53	0.86
Aaron Curry	9.5	45.5	51	1.08
B.J. Raji	12.5	32.5	49	0.92
Aaron Maybin	16	24.5	26	1.56
Brian Orakpo	23	34.5	49	1.17
Brian Cushing	8.5	27	44	0.81
Larry English	32	57	50	1.78
Robert Ayers	9	31.5	48	0.84
Peria Jerry	12.5	37	38	1.30
Clay Matthews	5.5	13.5	50	0.41
Evander Hood	15.5	22.5	50	0.76

In this formula, I'm looking for someone scoring 1.0 or better. Consider a guy like Larry English. His Explosion Number was slightly below 70, but when you consider he averaged nearly two plays behind the line of scrimmage over the course of a 50-game college career, a team can be confident that it's getting a playmaker. He spent his rookie season backing up Shawne Merriman, and missed half his second season with an injury. Still, there may be reason to think the Chargers have something to look forward to down the road.

At first glance, the low number for Clay Matthews would raise a red flag. Rather than dismiss him outright, however, a deeper investigation into his career would show that Matthews started only his last 10 games at USC. In his senior season, he made 13.5 plays behind the line in 13 games, a Production Ratio of 1.04. A late bloomer with an incomparable pedigree, Matthews proved himself right away. He posted double-digit sack totals in each of his first two seasons, and finished as the runner-up for the NFL Defensive Player of the Year Award in 2010.

Neither formula is definitive—there's no such thing as a surefire predictor of NFL success. But when you combine a prospect's Explosion Number with his Production Ratio—Ndamukong Suh's Explosion Number was an outstanding 76.4 and his Production Ratio was a gaudy 1.47—you get a snapshot of the kind of physical tools a player brings to the table as well as what he's been able to do with them.

TACKLING A PROBLEM

No matter what base defense a team runs, playing defense will eventually come down to one thing—tackling the guy with the football. That most fundamental skill for a defensive player is really becoming a big issue in today's NFL.

Ironically, you could probably trace the decline of tackling skills back to Ronnie Lott—one of the greatest players of all time. In his 14 seasons with the 49ers, the Raiders, and the Jets, Lott was a great form tackler but preferred putting his shoulder into ball carriers. Fans loved that kind of physicality, and *SportsCenter* and other highlights shows fed their appetite by featuring hits like those each and every Sunday evening. Young players would watch Lott and wanted to emulate him—only they didn't have his speed or ability to recognize a developing play. When those young players went to throw a "Ronnie Lott tackle," they'd miss their guy.

It's not unlike the way young basketball players stopped working on their jump shots after being exposed to endless highlights of Michael Jordan dunking the ball. And now we've got a lot of guys in the NFL who want to hit like Lott but don't have the basic technique to tackle properly.

I think tackling took a big step backward when we entered the salary cap era. All of a sudden, there were limitations on the number of players a team could bring to training camp and limitations on regular-season rosters. Do the math—a team brings 80 guys to camp, 53 will be on the roster, and eight will be on the practice squad. That's 61. One or two will wind up being placed on injured reserve during camp, so now the number's up to 63. That leaves only 17 guys who are going to get cut.

As a result, teams can't practice the way they used to because they can't afford to get anybody hurt. The GM doesn't want his $2 million safety hitting his $2 million running back in practice, so coaches started holding more half-speed practices and walkthroughs, which resulted in a deterioration of fundamental skills, tackling being foremost among them.

The rise of diversified offenses and defenses has also driven coaches to spend more practice time on schemes and not enough on those fundamentals. Coaches are spending their time installing page after page after page from the playbook, making players learn 9 million different sets. That leaves a whole lot less time to practice tackling.

I believe every team should have a form tackling drill every day in practice, followed by the one-man sled drill, open-field tackling drills, and live tackling in 9-on-7 drills. None of that goes on much anymore, but in the places that it does, you notice—the Bengals made a commitment to spending time on tackling in 2009, and they won the AFC North, in part because they tackled well.

The problem has permeated the college and high school levels as well. Back in the early 2000s, I worked with Bill Walsh on an instructional DVD for the NFL's Junior Player Development program, so we could teach tackling to junior high school players before it was too late for them to learn.

Other factors have also contributed to lousy tackling technique. Today's NFL teams tend to defend the pass first, so teams are running the ball against pass defenses. That gives the ball carrier more time in space, and the farther from the line of scrimmage he is, the harder he is to tackle. Plus, receivers are getting bigger and stronger, and tight ends are more athletic than ever before. Teams are asking their linebackers and secondary to hit ball carriers that are bigger and moving faster, and yet they don't practice open-field tackling.

Smaller, faster defenses designed to defend the pass and pressure the quarterback haven't helped matters. When a defense trades size for speed, that amounts to a lack of power, and a lack of power gets a guy run over.

As you watch the replays of a defender missing a tackle, there are several things you can look for to identify where the tackler failed:

- Did the defender close the gap to the ball carrier? That's called "reducing the field." If a defender winds up having to reach for a guy, the runner is going to bust right through that arm tackle.
- Did the defender make good contact with his shoulder pads? A tackler has to bend at the knees and make sure his head is up. Too often, a defender comes in bent at the waist with his shoulders and head down, a position that negates the power that comes from his legs and his posterior.

- Did the defender accelerate his feet through the tackle? As soon as you hear the contact of the pads, the tackler's feet need to be accelerating through the ball carrier. If they're standing still, they're not maximizing their power. Similarly, look and see if the tackler's feet are too close together. If they are, he had too narrow a base and lost power there, too.
- Did the defender know who he was tackling? Defenders must have a plan for every guy they're asked to tackle. They might be able to take down the 200-pound Chris Johnson with a high tackle, but if they try to tackle the 260-pound Brandon Jacobs up high, they'll get run over. For the most part, the best tacklers will tackle low. Vikings cornerback Antoine Winfield told me he learned to tackle low because he's been a little guy his whole life. He learned that to take on the bigger opponents, he basically had to rope 'em and tie 'em. And now he's one of the best tackling cornerbacks in the NFL.
- Did the defender take a bad angle of pursuit? If a tackler reaches the ball carrier and wraps him up with his head behind the runner, he's taken a bad angle of pursuit. He's only tackling with one arm across the front of the runner. If he gets his head across the bow of the ball carrier, he can get his hips and legs and lower body into the tackle.
- Did the first defender on the scene try to strip the ball instead of making the tackle? Coaches have done a great job of teaching the strip, but that shouldn't take the place of the tackle. The first guy in is the tackler; the *second* guy goes for the strip. If the first defender to make contact goes for the strip, he has not secured the ball carrier. If that player breaks free, the second defender is now out of position to make the tackle.

If you want to watch someone who knows how to tackle, watch Ray Lewis. He is a great "key and diagnose" player, which means he picks up his reads fast, sees what's happening, knows where the ball is going to go (thanks to both instincts and film study), then attacks that point and reduces the field at great velocity. A lot of bad tackles are the result of reading and reacting slowly. If a guy can't get off his block or is slow to diagnose what's happening, he can't get disengaged in time and winds up reaching and missing the play.

Patrick Willis in San Francisco is another example of a textbook tackler. He loves contact and he's fundamentally sound—largely because Ed Orgeron, his coach at Ole Miss, ran a lot of live tackling drills. He also understands how to control his speed. Willis can run the 40-yard dash in 4.3 seconds, but he understands that you can't apply 4.3 speed the whole time. Blazing speed is a terrific asset for reducing the field, but it can work against a player if he takes a bad angle of pursuit and winds up overpursuing the ball.

The best tacklers in the game, not coincidentally, are the guys who were tackling machines in college. Because coaches are not teaching or practicing tackling at the NFL level, the hard truth is that players need to have acquired that skill *before* coming into the league. Willis, Barrett Ruud, Brian Cushing, David Harris, and James Laurinaitis were all great tacklers in college. As pros, they're coached to read and diagnose faster, and they play in schemes designed to give them the best chance to get to the ball carrier. That's a great combination for a defense, no matter which scheme it's running.

BLURRING THE LINE

Coaches like to have a base identity—something that dictates what they do best and what they can turn to in tough situations. At the end of the day, they'll fall into one of two camps—the Monte Kiffin 4-3 or the Bill Parcells 3-4. Everything in the league today stems from one of those two philosophies.

Sometimes, a new coach will have to wait before implementing the system he prefers to run, as Mike Tomlin did in Pittsburgh. I remember talking to Parcells when he first went to Dallas, asking him when he was going to install his trademark 3-4. He told me that he simply didn't have the pieces to convert right away, so he retained Mike Zimmer as defensive coordinator and continued the 4-3 scheme the Cowboys had been playing. Parcells eventually converted the Cowboys to the 3-4 after bringing in Marcus Spears, DeMarcus Ware, and Chris Canty.

Too often, a team in transition will wind up with an ineffective hybrid system as it changes personnel from one scheme to the other. A defense can have components of both, but it won't have a clear foundation.

But then there are teams who are built to do both well. And that makes them a dangerous team to prepare for.

Some of Bill Belichick's most interesting work has been switching the Patriots from one system to the other over the course of a game or even a series. He built a roster with personnel versatile enough to jump from

Q: How long does it take to convert a team from a 4-3 scheme to a 3-4 or vice versa?

A: If a team is smart about it, it should take two years. Let's say the team is switching from a 4-3 to a 3-4. Maybe three of its front seven will have the skills that could translate into the 3-4; that means it needs four guys to fill out that front seven. A team should be able to make that conversion in two drafts and one free-agent period. It may cost $40 million, but that's a different consideration.

The bigger problem is finding the players. When most of the NFL played a 4-3 scheme, a 3-4 team like the Steelers faced little competition for their kind of player. Once half the league started running a 3-4, with everyone looking for their own massive nose tackle, it became harder to land the best players for that system. Eventually, so many teams will be playing the 3-4 that teams who stick with the 4-3 will regain the advantage.

a legit 3-4 to a legit 4-3. Willie McGinest was the ultimate wild card for him—he could play defensive end with his hand on the ground in a 4-3 front on one play, then stand up and rush the quarterback from a 3-4 on the next.

Guys like Julius Peppers can do for their defenses what McGinest did for the Pats. There aren't too many of them in the NFL, and when a team does find one, he'll claim a big chunk of cash.

Ironically, it was this hybrid approach that enabled the Giants to beat the Patriots in Super Bowl XLII. Defensive coordinator Steve Spagnuolo picked up a few things that the Ravens and Chargers—both 3-4 defenses—had done to Tom Brady and incorporated them into New York's 4-3 scheme. Most people were afraid to blitz Brady, but as Spagnuolo told me, "If we played it straight, we would've died a slow death."

SO WHICH ONE WORKS BETTER?

As long as a team is playing to the strength of its personnel, there really isn't a case to be made for one scheme over the other.

Consider the defensive rankings for the 2008 season. The Steelers and the Ravens—both 3-4 defenses—were the top two defenses in the NFL. The next four teams—the Eagles, the Redskins, the Giants, and the Vikings—all played a 4-3.

In 2009, six of the top 10 overall defenses, six of the top 10 rushing defenses, and six of the top 10 defenses in sacks all ran the 3-4. At the same time, however, seven of the top 10 individual sacks leaders played on 4-3 defenses. And the two Super Bowl participants—New Orleans and Indianapolis—were both 4-3 teams. In 2010, six of the top 10 overall defenses and rush defenses played a base 3-4. But both teams in the Super Bowl—Green Bay and Pittsburgh—played a 3-4.

That said, it might be advantageous to be the only team in a particular division playing a certain way. From 2008 through 2010, all four teams in the NFC South—Carolina, Atlanta, Tampa Bay, and New Orleans—played a 4-3. That means all the offensive linemen in that division got their practice reps before division games against the same look. One of those teams might've created an advantage if it had been able to switch to the 3-4, simply because its divisional opponents wouldn't be as familiar with it. That's what Green Bay did; they were the only team in the NFC North playing the 3-4, which made it tougher for the Vikings, the Bears, and the Lions.

Also, offensive linemen don't like blocking against a 3-4. Most prefer taking on a 4-3 front—even a very good one—because with four linemen on the ground, it's easy to know who they're supposed to block. Against a 3-4, the linemen have to figure out where the fourth (or fifth or sixth) defender is coming from, an element of surprise that often favors the defense.

Bottom line, there is nothing to suggest that one way or the other is more effective in today's game.

A quick glance at recent Super Bowl champions, though, shows that both systems work—as long as you have great players who fit that system. It's not the scheme as much as it's the players in it.

Just ask Mike Tomlin.

CHAPTER 9

FEEL THE RUSH
» *Pressuring and Protecting the Quarterback Is the Key to Success*

O f all the chess matches going on throughout a football game, perhaps the most interesting one to watch showcases two of the biggest players on the field in a display of size, speed, strength, and strategy. It's a physical battle with more of a tactical component than many fans realize, and you usually can tell who won by whether the quarterback is upright or flat on his back when the whistle blows.

The chess match, of course, is the ongoing battle between pressure and protection. You can tell when it's coming just by looking at the stance of the offensive tackle—if he's standing up in a two-point stance, a pass play (most likely) is on. And then you can focus your attention on the critical matchup between one team's best pass rusher and the other team's best pass blocker.

FINDING AN EDGE

If you saw the movie *Sherlock Holmes,* you probably remember the scenes where Robert Downey Jr.'s title character experienced his slow-motion premonitions. In his mind, he saw his opponent's weaknesses and developed the blueprint for beating him moments before it happened. Well, any lineman looking to win his own matchup requires a similar plan.

Different offensive tackles require different approaches. In baseball, a first-pitch fastball hitter is unlikely to get a heater on the first pitch.

Similarly, the more a pass rusher tailors his individual game plan to a specific opponent's tendencies, the more effective he's likely to be.

For example, any defensive end (in a 4-3 scheme) or outside linebacker (in a 3-4) would have watched tape of Jets tackle D'Brickashaw Ferguson early in his career and found an exploitable weakness. Ferguson hadn't shown real leg power or an ability to drop his weight, which made him susceptible to a bull rush. Ferguson's athletic ability and agile footwork, though, made him difficult to beat with a speed rush. Eventually, Ferguson became an accomplished and versatile pass blocker, but it took time—which is a commodity first-round picks get that lower-round picks do not.

Of course, any pass rusher requires more than one move. He can't attack any NFL tackle with one approach alone. One-dimensional rushers will be neutralized, no matter how skilled they are at that one dimension. You can't be a successful pass rusher in the NFL without at least two ways of beating your blocker.

There are four basic pass rush techniques that you'll see in today's NFL.

Speed Rush
A pass rusher has to be able to get off the ball and beat his blocker on the edge. This one is a mandatory skill, because in the NFL a speed rush is also a contain rush. It positions the end outside the tackle, which keeps the quarterback from escaping to the outside edge.

Bull Rush
This is simple mass against mass, strength against strength. The rusher needs to get his pads lower than his blocker's pads, and his hands inside his blocker's hands. Then he can power rush his man right back into the quarterback.

Crossing the Face
A defender will start with a speed rush but on his third step, he'll cut back across the face of the blocker and go inside. Basically, he's luring the blocker into stepping outside to take away the angle of a speed

rush, and as the tackle moves laterally, the rusher cuts back in the opposite direction. Early in his career, Jevon Kearse was great at this. This technique won't work against a disciplined blocker who stays on his "imaginary line"—in other words, a player who drops straight back instead of leaning toward the outside.

Conversion

This is the most popular and most effective technique in today's game—converting power to speed or speed to power. The first move sets up the second. Most pass rushers prefer to convert speed to power. They sell the outside speed rush, and when the blocker widens to carry his rush past the pocket, the defender redirects right at the blocker's chest and bulls him back into the quarterback.

Jon Runyan used to talk to me all the time about the trouble he had with Michael Strahan, who was a gifted, multidimensional pass rusher. Strahan could rush with speed or strength or convert from one to the other. But the mere fact that he was able to keep Runyan guessing was as big a weapon as any of his individual moves.

There's also a time and a place for using each technique. Tim Ryan, my radio partner, used to love the gamesmanship involved in setting up his man—a strategy he learned from Richard Dent, his onetime teammate on the Chicago Bears. A smart end might hold back his best move until a critical point of a game, then pull it out when he needs it most. For example, he might lull a tackle into a false sense of security by unleashing speed rush after speed rush after speed rush. But then on a key third down—when a sack might knock a driving team out of field-goal range or force a team to punt from its end zone—he lets loose the bull rush that his scouting report told him would work against his blocker. To an untrained eye up in the stands, it appears as if the tackle had been winning the battle all game long, but in truth, the end may have been toying with him, waiting for the most important moment to play his trump card.

Then again, the chess match does go both ways. The tackle also watches film to discern his opponent's strengths and weaknesses, and he too builds his personalized game plan. How much weight does a rusher in a three-point stance have on his hand? Does his stance tip off which rush move he's going to use? A tackle may decide that an undersized speed rusher is not strong enough to bull rush him, so he may overcompensate for the speed rush, inviting the end to try all the ineffective power-based moves he'd like all game long.

Blockers counter rushers with their own variety of protection techniques. From the location of the spot where he sets up to the timing of getting his hands on his man, each tackle has his own bag of tricks. He, too, wants to remain unpredictable, and the best blockers in the game understand how to do it. Paul Alexander, the Bengals' longtime line coach, said that Willie Anderson would never block two guys the same way.

There are other factors that impact a rusher's plan of attack. One consideration is the quarterback's mobility—or lack thereof.

A mobile quarterback helps protect himself by limiting the options available to a pass rusher. Against a player like Ben Roethlisberger, the end must respect the threat of the scramble and therefore will stick to a speed rush that will contain the edge most of the time. You may watch the best pass rusher in the league go an entire game without registering a sack or any other pressure statistic…but that doesn't mean he didn't do his job.

Look at the opposing quarterback. If he's a scrambler, the end may have been told by the coaching staff to speed rush all game in order to reduce the pocket and take away the quarterback's window of escape. As a result, the quarterback might wind up completing just one pass rolling to that side the entire afternoon. That's not something that will show up on the stat sheet (and there are no contract incentives for "contains"), yet it was a win for the pass rusher—without ever getting his hand on the quarterback's jersey.

Then there are quarterback statues like Peyton and Eli Manning, guys that aren't a threat to take off under pressure and run. Against a stationary pocket passer, defensive coaches are going to remove the contain responsibilities and turn loose their outside rushers. It's called a "two-way go," which essentially is a license for the defender to rush the quarterback with his full repertoire of moves.

Obviously, this creates tremendous stress on the tackle. He can't predict what's coming, and he can't prepare for the probability of seeing a particular move in a certain situation. A competitive disadvantage exists.

Even an immobile quarterback can assist in his own protection, however. He can help neutralize a speed rush simply by stepping up into the pocket. Peyton Manning is many things, but one thing he is not is a running threat. Still, once the tackle has carried the speed rusher farther upfield than Manning's back foot, he simply steps up in the pocket and that defender has been effectively taken out of the play.

Q: Would a good defensive lineman make a good offensive lineman or vice versa?

A: Most NFL linemen played both sides of the ball in high school. When they got to college, the explosive, aggressive types were put on defense. The others wound up on offense.

Usually, a faster lineman is going to wind up on defense. The dimension of pursuit is purely a defensive trait. A defensive lineman will run about three times as much as an offensive lineman over the course of a game. There are also elements of quickness and the ability to change direction that are assets in rushing the passer.

NFL scouts love finding a guard or tackle prospect who moved over from the defensive line a couple of years earlier. They think that he'll bring an aggressiveness that they like on offense, particularly in the attacking mind-set of the zone scheme. He may also bring a quickness that was applicable to playing defense.

INSIDE JOBS

An interior lineman—whether it's a tackle in a 4-3 or the nose tackle in a 3-4—has one primary job: collapse the pocket. Sacks are gravy for these guys (Tim Ryan had 20 sacks as a senior at USC, but most of those came on plays when he was lined up at defensive end). If they can collapse the pocket, there's nowhere for the quarterback to step up, keeping him vulnerable longer to that speed rusher he otherwise could have evaded.

Inside guys don't have the same menu of pass rush moves that the outside guys do. Outside guys have free body parts—a right defensive end lined up outside the tackle won't have a blocker on his outside arm or leg, for example. Those first steps before contact keep all his pass rush options open. Inside guys usually are lined up directly across from their blockers, so their body parts are all covered. That forces them to be bull rushers first and foremost. Defensive tackles have to be able to square up and go power against power, driving their blockers backward until their heels are at the quarterback's toes.

Even as bull rushers, though, interior linemen have to develop a repertoire of moves beyond what they had in college. Most guys come into the league proficient with the "swim move." But in the NFL, an offensive lineman is going to wait for a defender to lift his arm in a swimming motion, then he's going to put his hands in the guy's armpit and knock him right off his feet. So the interior guy needs to develop a "rip move." He needs to use his first-step quickness (a key trait for defensive tackles in a 4-3) and get his hands under the pads of the guard or center he's facing. Once he can get his heels next to his blocker's heels, he's beaten his man and can go after the quarterback.

Some defensive tackles (like Albert Haynesworth in his days with the Titans) are such dominating bull rushers, they can be moved outside to defensive end in obvious pass rush situations.

More common, though, are the situations where defensive ends are brought inside to play tackle on passing downs. Instead of lining up head-to-head against a blocker and having their options limited, these converted ends will shade a bit—they'll line up on the outside shoulder of the guard, not straight across from him. The guard will have to step out to protect the B gap that the end is threatening to bull rush through, which makes him vulnerable to a cross-the-face move.

You'll also see teams get everyone on the line involved by running a line stunt, which Tim Ryan calls the best example of teamwork you will see in terms of rushing the passer.

For example, you might see a defensive end take two hard steps upfield to sell the offensive tackle on an outside speed rush. That draws the tackle out and vertical (back), expanding the B gap and giving the defensive tackle room to penetrate between the guard and the widened tackle. As soon as the defensive tackle is inside that gap, the end plants his cleats, cuts back across his blocker's face, and shoots into that B gap as tight to his teammate's backside as possible. The geometry is simple—the defenders are looking for the shortest distance between two points, which is a straight line. The bigger the loop, the more time the quarterback has to react, recover, and get rid of the football. It's paramount, as Tim says, for the end to cut that arc and make a beeline to the quarterback; that way, if the guard responds and picks up the end, the defensive tackle now has a quick path to the quarterback.

Whether it's a stunt or a straight rush, the battles that go on in the trenches on every pass play provide some of the best action on the field that most fans never see. A pass rusher may get 500 chances to rush the quarterback over the course of the season; if he manages 10 sacks, he's a star. A pass blocker also gets 500 chances to protect the quarterback; if he gives up 10 sacks, he's going to be replaced. Clearly, there is a lot at stake—with immediate and long-term ramifications—on every pass play.

» HANDS UP

There comes a time on every pass play when the rushers know they're not going to get to the quarterback. But there is still a way for them to affect the play, and it's very easy for you to see from the stands whether they're diligent about doing it.

As soon as the quarterback takes his non-throwing hand off the ball, he's made up his mind where he's going to throw. Pass rushers are watching both of the quarterback's hands as they fight to get off their blocks. The moment he sees that hand come off the ball, the rusher must stop and throw up his own hands. That's when a defender stops rushing and starts blocking, and he can still disrupt the play by closing off throwing lanes or knocking down the pass.

If you're watching your team and they're not getting to the quarterback, make sure they're at least getting their hands up to try to make a play.

THE FIRE ZONE: SIMPLE MATH, BIG PROBLEMS

Defenses are always looking for new ways to bring pressure, and no one has been more influential than Dick LeBeau, the inventor of the Fire Zone blitz.

The Fire Zone is different from the reckless blitzing we saw in the 1970s and '80s, blitzes that left defenses susceptible to the big play. Joe Namath made it to Canton beating the blitz with the bomb. Nowadays, it's not about creating chaos. It's about creating confusion.

LeBeau's innovation was finding a way to make an opponent waste its best blocker. In LeBeau's preferred 3-4 defensive scheme, one of the outside backers comes on a blitz on almost every play. On a Fire Zone call, one of the rushers jumps at the tackle as if he was a blitzer. Simultaneously, another linebacker or a defensive back blitzes from somewhere else. Then, that first rusher suddenly stops his forward progress and drops back into coverage. As a result, the tackle—often the left tackle and the team's best pass blocker—is left with no one to block. The man he was assigned to block one-on-one is no longer rushing, and it's too late for him to pick up the man who is.

It's a system that paralyzes an offense's best blocker, gets hits on the quarterback, and, because it is played under a three-deep zone, doesn't

FIRE ZONE BLITZ FROM THE 3-4

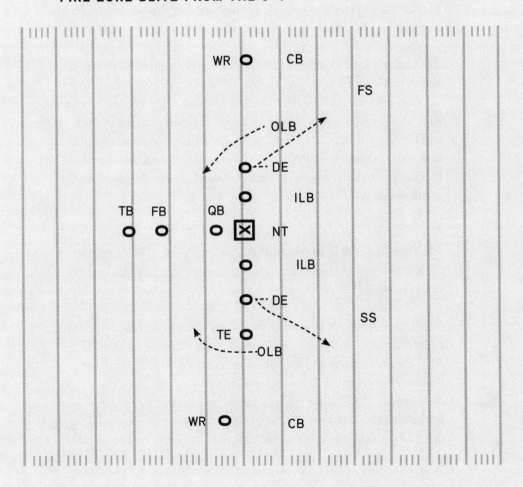

allow the deep ball. It's no wonder everyone in the league loves it and why everyone continues to use some form of it.

Even 4-3 teams.

Jim Johnson, the legendary defensive coordinator in Philadelphia who passed away before the 2009 season, found a way to do with his defensive end what LeBeau was doing with his outside linebacker. The end, who begins every play with his hand on the ground, would stab at the tackle and then drop into coverage, taking the tackle out of the play. Meanwhile a blitzer was coming through another gap and would likely be picked up by a running back, if at all.

Remember what I mentioned about teams playing an extra defensive end at tackle on obvious passing downs? When Steve Spagnuola (a Jim Johnson disciple) was the defensive coordinator of the Giants, he would have some combination of Strahan, Mathias Kiwanuka, Justin Tuck, and Osi Umenyiora on the field at the same time. Spagnuola would slide one of them—usually Tuck—down to tackle, and then he'd have that tackle drop and blitz a linebacker instead, a man the guard would usually miss.

At its essence, a pure blitz is about simple math—the defense is sending one more player than the protection is able to block. The Fire Zone takes it one step further. It convinces a lineman that he's blocking the right man and then sets another man free.

You can see the math at work at the start of every play. Before the snap, count the number of defenders in the box who may be rushing. That's what the quarterback and the offensive line are doing. The defense is almost always going to try to make them count one more than their personnel will allow them to block. You see this all the time—linebackers showing blitz but then backpedaling, or safeties sneaking down into the box before scrambling back into position. That kind of sugaring is designed entirely to create mistakes in the offense's math.

FIRE ZONE BLITZ FROM THE 4-3

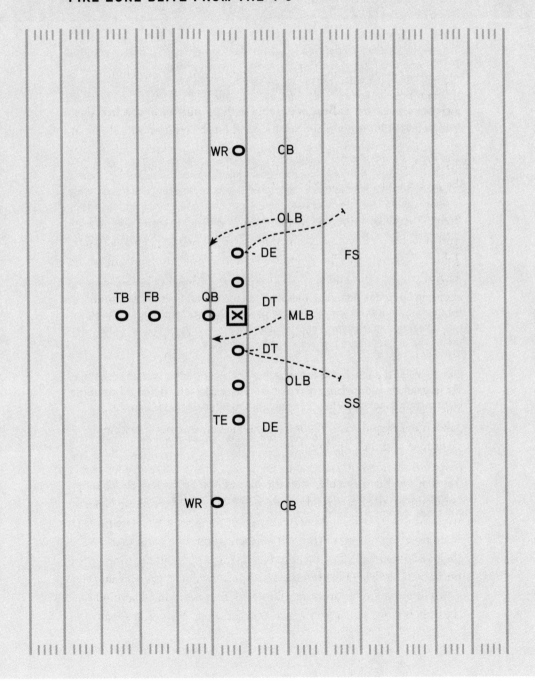

» BACK ON THE RADAR

In Green Bay, Dom Capers called it the Packers' "Psycho" defense. In the 1960s, when Hofstra was using the same defensive formation, it was called "Radar." Whatever you want to call it—and they used to call the Hofstra coach Howard "Howdy" Myers "crazy" for using it—the 1-5-5 defense (one lineman, five linebackers, and five defensive backs) made a prominent return late in the 2009 season.

The Radar defense is not designed to generate pressure as much as it is to create confusion. With only one man down and nine or 10 standing up, there's no way offensive linemen can declare who they're blocking. All the defense is telegraphing is a one-man rush, but it can blitz one man or three men or five men or no one else, and the offensive tackles don't know who they are responsible for blocking. Whatever pressure is coming will have the element of surprise.

Basically, the return of the Radar was prompted by offenses getting too good at calling out protection schemes. Many centers have become exceptional at making the right read and getting the pass rush blocked properly. The Radar was a reaction to that, forcing offensive lines to become generic and making them wait to see where the rush was coming from.

Like the Wildcat offense, this throwback wrinkle created a matchup advantage. The pendulum had swung too far in the favor of the offense, so defenses went to an old-school scheme to counter the offensive evolution.

It's something you're likely to see more 3-4 defenses doing—and something you saw the Packers do in Super Bowl XLV—since they already have one fewer guy playing with his hand on the ground than a 4-3 team does. A 4-3 team like the Vikings would have to think long and hard about asking Jared Allen to stand up on an obvious passing down. But believe me, those teams will study it and consider it.

RADAR DEFENSE

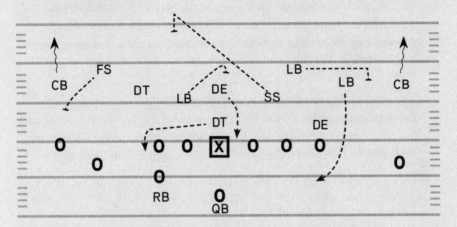

In the Radar, defenders delay lining up in an effort to confuse the offense. It is best utilized in third-and-long situations.

The Fire Zone doesn't tip its hand. Because the Fire Zone can replace any of the rushers, the offense can no longer count on the four down linemen in a 4-3 coming with any certainty. The problem is they have to prepare to block them as if they are; otherwise, they're letting a guy come straight into the backfield with a clean shot at their quarterback.

If the offense is in 11 personnel, they have seven men to protect the quarterback. The defense might show eight men in the box, but the offense has no idea if they're all coming. If the defense does send them all, someone is coming unblocked; if the pressure doesn't result in a sack, it's likely to force the quarterback into a bad decision, which can be just as effective.

If you're sitting in the stands or at home watching your team get Fire Zoned to death, start watching where the dropper goes after he drops into coverage. Remember, in a 4-3 front, that guy is probably a lineman, so playing in coverage is not one of his strengths. Even if he is athletic enough to cover a receiver, he's going to be getting to his zone late; he has to sell the tackle on his rush first, which necessarily means he'll be late into coverage. So if I notice that Justin Tuck is dropping back into the hook zone, I'd want my team to send a receiver on a 15-yard curl route right behind him. No way can the defender get there in time.

The three-deep zone being played in the secondary, compounded by the defender coming free on the blitz, makes it nearly impossible to make a big play against the Fire Zone. But an offense can complete short passes against it, especially if it can get a receiver beating the dropper to his zone.

CHAPTER 10

GOTCHA COVERED
» How Defensive Backs Do Their Thing

In 1994, I was with the Jets as we prepared for Pete Carroll's first draft as the team's head coach. Pete believed in the principles of man-to-man coverage, so we spent a lot of our draft preparation looking for cornerbacks who could line up in a receiver's face, force him out of his route, and blanket him all over the field. Press corners need to have the agility to mirror a receiver's cut and the speed to turn and run with the fastest deep threats in the game, and our job was to find one.

We got our man with the 12th pick in the draft: Aaron Glenn. He was ideal for the scheme Pete wanted to play, and he wound up having a solid 15-year career.

Fast-forward five years. By 1999, Pete and his successor Rich Kotite had come and gone. The Jets were in their third season under head coach Bill Parcells and defensive coordinator Bill Belichick. Glenn was an established veteran coming off back-to-back selections to the Pro Bowl, but he was no longer the ideal cornerback for the Jets. Belichick loved Aaron as a person and appreciated his skills, but he was looking for something different. Belichick preferred more of the prototypical Cover 2 corner—in other words, someone bigger and stronger—and he was willing to sacrifice speed for someone better suited for run support. As for Glenn, the player who was a cornerstone in one coach's defensive system was just a square peg in another coach's scheme.

Glenn's situation represents the classic philosophical difference in defensive back play: man-to-man versus zone coverage. Similar to the fundamental differences between a 3-4 and a 4-3 front, the principles a coach believes in regarding the four-man shell in the back of his defense will dictate what kind of players he needs on his team.

MEN ON THE CORNER

Let's look at the different job descriptions for cornerbacks in the two schemes. On the snap of the ball, a man corner will turn his back to the quarterback and run with the receiver. Run support is secondary; shutting down his man is the priority. In a zone scheme—especially the Cover 2 popularized by Tampa Bay—the corners always face the quarterback so they can be heavily involved in run support. The man corner turns and runs, while the zone corner relies on backpedaling so he can react if the offense calls a run.

In man coverage, the cornerback shadows his man wherever he goes, which is a unique ability, especially in a era when the rules allow little chance to be physical with a receiver. It's tough to be a lockdown corner

Q: A defender can't bump a receiver after 5 yards. How can he overcome rules that seem to favor the receivers?

A: The defender has to use those 5 yards to his advantage. He has to be able to press his man, get his hands on the receiver, jam him, and funnel his release. If a cornerback can affect a receiver's get-off, he throws off the timing between the receiver and the quarterback. Plus, he's eliminated a set of routes the receiver could potentially run. Once the receiver has been funneled outside, the defender no longer has to worry about the square in, the curl, or the slant. He can focus on, say, the fade or the out route. He knows what the receiver can't do, so he can overplay what he thinks his man has to do.

with your hands tied, and so the truly great press corners are extremely rare and extremely expensive.

Lester Hayes and Michael Haynes played at a time when corners could put their hands all over receivers all over the field. Today, life on the island for a guy like Nnamdi Asomugha is vastly different. After the 2008 season, the Raiders made Asomugha the most expensive blanket in history, signing him to the richest contract ever given a defensive back. His talent and reputation grew to the point where opposing quarterbacks would rather climb into the Black Hole to mingle with the rowdiest Raiders fans than look in Asomugha's direction. In the two seasons after signing his record deal, Asomugha was thrown at so infrequently, he had one interception and 10 passes defended—all for the price of $15 million a year.

By comparison, zone corners pass off their receivers, either inside to a linebacker or deep to a safety. And this is where a lot of fans get confused. You need to understand which principle your team is playing, if for no other reason than knowing who to blame when the opponent completes a deep pass against it.

Let's say your team is playing a Cover 2 zone—which means two safeties line up deep and each is responsible for half the field. The corner faces the line of scrimmage and backpedals, carrying the receiver vertically until a second threat appears in the flat. The corner then releases the first receiver, expecting the safety to pick him up, and comes back to cover the flat. If the quarterback hits that first receiver in stride along the sideline, many fans think the corner got beat deep; in reality, he passed the receiver off to the safety who didn't close the gap quickly enough to defend the pass.

Some coaches prefer a man-to-man scheme because it's so easy to see which players are making mistakes. There's no gray area in man coverage the way there is in a zone scheme. You know who got beat.

It's easy enough for a fan in the stands or at home to identify which coverage a corner is playing before the ball is even snapped. Just look at

COVER 2

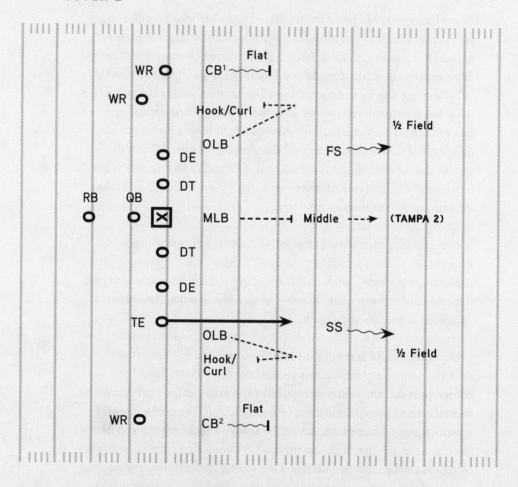

In a Cover 2 defense, each safety is responsible for half of the deep field. The cornerbacks and three linebackers are responsible for five "underneath" zones. (In the Tampa 2 defense, the middle linebacker drops back to cover the deep middle of the field.)

the hips of the cornerback: if his ass is toward the sideline, he's playing zone.

Zone corners line up to the outside of the receiver, funneling him inside where the safety or linebacker can pick him up. Man corners line up inside the receiver and try to force him outside. They use the sideline as a second defender and try to lure the quarterback into throwing a deep fade or other lower-percentage passes. The cardinal sin in man coverage is a corner allowing the receiver to cross his face on the snap of the ball and get inside, which compromises the integrity of the coverage. That receiver is going to be open, and there's no help coming from anywhere else.

Of course, if fans can read coverage that easily, you better believe that quarterbacks and receivers will figure it out, too. Wide receivers these days are trained to read coverage as early as high school, and they have routes specifically designed to beat both zone and man coverage.

Against a zone, receivers will look for holes in the coverage; when playing against man, the goal is to gain separation. They're often given option routes so they can find a way to beat the coverage they identify: if the corner squats in the flat, they'll run a slant; if the corner backpedals, they'll run a 9-yard stop route.

Those option routes are why most teams in today's NFL play a combination of coverages. Even Monte Kiffin, the iconic defensive coordinator in Tampa Bay, played more man-to-man coverage with his cornerbacks than most fans realize. Sure, he played it mostly on run downs when the probability of a pass was low. But that added dimension to his defense gave receivers and quarterbacks something they had to think about.

Coaches and coordinators can and must play both man and zone—they just need to be aware of which players they have on the field at any given time. Dan Marino has talked to me about waiting for the occasions when Ty Law, a top-tier zone corner, would sneak into man coverage. Marino took advantage of Law's limitations whenever he could.

CORNERBACKS: MAN COVERAGE

Man coverage: The corners face the receiver, not the quarterback. It is critical for them to jam or push the receiver outside, using their inside hand.

CORNERBACKS: ZONE COVERAGE

Zone coverage: The corners face the quarterback, not the receiver. Most of the time, their job is to funnel the receivers toward the inside where other defenders are waiting, and then play the zone they're assigned.

Q: Is switching between man coverage and zone as hard for a cornerback as the adjustment a lineman would make switching between a 3-4 and a 4-3 scheme?

A: It might be harder. There's such a difference in the skills needed to play cornerback in one system or the other.

Zone corners like Ty Law, Ronde Barber, and Asante Samuel have made their living squatting in the flat. But asking them to turn and run with a receiver, to mirror him around the field, is a whole different ball of wax. Instead of looking in on the quarterback, they now have to watch the receiver's face. All the old cues that they used to use to gain an advantage no longer apply.

In zone, the corner would play his area and pass his man over to the next defender. But in man, a corner has to cover a receiver like Lee Evans, who has 4.2 speed. When he takes off on a 9 route, that corner is going to need a burst of speed he's never needed before.

This chess match is much more complex than simply shifting coverages from play to play. A tremendous amount of gamesmanship goes on before the snap as the cornerback tries to disguise the coverage he'll be playing. He may line up with his back to the boundary, showing zone, but then jump inside just before the snap. That simple move might be enough to make the receiver run a route that doesn't match up well against the actual coverage.

Ultimately, there are several factors that will dictate the kind of coverage a defense will call on a particular play, perhaps the most overlooked one being the mobility of the quarterback.

When I would present a scouting report to a defensive coach, the first thing he'd ask about was the quarterback's ability to escape the pocket. Was he a full-fledged runner who would take off and run? When Donovan McNabb was young, his mobility limited the kinds of coverage you could play against him. He'd spot the corners in man coverage under two safeties back in a Cover 2 zone, send his receivers on routes that would clear out the corners, and then run for a first down. A guy like Ben Roethlisberger is more of a mover than a scrambler—his intent is to elude pressure but not to cross the line of scrimmage; his top priority is always throwing the ball. A quarterback who is a statue allows a defense more coverage opportunities because it doesn't have to worry about getting beat by his feet.

Other factors that affect going man or zone include offensive formations (against an I formation, the defense doesn't have to worry about either the fullback or tailback as an immediate pass-catching threat); personnel groupings (a team's pass-run ratio when 21 personnel is in the game might dictate the coverage); down and distance (a coach may choose to play zone in a 3rd-and-long situation); and, of course, the skills of the receivers (a double team may be required if the offense has a true No. 1 receiver).

A relatively new coverage dictator is the potential vertical threat of the tight end. When the 2008 Patriots came out in 11 personnel, teams had to identify whether the one tight end was Benjamin Watson, a prominent target for Tom Brady, or David Thomas, who was more of a traditional blocking tight end. Watson caught 22 passes in 2008; Thomas caught 21 in his first three seasons combined.

The evolution of the tight end is reason enough to put Shannon Sharpe in the Hall of Fame. He changed the way the position is played and how tight ends have to be defended. When guys like Tony Gonzalez, Dallas Clark, Antonio Gates, Owen Daniels, and Vernon Davis are in the game, a defense may be facing 11 personnel but, in reality, the presence of that receiver makes it a 10 personnel grouping (one back, no tight end, and four receivers). The defense has to be prepared to substitute accordingly.

Most teams defend 11 personnel with a nickel defense (five defensive backs) and defend a 10 personnel with dime (six defensive backs). One key for a defense is whether the tight end is lined up next to the tackle or in the slot. When your team is facing a tight end with great receiving skills, watch to see where he lines up and then count how many defensive backs your team has on the field. You should be able to tell before the snap of the ball whether the matchup favors your defense or the tight end.

Q: Can you have a great secondary without a great pass rush or vice versa?

A: Everyone has heard of coverage sacks—when the coverage in the secondary prevents the quarterback from going to his first or second read, forcing him to hold the ball long enough for the rush to get to him. But the flip side of the coverage sack is the pressure pick. Sometimes a quarterback knows he can't get a pass rusher blocked, so he takes a three-stop drop and gets rid of the ball before the pressure gets there. The cornerback anticipates a quick throw and jumps the route—that's exactly what happened in Super Bowl XLIV, when Tracy Porter's pick of Peyton Manning sealed the Saints' victory.

The secondary and the pass rush really have to work hand in hand. If I have a great coverage team and force the opposing quarterback to make his third read, the rush still must get there. If it doesn't, the quarterback is going to find that third option is open. That's what happened during the Giants' run to Super Bowl XLII: teams rolled their coverage to Plaxico Burress and jumped Jeremy Shockey, but they couldn't get pressure on Eli Manning, who regularly found third option Amani Toomer.

Basketball fans can tell when their team is playing a 2-3 zone defense. Baseball fans can see when their middle infielders are positioned at double-play depth. Football fans can look for similar clues and anticipate the action; you can sit in your seat and look at the matchups on every play to see whether your defense is using the right coverage.

When the opponent comes out in 21 personnel, you know your team shouldn't be in the traditional Tampa 2 zone coverage. You should also check to see if one of the safeties has dropped down into the box (essentially becoming an eighth man in the defensive front) to defend against the increased probability of a run.

SAFETY CONCERNS

That brings us to the role of safeties, a position undergoing a radical change from its roots. In the past, a team used to have four safeties on its roster—two strong safeties who could come up and support the run (Ronnie Lott and John Lynch, for example), and two free safeties who could play deep coverage either alone in the middle of the field or covering half the field in a Cover 2 scheme (players like Ed Reed and Brian Dawkins).

Today, a team must have a contingent of safeties on the roster who as a group can perform these four functions: drop into the box to support the run; play deep middle coverage; cover half the field in two-deep coverage; and blitz.

If a team can find a guy who has three of those traits, it will probably try to lock him up with a seven-year contract. A guy with two of those traits will still be very useful, and he'll probably get a four-year deal.

The more versatile the safety—and the more of those jobs he can do— the more time he'll see on the field and the more effective a weapon he'll be. The best-case scenario is a single safety who can do all four things, but exceptional athletes like Troy Polamalu and Bob Sanders are rare. A player of that caliber never has to come off the field, regardless of the game situation or the offense's personnel group. Teams must keep their eyes open for special players like that, even if they're currently playing another position. Consider a guy like Malcolm Jenkins, who the Saints took with the 14th pick of the 2009 NFL Draft. He won the Thorpe Award as a cornerback at Ohio State, but he came into the league at 6'0" and 204 pounds. He can cover a wide receiver, defend either the deep middle or cover half the field in a two-deep zone, and he's stout enough to play the run. That's why the Saints moved him to safety in his second season, and he's the model for the kinds of safeties we'll soon see in the NFL.

The flipside of the multidimensional safety is a safety who can check only one of those boxes. That guy is going to get cut because he'll be exposed too easily. Look at Roy Williams. The guy made five Pro Bowls from 2003 to 2007 with the Cowboys and was one of the league's best in-the-box strong safeties. Once they realized he was unblockable, however, teams in the NFC East found a different way to neutralize Williams. They all deployed vertical threat tight ends—Jeremy Shockey (Giants), Chris Cooley (Redskins), and L.J. Smith (Eagles). They would flex their tight ends and force Williams out of the box and into coverage. As dominant as he was against the run, his one-dimensionality eventually forced the Cowboys to cut him.

Being a one-dimensional safety is also exploited by true hybrid running backs—guys such as Chris Johnson and Ray Rice—who are as good at catching passes as they are running the football. If a team has a back with the receiving skills of a Reggie Bush, it sends him in motion to the tight end side and there's nowhere for an in-the-box safety like Williams to hide. He has to cover someone.

Fortunately, safeties are developing more versatility at the college level than ever before. The traditional offenses you used to see at the college level—the two-back running game of the Big Ten or the triple-option three-back attacks of the old Big Eight—forced a particular style of defense that bred the wrong kind of safeties for the NFL game. With the spread offense having taken over the college game, college defenses need safeties who can do it all as much as those in the NFL do.

Of course, no new trend is without its flaws. As Jeff Fisher always tells me, the problem with safeties who can cover and provide you matchup advantages is that they're smaller than their predecessors. These new safeties are faster but less sturdy, they tend to break down faster, and they predictably have problems matching up against the few teams that still play power football in the NFL. Miami head coach Tony Sparano loved to send out his 22 personnel—with 230-pound backs Ronnie Brown and Ricky Williams, and two mammoth tight ends in 255-pound Anthony Fasano and 270-pound Joey Haynos—and ram the ball down the throats of smaller defensive backs.

That is why teams need a collection of safeties who complement one another's strengths and cover up their weaknesses. When a coach sees 21 personnel with a pass-catching tight end and a back who can catch the

Q: If prevent defenses never seem to stop an offense's momentum, why are they used so frequently?

A: The prevent defense has the clock on its side. All the defense has to do is keep the play in bounds and keep the clock running. Coaches know the offense will take shots deep against them, so they'll protect deep against the quick score, and they'll defend the sidelines. They can do that because they don't really have to defend anything in the middle of the field.

A lot of fans prefer that their team just stick with the defensive scheme that put it in position to win the game. But you have to remember that your team was playing that defense when the offense was in a different set of circumstances. When your defense was working, the offense was still trying to run the ball. Now, the opponent is probably going to abandon the run and is in four-down territory. What your team had been doing all game long no longer applies.

ball on the field, the Roy Williams–style strong safety goes right to the sideline in favor of a smaller, faster safety who can play the pass. When the Dolphins load up their 22 personnel, in comes the traditional headbanger of a strong safety.

Safety had never been a position where we saw much situational substitution in the past. Defenses substitute cornerbacks for linebackers in nickel and dime coverages, and they pull out the big, slow defensive tackles in pass rush situations. But as safeties continue to evolve to match the evolving offenses they need to defend, we will begin seeing situational safeties to counter specific personnel groups in certain down-and-distance situations.

CHAPTER 11

WHAT'S SO SPECIAL?

» The Strategy Behind Special Teams Deserves
Your Attention

To most football fans, special teams are like air bags or cholesterol—nobody pays attention to them until there's a problem.

Special teams became back-page material for the New York newspapers in December 2010 thanks to Sal Alosi's sideline trip and DeSean Jackson's last-second punt return against the Giants. But despite its name, special teams is usually not where fans turn for the sensational and the scandalous.

Too many fans, in fact, view them as a chance to hit the fridge or beat the line to the men's room. Too few realize that special teams plays—kickoffs, punts, field goals, and extra points—account for 20 percent of all plays in an average NFL game. A team runs about as many special teams plays in a game as it does running plays.

The truth is not enough coaches devote the necessary time and attention to special teams. You can tell the coaches who do; they're the ones who practice special teams right in the middle of practice, with everyone involved. The less successful teams tend to relegate special teams sessions to either before or after practice, and they don't involve their offensive or defensive starters.

In part, that's because the bulk of special teams players aren't specialists the way they used to be. Coaches like Bill Belichick always like to keep a small core of guys for their special teams. Since the advent of the salary cap era, teams have not had the luxury of dressing—or even carrying—a core of players who are special teamers first and foremost. Aside from the punter, the kicker, and perhaps the long snapper, the rest of the 53-man roster consists of players whose primary jobs are either on offense or defense.

The caliber of special teams play across the league—particularly on the cover teams—reflects that.

Typically a special teams coach is handed a bunch of rookies and young players who didn't play special teams in college, guys who were told that if they wanted to make the roster, they'd *have* to play on special teams. The special teams coach has to start from scratch, teaching those players everything he can over the course of the preseason at the same time they're also learning their regular positions. Inevitably, the players go into the regular season unprepared for everything they will see. They're destined to stray from their lane assignments, overpursue returners, and make fundamental tackling mistakes. That's why you often see a flurry of punts and kickoffs returned for touchdowns the first three weeks of the season.

The special teams coach continues to work with his young players, and by October they begin to show signs of improvement. But by November, starters have gotten hurt and those young guys are pressed into playing more snaps on offense or defense. They'll either have their special teams duties removed entirely or they won't get as many practice reps during the week, since their time is now spent getting up to speed at their regular position.

Jason Pierre-Paul was a great example in 2010. The Giants' rookie was just learning how to play special teams when Mathias Kiwanuka got hurt. Pierre-Paul had to focus on the position the Giants drafted him in the first round to play. Instead of being reminded about blocking out by the special teams coach on the sideline, he was on the field playing defense. He was out there when the Giants defense forced an opponent to punt, and then he had to turn around and go rush the punter.

So the Giants had a player who was physically exhausted, mentally stressed, and more prone to making mistakes. Eventually, the Giants put Kiwanuka on injured reserve, committed Pierre-Paul to seeing significant defensive snaps, and had to replace him on special teams. In cases like that—which happen all the time—the replacement tends to be a guy off the practice squad or a free agent off the street, and the special teams coach is back to square one again.

It doesn't help that the composition of most 45-man active rosters is lacking guys with the size, speed, and skill set that used to make them special teams stalwarts. The extinction of the traditional fullback has cost special teams its prototype player, as has the evolution away from the blocking tight end. Now, special teams are filled predominantly with receivers and running backs—who aren't trained tacklers—as well as linebackers and safeties. There's an abundance of those players, especially on teams that play a 3-4 defense.

A team that plays a 4-3, though, will dress five linebackers for a game instead of eight. If you look at a team that plays a 4-3 defense, runs a spread offense out of primarily 11 personnel, and has a vertical threat tight end, you can predict they're going to suffer some special teams issues.

THE PUNT GAME

Instead of making the mad dash to the beer vendor, fans in the stands should focus on a few factors as soon as the punt units take the field.

First are the basics—wind and weather. You can tell immediately whether the conditions are going to play a factor.

Then look at where the returner is lining up to field the punt. Usually, he will line up as deep as the deepest ball he expects to get. In other words, he prepares for the punter's best effort, since he doesn't want to be backpedaling to field a punt. So, if a team is facing Shane Lechler, and he's averaging 47 yards per punt, you can expect the returner will line up about 55 yards deep (unless the wind is an issue, one way or the other).

Next, turn your attention to the guys lined up wide on both sides of the field for the punt team, known as "fliers" or "gunners." Does the receiving team have two men on the fliers or one? If they have two on each flier, they're setting up for a return; if they have one, they're setting up for a block.

Finally, count the men on the line of scrimmage. If the block is on, the returning team will have eight men up front. Try to determine if they're lined up 4 by 4 (four men to either side of the ball). If they are, they're probably setting up for a middle return, since there's no advantage created by rushing 4 by 4.

When the receiving team is going for the block, there will be an overload to one side or the other. You can also look for their best rusher. Is he on the overloaded side or not?

Sometimes, the overload is designed to put pressure on the snapper. If a team overloads to its right, the center will have to step to his left on the snap of the ball. When a guy has to worry about snapping the ball 15 yards deep and then sliding to protect, he can become real average in a hurry or miss the punter altogether.

All that information can give you a much clearer picture of what to expect on the ensuing punt. But there's more you can look for before the snap.

For instance, where is line of scrimmage? If the ball is inside the 14-yard line, the punter is going to be kicking out of his end zone, and that forces a change to his delivery.

Most guys are three-step punters. That means they catch the ball, step right, step left, and then punt. But when they're in their end zone, they don't have the space to take their usual approach. So, they're forced to become two-step punters: catch, step left, and then punt.

When a team is punting from its end zone, it's usually a pretty good time to go all out for a block. No team will fake a punt from its own end zone. The punting team will bring its fliers in tight, diminishing the rushers' angles to the punter and making them easier to block. Of course, that means they don't have fliers getting upfield to cover the kick, which usually leads to a directional punt out of bounds.

The strategy of directional punting became a point of considerable debate during the 2010 season, especially after DeSean Jackson and Devin Hester returned punts for high-profile touchdowns on consecutive days in Week 15. A lot of coaches agonize over kicking the ball out of bounds. Ironically, these coaches have no problem instructing their quarterback to throw the ball away instead of taking a sack. But there's something that makes them too proud to admit they can't cover game breakers like Hester or Joshua Cribbs.

It doesn't help that special teams coaches reinforce their head coaches' stubborn contention. "Of course we can cover him," they'll say, which is exactly what the head coach wants to hear. It's hard for an assistant coach to tell his boss that the unit he's responsible for can't get the job done.

Another complicating factor is the kicking style of the punter.

There are two kinds of punters. One is in the Sean Landeta mold—long yardage, short hang time. His punts go 55 or 60 yards, but they're line drives. These guys tend to outkick their coverage, giving a guy like Hester time to catch the ball without any pressure, plus an extra 10 yards to set up his return.

The second kind of punter makes a living on his hang time. His punts travel 40 yards or less in the air, but they're so high, there's no chance for a return. These punters don't like to kick the ball out of bounds.

Against hang-time punters, the return team doubles the fliers and prevents them from getting upfield. Then, the guys on the line hold up

PUNT BLOCK

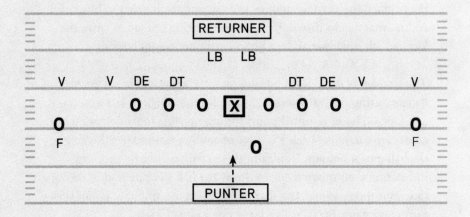

PUNT RETURN

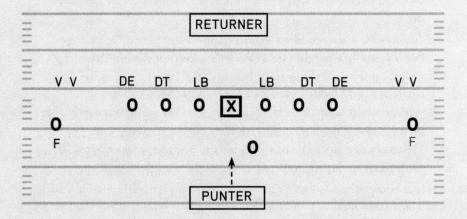

If the return team has two defenders on each flier, it is likely setting up for a punt return rather than a punt block.

the front, essentially becoming blockers at the line of scrimmage instead of actually rushing the punter. That allows the returner to set up 40 yards away rather than 55, and now he's in position to return a punt even after substantial hang time.

When a coach does decide to kick away from certain returners—as more are grudgingly doing—there are a few mitigating factors he must consider. Most teams like to punt the ball toward their own sideline. That's for a variety of reasons, not the least of which is that receiving teams like to return the ball up their own sideline. Coaches feel that officials are less likely to call clipping on a return right in front of the returning team's bench.

But what if the wind is blowing the ball back toward the middle of the field, away from the punting team's sideline? That will complicate a punter's ability to take the wise, conservative approach.

A team planning to punt the ball out of bounds may need to call a third-down play to set up that punt, which coaches are reluctant to do. To give the punter the best opportunity to get the ball out of bounds, the coach needs that fourth-down snap to originate from a specific part of the field. It sounds like a defeatist approach to offensive strategy, but if you're beating the Bears by a touchdown in the fourth quarter, why wouldn't you be thinking that way? Bill Parcells played the field-position game like that his whole career.

Ultimately, the decision comes down to a coach's confidence in his coverage team. Against most punt returners, a coach shouldn't be afraid of giving up a touchdown. There were only 13 punts returned for touchdowns in 2010 (as opposed to 23 kickoff returns), three of which were by Hester.

The more prevalent concern is the 20-yard return. That's two first downs' worth of field position lost on the change of possession. Hester led the league in 2010 with nine returns of 20 or more yards. Danny Amendola had seven, and Brandon Banks and Captain Munnerlyn had six apiece—though none of them broke one for a touchdown.

Do you kick away from Antoine Cason, who averaged 16.5 yards per return, or Julian Edelman (15.3)? Probably not.

What about a guy like Mike Thomas? In 2010, he averaged 10.5 yards per return; anything over 10 yards is noteworthy. He had three returns of 40 or more yards, including a 78-yard touchdown. That's enough evidence to suggest teams should consider punting away from him in critical situations.

But Thomas also fumbled three times in his 34 returns. Davone Bess averaged 11.4 yards per return, but he fumbled three times in 25 attempts. You have to respect the threat, but I'm punting to guys like that. When punting to a fumble-prone returner, watch the first guy down on the coverage unit. When the returner calls for a fair catch, that guy will go right behind him, hoping for a fumble. But why would you put the ball in the hands of someone like Hester—who had five returns of 40 yards or more, three touchdowns, and never fumbled—when you don't have to?

One last thing to watch for in the punt game is the fake. Obviously, fake punts are most successful when the opponent doesn't expect one. But there are a few indicators that should alert a team to the possibility.

When a team has the ball close to midfield and it's 4th-and-short, the defense has to be prepared for the fake. Gary Zauner, the former special teams coordinator for the Vikings, Ravens, and Cardinals, wouldn't even have his team in return formation in those situations. First off, the chances of getting a solid return are not great. Instead, the returner is focused more on setting his heels on the 10-yard line and not touching anything over his head. Zauner often would keep the regular defense on the field to protect against the fake, and he'd call for only a token rush to make sure the offense actually kicked the ball.

It becomes even more likely when the punting team has a great defense. A guy like Rex Ryan feels so confident in his defense, he's much more likely to try a fake punt. He feels like even if the Jets don't succeed, his defense will stop the opponent anyway.

SIDELINE PUNT RETURN

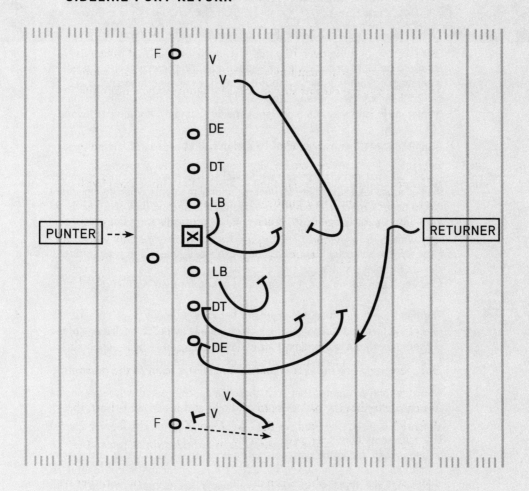

Teams prefer to set up a punt return to their side of the field whenever possible, hoping officials might be dissuaded from calling a clip or a block in the back in front of their own bench. For sure, coaches from the opposition will be pointing out every infraction when a punt is returned up their sideline. To set up the actual return, the returner will catch the ball, drive five yards upfield to sell the middle return, then cut behind the wall being set up by his return unit.

» WHEN THEY LEAST EXPECT IT: THE SURPRISE ONSIDE KICK

Most onside kicks occur under one specific set of circumstances. It's late in a game, one team is trailing, and it doesn't have enough timeouts to get the ball back through a defensive stop. The linemen come off the field, the hands team goes in, and they run a declared onside kick that's not fooling anyone.

A better time to run it? The other 59 minutes or so.

I wish we had more surprise onside kicks. There are more opportunities than coaches take advantage of, unconventional moments when the opponent would never expect it. Sean Payton opened the second half of Super Bowl XLIV with a surprise onside kick. Andy Reid has used it to start games, too.

First off, it's perfectly disguised. The kickoff unit lines up like it's a normal kickoff, five players on each side of the ball, same personnel. There's nothing to suggest something's up, so opponents set up for their normal return.

The opportunity is presented regularly because so many guys on a kickoff return unit turn and run before the kick is actually made. Often, it's one of the slower guys who has a landmark he needs to get to, so he bails early to make sure he's on time to be in position to block for the returner.

When that player vacates that spot, there's a space created where an onside kick can be targeted.

This isn't something coaches will decide to try spontaneously. The surprise onside is included in the game plan. The head coach will turn to the special teams coach during the week and say, "Be ready for me to call one at an unconventional moment." Or maybe the special teams coach noticed on film that a player on the opposing team bailed early. Then he looked at several games' worth of that opponent's kickoff returns and he determined that was the player's tendency, not an aberration. After he presents his findings to the head coach, they might decide the onside is worth a try.

Once they've identified their target, they will practice that onside kick during the week. They want to make sure the kicker can put the ball in that area without changing his approach to the ball. The second a kicker's approach changes, everyone on the receiving team yells, "Alert! Alert!" They've scouted the kicker's approach. They even know how he sets up the ball on the tee. If he likes it straight up and down and they notice he has set it up slightly tilted, that triggers an alert for an onside kick.

The kicker will also have to decide whether he's going to pop the kick high in the air—like hitting a wedge shot in golf—or squib it. The pop requires kicking underneath the ball, while the squib requires making contact with the top of the ball. The kicker has to determine which one he's most comfortable with, and which one he can do without changing his approach. Then he has to convince his coach he can do it consistently.

The head coach will watch the kickoff unit during practice and evaluate the execution. He's not going to consider using the onside in a game until he's confident his guys can do it. A call like that is all on the head coach, and not every head coach has the right temperament to make that call. You might expect it more from an offensive-minded coach (like Payton and Reid); they tend to risk more in order to get an extra possession of the ball. A defensive coach sees special teams as an opportunity to win the field-position battle; he'd rather put his opponent on a long field as often as he can.

But you can look for situations where a surprise onside would be a great idea. Watch to see if someone along the front line bails. Hint: players do it all the time.

Then, look to see if the opponent is a "wall return" team. Teams with particularly speedy runners might be looking to set up a wall return and run it toward their sideline (where most returns ideally are run). You may notice that the guy routinely bailing is lined up on the far outside, opposite his team's sideline. You know he has the farthest to run, so he's more likely to turn and run early. That's the perfect opportunity for a surprise onside kick—which, ideally, would be headed toward your own sideline.

Remember, officials rarely call offside on a kickoff, even though the kicking team is offside fairly often. If I knew I could get away with crossing the line early, while the opponent is bailing out of an area at the same time, I'd call a surprise onside kick every week.

» A RETURN TO THE PAST

It's not often that a progressive league like the NFL takes a step backward. But it did just that with its decision to move kickoffs to the 35-yard line, back to where they used to be in the early 1990s.

In doing so, the league reduced one of the most exciting plays in football—the kickoff return—to near irrelevance.

The move was made with an eye toward safety, and that aspect can't be criticized. Still, the decision is not without collateral damage, the primary casualty being the game-changing return.

There were 23 kickoffs returned for touchdowns in 2010—one every 11 games, or essentially one every week. Back in 1993, when kicks originated from the 35, there were only four. That's one out of every 64 games. Instead of one a week, you're now looking at one a month. The new rule might cost teams 20 touchdowns a year.

It's not just the returns for touchdowns we'll be losing but the return that flips the field immediately. In 2010, there were 113 kick returns of 40 or more yards (one every 2.2 games). In 1993? Only 57 (one every 4.5 games).

This rule will dramatically change the role of the kickoff returner. First off, teams won't be able to keep a player unless he can also return punts or contribute on either offense or defense. Players like Leon Washington—who returned three kicks for scores in 2010—could be facing extinction.

When those players are no longer on the roster, someone else will be forced to fill that position. And if those players don't display the kind of game-breaking abilities of Washington or Devin Hester or Brad Smith, other teams will pooch punt and force these lesser talents to return the kick. That's not exactly a recipe for excitement.

The new rule will also force a kick returner to decide when to take the ball out of the end zone. It used to be that a returner would take a knee if the kick went two yards deep into the end zone. Now, returners will have to determine whether the hang time (or lack thereof) dictates that they return a ball kicked into the end zone. Special teams coaches will spend a lot of time with their returners, firing balls at him with the JUGS machine, and the returner will have to learn to judge which ones he needs to bring out.

THE KICKING GAME

There's a perception that the placekicker is the loneliest guy on an NFL team. That's because his job is so specialized, he rarely has the opportunity to interact with his teammates on the practice field.

It's also because in the NFL, 25 percent of the games are decided by three points or less. Kickers don't get too many opportunities to take the field; when they do, it's often at a critical moment.

But contrary to what the caricature might suggest, kickers are not fragile. It's helpful if you look at them like golfers. They are slaves to their routines, so exacting and precise that if any part of their approach is disrupted, the results are predictably disappointing.

That's why it's so important for a kicker to be comfortable with his holder and his snapper. Ideally, the snapper delivers the ball with the laces in perfect position so the holder can put it down according to the kicker's preference. That's something they will have discussed and practiced together thousands of times: the kicker wants "perfect laces" (laces out) and the ball tilted 6 degrees to the outside. And when teams make changes to any part of the snapper-holder-kicker formula, it can take a long time to get everyone on the same page.

It's never as simple as snapping the ball, getting it down, and kicking the ball through the uprights. The tiniest of issues can throw off the routine. You can see it on the replay when the snap is high or off-target. You can see it when the holder is marking the spot with his fingers, and then that spot suddenly moves. Maybe the snapper is also the starting center, and maybe he's tired after a 10-play drive that set up this particular field-goal attempt. Anything that throws off the mechanics even slightly is a problem.

When things go bad, it can often be traced back to the kicker's head—not the inside as much as the outside. A placekicker needs to keep his head down through his entire leg swing, just as a golfer needs to keep his down during his backswing. A kicker's head comes up early when he is anxious to watch the flight of the ball, and usually he's not going to like what he sees.

Getting into their heads, though, is one of the most common ways a coach will attempt to defend against a kicker. Opposing coaches like to "ice" the kicker, calling a timeout an instant before the ball is snapped and after the placekicker has gone through his whole routine. The idea is to get the kickers to dwell on their kick, to let the pressure get to them. Problem is, it doesn't work nearly as often as you'd think.

Veteran kicker Neil Rackers told me that good kickers actually like the icing. When an opposing coach calls a timeout just before the ball is snapped, the kicker often will continue through with his kick. That gives him a chance to gather some information he didn't have before.

Against veteran kickers, sometimes the threat of icing is more effective than the icing itself. If I was a coach, I wouldn't call timeout against certain kickers because I wouldn't want to give them the chance to figure out the wind or the field condition. But I would be animated on the sideline, yelling at the officials, and make it appear like I'm about to call a timeout. Maybe the kicker will anticipate the timeout and not be fully prepared to kick it clean when it counts.

I know a lot of fans hate icing and would prefer it wasn't part of the game. To me, if it has even a slight chance of working, a coach might as well try it in certain situations. If it's the last play of the game and he has one timeout left, why not?

CHAPTER 12

FBI: FOOTBALL INTELLIGENCE
» *Teaching the Game at the NFL Level*

By now, you can see that quarterback isn't the only position on the football field that requires a sharp intellect. Linemen, skill position players, defensive backs, and the entire defensive front all have things to consider before every play. Yes, football often comes down to whipping the ass of the guy in front of you, as my radio partner Tim Ryan likes to say. But he'll also be the first to admit that if it was just about physical play, there would be a lot more players finding it easier to keep their jobs.

To make it in the NFL, players need to possess football intelligence—FBI—and teams are regularly being forced to let go of great athletes who don't have it. So I think it's worth exploring how the mental part of preparation impacts the physical play on the field.

TESTING FOR FOOTBALL SMARTS

Everyone knows about Bill Belichick's FBI. He has one of the NFL's best football minds and has been one of the game's great innovators. But he knows as well as anyone that ideas alone don't equal victories. It's not what Bill or any other coach knows—it's what the *players* know. That is why Belichick places such a high priority on finding players who are smart enough to execute the scheme he's running.

When Belichick is evaluating college players, he likes to give them a quiz. He'll meet a prospect in a classroom on campus or in a hotel room at an all-star game, put the player in a chair just like a student, and talk through five or six or 10 things that the Patriots do. He'll tell a defensive lineman, for example, that he'll be down in a three-point stance on first and second down, and in a two-point stance on third down. He'll diagram it all for them on a white board. Then they'll take a break. When they reconvene, Bill will sit down, send the kid to the board, and say, "Now, tell me everything I just told you."

From there, he can make a judgment call on whether the player has shown the requisite FBI to succeed in his system.

When he went out on his college tour before the 2008 NFL Draft, Belichick ran Jerod Mayo through that classroom drill. Mayo went to the board and repeated everything he'd been told right back to Belichick. He could envision himself and identify his responsibilities in every play. Sold: Belichick drafted Mayo with the 10th pick of the first round. Mayo became the NFL's Defensive Rookie of the Year and was voted New England's defensive captain before his second season.

More often, players reveal something during a Belichick test that makes them radioactive to him. I remember being with him at the scouting combine, sitting in a hotel room and waiting for prospects to show up for their interviews. A player would show up and Bill would welcome him into the room with a short "Nice to see you, have a seat," never giving the kid a chance to build rapport. Immediately, he'd shut the lights off and turn on the tape of the player in college, usually footage of the guy not playing great. He'd ask the player, "What was the call here?" He was testing the player's ability to recall specific situations, a skill that is essential in the NFL.

The player would have no time to prepare. He'd answer the question off the cuff, then Bill would watch another play and ask, "Okay, what happened here?" He was trying to determine how the kid handled adversity. Was he going to admit he made a bad read, or was he going to blame someone else?

I remember one prospect in particular who blamed his coaches for one of his bad plays. When the interview was done, the kid left the room

Q: If football intelligence is so important, why are smart players so often passed over in favor of athletically gifted players who don't know how to play?

A: There are a ton of guys in the NFL with brains but not the physical skills to play the game. They're called coaches.

Before a team cuts a player for being dumb, it has to examine what he's being asked to do. Is their terminology counterintuitive? Are the coaches putting 300 plays on his plate and overwhelming him with information?

Take a guy like Braylon Edwards. Sure, fans get frustrated with his drops. But coaches feel they can teach him to catch the ball; what can't be taught is the ability to get down the field and get as open as Edwards can.

and Belichick crossed him off his list of candidates. Bill knew that sooner or later, he would wind up having to correct that player in the locker room at halftime or make an adjustment on the sideline, and he already knew how the kid would respond.

Belichick is not alone in this quest to measure FBI. Everyone wants smart players. It's just that some guys are better at identifying them than others. On the other hand, a good evaluator knows when to discount FBI a little relative to a player's position. Playing running back isn't rocket science, but playing quarterback, offensive line, and middle linebacker is harder than it appears. If you're a team playing multiple zone looks on defense, it might help to have cornerbacks with a high football IQ. But if you're a team playing press coverage on every play—like the Packers did throughout the 2009 season—you may look at a prospect differently. That guy needs speed, long arms, and the ability to change direction more than FBI. A coach can just tell that corner "Go cover that guy," and that's all he needs to know.

But for the most part, FBI is an important consideration for any position, and for many reasons.

First, there's the playbook. It's 400 pages. Is a player going to be able to read and understand the entirety of what his team is trying to do?

Then there's the installation pace. One day at practice, a coach will teach Cover 2, then the next day he's teaching Cover 3. Can a player absorb all the things he's being asked to learn at a breakneck pace? Can he find ways to connect the different principles and make it easier for him to remember his responsibilities?

Can he read and retain a scouting report? Let's say he gets a tip sheet on Saturday night telling him that when the opponent is in 21 personnel and an I formation, it runs 90 percent of the time. Will he remember that in the heat of the moment?

Can a guy learn two positions if necessary? He may go into the game as the starting Sam linebacker, but injuries might dictate that he's got to move over and play the Will. Likewise, can a guard learn to play tackle without getting any reps at practice?

How good is his recall? In the first quarter of a game, an opponent may be doing something the team hadn't practiced for, so the coach says, "We're going to go back and do what we did in Week 6." Can a player recall that old game plan? Bill Cowher had a strategy for short weeks that relied heavily on his players' ability to recall information. If his Steelers were playing a Thursday night game, he felt there wasn't enough practice time to install a whole new game plan. Instead, he'd dust off a game plan from earlier in the season and expect recall to take over.

As a defensive coach, the late Foge Fazio used to do a great job of staying on his players about all the things they'd need to remember.

He'd tell them, "I know we're not practicing the 'Cat' blitz at all this week, but I've been with these coaches a long time and I know that against this opponent, the head coach is going to call a 'Cat' blitz." He'd make sure to refresh his players' memories. I used to warn players with the Jets that Foge was not going to be their coach forever, and that they weren't always going to have someone reminding them what to review. They needed to start thinking like Foge and ask themselves, "What do I need to refamiliarize myself with, just in case?"

FBI plays a much bigger role in the game today than it used to. If you watch films from the 1970s and '80s, you will see simple offenses and even simpler defenses. Now, offenses are coming out in 10 different personnel groups in the first 10 plays, and they're facing defenses with 9,000 variations—base, big base, nickel, dime, fast dime, and so on. What used to be a checkers game is now a chess match, and FBI is a necessary trait if a team wants to stay in the game.

You always hear from rookies that the biggest adjustment to the NFL from the college game is the speed. They're not talking necessarily about the physical speed of the game, that a linebacker used to face a guy who ran a 4.6 and now he's facing guys who run a 4.4. It's the *mental* speed of the game—the speed at which they need to respond—that kills young players. A player can't react physically until he understands what he's seeing.

Veteran running back Thomas Jones told me that it wasn't until his third year in the NFL that he learned what it took to be a professional every single day. It wasn't a matter of commitment; it took him that long to understand how to make the most out of a scouting report, how to watch film, and how to pick up tips that enhanced his own plan of attack.

It's a big reason veterans are so important to a team's development. The Patriots called Junior Seau out of retirement midway through both the 2008 and 2009 seasons. Sure, he was an insurance policy in case one of their younger linebackers got hurt. But his greatest contribution was teaching the young guys how to prepare and how to learn.

That may be one of the most overlooked elements of Peyton Manning's greatness. When Marvin Harrison retired before the 2009 season, Peyton knew the development of the Colts' young receivers—Austin Collie and Pierre Garcon—would be critical. To get them up to speed, Manning became more than their quarterback; he was their professor. He was the private tutor you go to after class when you realize listening to a lecture wasn't going to be enough. And when Anthony Gonzalez went down, Collie and Garcon were ready to step into the sophisticated Colts offense, thanks to all the one-on-one work Peyton put in with each of them back in the spring. All the extra attention paid off: the Colts reached the Super Bowl that season.

Q: What do teams do during their bye week?

A: The first priority is to get players healthy. Most coaches will give their players three to five days of downtime, especially if the bye comes late in the season. If a guy is even slightly injured, he'll shut down completely. Some players even use the bye week to get minor surgeries—they go straight to the hospital on Sunday night after their game is done to get a scope or clean out a joint—and then they have extra time to recover without missing a game.

It's also a great time to get back to basics. Most coaches don't introduce a game plan during the bye week, so they spend their time reviewing. And if the bye is early in the season, some coaches use that time to install things they didn't have a chance to do during preseason.

Once the bye week is done, teams go right back to their regular week of practice.

TEACHING NFL PLAYERS

There have been plenty of studies done about learning styles, not just of football players but of students in general. The three prominent entry points for information are auditory (hearing), visual (reading or seeing), and tactile (touching or physical demonstration). It's always interested me that coaching staffs don't take the time to figure out how their players learn.

I did a workshop in Green Bay once, and I asked all the coaches to bring a list of the players they were responsible for. Next to each player's name, I asked the coaches to write down the type of learner that guy was: auditory, visual, or tactile. Nobody knew for sure what any of their guys were.

I asked them, "You're the communicator of the information, and you don't know how your guys learn? How can you possibly expect them to process what you're telling them?"

In presenting the game plan during practice each week, coaches use all three methods. They start by talking through the game plan (auditory), follow it with film study (visual), and then hold practices and walkthroughs (tactile). It hadn't occurred to these coaches that there are a lot of guys who learn better via one method or another. A player might arrive at the walkthrough still not clear about what he's doing, and the coach's first reaction is to chew him out without realizing that perhaps he's not an auditory learner.

I asked those coaches if they had good players who fell asleep in film study. Every one of them raised his hand. Well, those players may be auditory learners or tactile learners; film study isn't as effective with them.

Perhaps a team has a group of guys who had 3.0 GPAs in college. College is primarily an auditory experience; those guys learned from lectures. Another team might have a bunch of guys who struggled in class but were pretty good in their labs. Those are tactile learners.

Coaches need to do a better job identifying how their players learn, and many of them may need to rethink their teaching strategies.

Let's say you're a receivers coach and you realize all five guys are tactile learners. Why wouldn't you take them out on the field in sweats at 8:30 AM and walk them through your teaching points? Then they can go into the 9:00 AM meeting with a better chance of picking up the game plan.

Most players don't realize what kind of learning suits them best, and most coaches don't know what kind of learners they are either. Most coaches tend to teach the way they themselves learn, so they may spend 15 minutes in a meeting and then watch film for hours and hours because that's how they figure things out. Those coaches can't be truly effective if they can't teach their players in all three modes.

THE SIDELINE CLASSROOM

It's critically important for coaches to know how to reach their players when it comes to game day. It's one thing to have the capacity to digest information in a classroom or back in the dorm room during training camp. But when the game's going on, and a player is under fire and trying to make adjustments on the sideline, how can a coach best communicate with his guys?

As we've discussed, two pictures are taken on every play, and pictures obviously are a form of visual learning. Guys who respond to that method should be able to make their adjustments by what they're seeing in the pictures.

Often you will see a group of offensive linemen sitting on the bench while their coach is yelling and diagramming like a lunatic in front of them. That's both visual and auditory learning.

But how many times have you seen a coach grab a player and physically work with him on the sideline? Imagine you are the receivers coach and your X receiver just went down with an injury. His backup is in the game, the cornerback is pressing him, and this receiver can't get off the line. If he's a tactile learner, showing him pictures or explaining to him how to get off the press isn't going to help. Instead of threatening him or begging him, you'd need to get physical with him. A coach should put his hands on the receiver the way the corner has been, or get another receiver to demonstrate it for him.

I love watching offensive line coach Alex Gibbs on the sideline. He may be the best line coach in football. He'll stand up with a guy and show him why his hips aren't sinking. He knows how to get his players to respond.

Think about your own learning experiences. What do you pick up from listening to the game announcers? Do things only become clear for you when the analyst draws it out on the Telestrator? I'm amazed at how many fans have doubled their football knowledge by playing video games like *Madden NFL*. They may not understand the strategy behind it, but they know what plays work against man-under and what works against two-deep coverages because they've figured it out playing video games.

When you see a player on your team struggling to make plays, you should ask yourself, "Does this coaching staff know how to get through to him? Do they know how to teach him?"

They better figure it out because an NFL team can't afford to flunk its students. In the world of the salary cap, a team has to make it with the guys it has. So the coaches better know how to get the best out of them.

CHAPTER 13

GETTING ORGANIZED
» *The Ideal Chain of Command in Today's Front Offices*

The first act of Mike Holmgren's tenure as president of the Cleveland Browns after he was hired in late 2009 surely was going to be firing head coach Eric Mangini. That was the prevailing wisdom in anticipation of Holmgren's hiring—that a man with his NFL pedigree would want his own guy molding his new team in his image.

As is the case with most foregone conclusions, it turned out to be wrong.

Holmgren retained Mangini for a second season so he could evaluate the coach for himself. That reinforced a point I've been making for years: the top decision maker in an organization needs to be a football guy.

When a man in Holmgren's position needs to make a critical call—and it doesn't get more critical than picking the head coach—it's invaluable that he understands what it means to be a head coach in the NFL. Holmgren came to Cleveland's front office with 161 wins under his belt—including a Super Bowl ring—and the self-assurance that comes with them. He recognized what Mangini had tried to do in his first year with the Browns, and he knew that the plan needed more time to play out before it could be evaluated fairly.

When Holmgren fired his coach, it was after doing his due diligence. A football decision made by a football guy.

Team presidents don't need to have Holmgren's résumé (few men in football history do). But if they didn't cut their teeth on the practice field or walk miles of sidelines in a coach's shoes, then they need to hire a head coach who they can entrust to make all the football decisions.

Two other organizations brought in new leadership in the aftermath of disappointing 2009 seasons. Both hired new head coaches—Mike Shanahan in Washington and Pete Carroll in Seattle—and gave them final say. The main reason Pete left USC to return to the NFL was because Paul Allen was willing to give him control of all football decisions. He'd been in systems set up the other way twice, and they didn't work.

I've talked about Pete's experience with the Patriots many times with their owner, Bob Kraft. Bob's first experience in the league was with Bill Parcells, who was trying to mold Kraft into the kind of hands-off owner every head coach loves. When Parcells left—after famously asking for the right to buy the groceries for the meal he was being asked to cook—Bob replaced his gruff former coach with Pete, a guy he liked personally, a guy who reminded him of his son, and a guy he would have fun working with. But he didn't give Carroll the keys to the kingdom; instead, he set up a three-headed monster, with power evenly divided between the coach (Carroll), the personnel guy (vice president of player personnel Bobby Grier), and the business guy (COO Andy Wasynczuk). When the head coach can be outvoted 2–1 in matters of football significance, a team has a fundamental problem.

Kraft's structural experiment didn't pan out, and he's still quick to admit it. To Bob's credit, he learned from that mistake. He brought in Bill Belichick and gave him all the power, and we all know how that turned out.

That's the model I fully endorse—give the coach the last word in decisions regarding his team. Whether the team president hires the coach and then hands him the reins or the coach is hired directly by the owner (as was the case with Shanahan and Carroll), the head coach needs to be sitting atop the football food chain.

In the case of a young, unproven, or first-time head coach who isn't yet ready for that level of control, it certainly helps if the team president is a former coach, like Holmgren in Cleveland. For a coach to prove to me that he's ready for full control, he'd need to demonstrate to me a passion for the personnel side of football. A lot of coaches pay lip service to the importance of personnel, but they find it tedious to be in those personnel meetings. I believe he has to understand it, appreciate it, and, ideally, be passionate about it, and then he needs to be able to communicate clearly to the scouts exactly what he is looking for.

In an ideal situation, then, the general manager should support the head coach. His job should be to run the daily functions of the building. Again, he should have enough personal football experience that he can be a valuable contributor to the head coach's vision. Too many GMs come up from the financial end of the business and have little football sense.

Ultimately, the GM's role should be to take care of everything that doesn't land on the head coach's plate, from handling the complexities of contract negotiations to hiring the non-football staff (coaches should maintain control over their coordinators and assistants). He can't be seen as outranking the head coach, especially in the eyes of the team. Players look at the front of the room and decide for themselves who the boss is, and that impacts the coach's ability to manage his players. Players need to know who they are accountable to.

Once you have the top of your front office pyramid in place, you have to determine what your management philosophy is going to be. To me, there are three models that have proven successful during the 2000s. These teams are not necessarily alone in doing business this way, but in my opinion, they are the archetypes.

The Eagles Model—Buy Early and Often
As soon as the Eagles identify that a player is going to be good, they lock him up to a big deal. They never let a player approaching his prime test the free-agent market. A guy in the second year of his four-year rookie contract hasn't seen big money yet, so he's more likely to sign a

contract extension out of fear he'll get hurt and will never cash in. It may seem like a big deal at the time, but two years down the road, the player's still locked up and the deal is much more reasonable.

The Eagles have done a great job of projecting how much cap space they'll have to work with in the future. I can ask Eagles president Joe Banner "How much cap room do you think you're going to have in 2014?" and he'll say, "Think? I know exactly what I'm going to have."

Part of what makes this model so effective is that the Eagles tend to not offer signing bonuses. Instead, they give players higher salaries and roster bonuses. After all, why buy a car on credit and incur all those hidden costs when you can pay cash up front? In other words, they don't get hit every year with signing bonuses that count against their cap; instead, they pay the roster bonus and clear their books every year. That's why they never find themselves in cap jail down the road.

The Patriots Model—Make the Tough Calls

Bill Belichick is the best there is at making hard decisions. The Patriots simply don't allow themselves to get emotionally attached to players. They make business decisions and let guys go if they think they won't be worthy of their next contract. Do they sometimes give up too early on a player? Sure. Ty Law was let go after 10 years in New England; five years later, he was still **in** the league. But the Pats knew the next deal he would sign would be too much for them to commit to an aging player, so they said good-bye to a productive and popular member of their franchise.

To be able to make those tough calls and succeed, a team has to consistently excel with its draft picks. The Patriots have been able to back up their stars with future stars. They coach the young guys for a year or two, then cut the veteran, replace him with the guy they've been grooming, and then draft the new guy's eventual replacement.

Sure, there are guys who the Patriots never had to say good-bye to. Tedy Bruschi played 13 seasons in New England. The 2010 season was Kevin Faulk's 12th with the team. These guys defied the fate that so many of their teammates faced because they never priced themselves out of town. Belichick told them, "We'd love to keep you, but only at this price." And the players came to realize that he meant it.

The Ravens Model—We Want What's Best For You

When a player is about to enter the free-agent market, some GMs will tell him, "I think your market value is X. So, I'm prepared to offer you X." But players don't like to be told what they're worth; they want to find out for themselves. That's why Baltimore GM Ozzie Newsome tells his players to go test the market and find out what their value truly is. He'll say, "Go out and find the best deal that you can, then give us a shot to match it. If the money turns out to be equal, we assume you love being a Raven and that you'll want to be here."

Doing it that way, Newsome never offends anyone. Essentially, he secures a handshake right of first refusal with every player about to hit the open market. It worked with Ray Lewis, and now players believe Ozzie's word is worth its weight in gold. They know the team will bring a player back if he deserves it, but if some other team is willing to overpay, Newsome won't break the bank to bring back a good player with a bad contract. He'll congratulate his former player for the big score and move on to the next negotiation.

PERSONNEL RESPONSIBILITY

After the president, head coach, and GM, the next two most important football positions are the directors of the college scouting and pro personnel departments—two of the most vital and underappreciated parts of any franchise. If a head coach has the final say in all personnel matters, these are the guys who make sure he is completely informed before making his decision.

The director of college scouting isn't someone who spends a lot of time around the team's headquarters. When Phil Savage was the GM in Cleveland, he was a familiar face in the facility. But when he was the scouting director in Baltimore, he actually lived year-round in Mobile, Alabama. He spent 250 days of the year on the road. The pizza delivery guy was more of a presence at the team's headquarters than Phil was. Any director of college scouting needs to be in the field, investigating exactly who's out there and gathering any information that will make his boss' decision easier.

He also has to be organized enough to manage a staff of about eight scouts and the inconceivable amount of information they collect. The one thing I'd want in a director of college scouting is someone who recognizes the value of football experience in his scouts. Too many teams nowadays are trending toward younger (aka cheaper) scouts. Yes, they're gung ho and energetic and comfortable with technology, and those are all advantageous traits. But scouts have to be more than information gatherers.

Too many inexperienced scouts are willing to say, "Just give me a stopwatch and a credit card and I'll go find who's out there." But information is no substitute for football acumen and experience. That's why I'd want at least half of my scouting staff to have football backgrounds, preferably as coaches. If a team sends an inexperienced guy to a campus, the team's head coach is going to say to him, "Here are the films, good luck." But if a team sends a scout with a football background, someone who can speak the coach's language, that scout is going to learn a lot more about a prospect than he can find out on film.

The director of pro personnel plays a similarly vital role. He needs to be able to advise the ultimate decision maker on pretty much every single player in the NFL. When free agency began in March 2010, there were 531 players available. The pro personnel director needs to know every single one of them, in addition to which guys are likely to be signed immediately and which guys a team can afford to wait on before acting.

Perhaps his second-biggest task is managing the emergency list. The director of pro personnel must always stay on top of players looking for a home in case one of his players gets hurt or a coach wants to cut someone during the season. There's a pool of free agents that few fans ever think about—guys who have never been on an NFL roster, guys who went to someone's training camp and got cut, and guys who played in Canada, the Arena League, or in Europe. At the end of the day, the head coach will decide who to pick up in an emergency situation, but it's the director of pro personnel who needs to make sure the coach is fully informed.

Amazingly, the pro personnel department used to be a one-man job. When the salary cap was introduced in 1993, every team added a second body—the assistant director of pro personnel. Now, most teams have a third guy on staff, someone who understands the cap and players' values in the marketplace (this is a role I filled for three different head coaches in three years with the Jets: Bruce Coslet, Pete Carroll, and Rich Kotite).

There's another rung in the hierarchy that is far more important than most people realize. There are three people who are in contact with every player, every day: the strength coach, the trainer, and the equipment manager. So the guys in these three positions need to be salesmen for the front office's vision. Frequently, they're the ones who have to explain to a player what's going on; why, for example, losing 10 pounds or switching to a new position would be a good idea.

The strength and conditioning coach is particularly important. If the players don't buy into his system, it can destroy a team's football program. That's why I wouldn't be interested in hiring someone for this position who hasn't already proven himself at the pro level. I want a guy who has gotten the job done with grown men. Players need to have motivational techniques sold to them, and it's a much easier sell coming from a guy with pelts on the wall, someone who has trained a bunch of All-Pros. If the players like the strength and conditioning coach, they're more likely to be around during the off-season. If they don't, they head home and hire a buddy to work out with, which is often a recipe for gaining weight or getting injured.

As you can see, one job requirement remains consistent at every level of the organizational chart: real football experience. If you want to build a football team, you're going to need football people.

THE SEASON STARTS ON MARCH 1

The one date that every football fan must keep an eye on is March 1—the day free agency and the hard work of building an NFL dynasty begins.

It's the day when a team's roster for the new season officially starts to take shape, when fans can start to see how the identity of their favorite team will be tweaked, refined, or overhauled. In that way, it's really the day the new season begins. Your team gets better or worse before it ever puts the pads back on, and it all begins March 1.

To understand how rosters are put together, you have to understand all aspects of the personnel process. Here's an overview of what happens throughout a calendar year.

March
As the first phase of free agency unfolds, teams will fill as many positional needs as they can—though they're at the mercy of salary cap limitations and the interest level of players wanting to come play for them. And what they can't solve, they'll address in the draft.

Don't buy into the myth that free agency has killed the possibility of building a dynasty in the NFL. Teams that write good contracts and evaluate free agents properly can still keep their own players and sign the right free agents. It's how New England managed to win three championships in four years.

All the while, contingency plans are being made in case they aren't able to sign a free agent they had targeted and also wind up missing out on their Plan B in the draft.

April
You can assume your team won't fill every hole with its draft. Ideally, a few key ones will have been addressed, but teams are still shopping after the draft, when the second phase of free agency starts.

A lot of players get cut after the draft. A lot of players also reenter the process—including guys your team may have cut but is looking to recall.

May-June

This is the slowest period in terms of personnel acquisitions. Once training camp begins, the personnel staff has lost the attention of the coach. He knows that if he's forced to acquire someone he hasn't coached throughout training camp, he's probably better off without him. If the player came from a system similar to what a coach is running, he might consider it. But rarely will the personnel staff try to tell a head coach in July or August that they've found the answer to a problem area—and that answer was just cut by somebody else.

July-August

As coaches and players are preparing for the season at hand, the college scouts are dispatched to campuses to start evaluating draftable prospects, and the pro scouts head out to preseason games. They are responsible for evaluating players on other teams who may get cut, as well as any players the team might consider acquiring through a trade. They'll spend extra time evaluating guys who are in the final year of their current contract and will become free agents after the season.

September-December

Throughout the season, the pro personnel staff builds and maintains a board—just like the board teams create for the draft—ranking every player in the league, including its own. A team will list, for example, all 32 starting centers in the league. Knowing that its own center is 12th on that list provides an important jumping-off point for decisions the team might face after the season.

January-February

If there's going to be any change in the coaching staff or front office, it's probably going to happen right after the end of the season. Teams heading in a new direction need people in place to steer them accordingly as soon as possible.

This is when the general manager, the player personnel director, and probably the head coach combine the research and scouting reports being compiled for both college prospects and NFL players. Those two distinct sides of the personnel department have not intersected all year, but this is the point they literally come together.

Teams spend the five weeks leading up to March 1 finalizing their courtship priorities—identifying the players they want to bring in for a visit and those they want to start negotiating with at 12:01 AM, as soon as free agency begins.

CHAPTER 14

TAKE YOUR PICK
» *Mastering the NFL Draft Can Make or Break a Franchise*

Fifty million people watched the 2010 NFL Draft on ESPN. More people tuned in to watch Sam Bradford hold up a Rams jersey than saw any NBA, NHL, or Major League Baseball playoff game. In other words, there was a greater audience for an off-season football event than a postseason game in any other sport.

The first day of the draft is a huge day on the calendar for any NFL fan, but for NFL teams, it's the culmination of a year's worth of work, the end of an intense period of scouting, scrutinizing, investigating, and identifying the next generation of impact players.

Preparations for one draft begin literally as soon as the previous one ends. Even sooner, in some cases. I know teams who dispatch their scouts *during* the draft because there are spring games on college campuses that same April weekend. But the process begins in earnest during spring ball, and the college scouting staff is on the front lines of all eventual draft decisions.

Most teams have somewhere between eight and 10 scouts in the field doing the critical legwork. There are a few oddball teams, like the Bengals, who send out only one or two scouts; they prefer their coaches do the work after the NFL season and feel that allowing non-decision makers to gather information is not the right way to do business. But teams like that are the exceptions.

Typically, a scouting staff will have three senior-level guys, each with more than 20 years in the business, and then a bunch of young guys looking to break into scouting. Each scout is assigned a region of the country. Eventually all of their evaluations funnel up to one super scout—either an assistant general manager or the GM himself—who will personally scout each of the top 50 or 75 players on his team's list.

The scouts initially hit the road (they usually live in the regions they cover, but they live more out of suitcases than their home address) from April through May. They're gathering initial information on the top 100 draftable players in their region as determined by an initial list circulated each spring by the various scouting services employed by the NFL.

For the most part, they're off the month of June—at least off the road. Then they report to NFL training camp in July to watch the players the team just drafted and learn what the team is doing on offense and defense. A scout can't gather truly relevant and helpful information if he doesn't understand how the team will utilize players at every position. When the Green Bay Packers switched from a 4-3 defense to a 3-4 prior to the 2009 season, the shopping list for their scouts changed dramatically.

A scout also needs to recognize what the team's needs are and what they will be. He'll build and maintain a database that will remind him, for example, that his team has three centers on the roster, what their contract status is, and how the coaches and pro personnel department feel about them.

As soon as colleges begin practicing, the scouts then hit the road for the long haul; they'll remain on the hunt until early December and the end of the college season. They'll take a comprehensive list of draftable players in their region and start watching them in their preseason camps. They'll wind up at some practice or another virtually every day of the week and be at games every Saturday, so they'll get to evaluate prospects both at practice and in game situations. They'll try to see everyone once early in the season and then again in the second half. This way, they can observe how a player is developing, how he's recovering from an injury, or how he's answering questions that might have been raised earlier about his skills. For example, a scout may have found out back in spring practice that a certain player hardly ever hit the weight room; in the fall, a scout will revisit that strength coach to see if the kid's work ethic has improved.

Remember, scouts are not decision makers; they are information gatherers. It is their job to provide the super scout all the conceivable data he needs to figure out which players he should see in person as the season goes along.

Once the college regular season comes to an end, scouts have numerous bowl games and all-star games to attend. The last stop on the college calendar is the Senior Bowl, which marks the first time that the NFL coaches will get to see players for themselves. The director of college scouting will put together a book of scouting reports for each assistant coach, who will then hit the practice fields in Mobile, Alabama, armed with rankings and grades for all of the players the team is following.

The coaches will watch as the prospects go through drills conducted by the NFL staffs coaching the two Senior Bowl squads—typically, they are the staffs of the last two teams eliminated from playoff contention. And that's pretty much when the coaches start to disagree with the scouts' assessments. In the best organizations, there are fewer disagreements because the scouts have been trained by coaches and scouting directors what to look for. One of the troublesome issues created by frequent turnover—either in the front office or the coaching staff—is that the scouts become less clear on what they're looking for because their team's priorities are changing all the time. In stable places like Pittsburgh— where Kevin Colbert always knew what Bill Cowher was looking for— the scouts do a better job than most at finding players who can do what the Steelers like to do.

After the Senior Bowl, the entire scouting staff will gather for the first of many meetings to start fine-tuning their analyses. Coaches will have begun formulating their opinions based on what they saw at the Senior Bowl practices, and then they start watching tapes of games, where they pick up even more information.

There's a tremendous difference between seeing a guy on the practice field and watching him in game action. Seeing a guy making plays when it counts is a lot more influential than seeing him light up teammates during the week.

Evaluating a player in game conditions makes it easier for the coaching staff to compare him with someone they're already familiar with. The way the concept for the movie *Speed* was pitched in Hollywood ("Picture *Die Hard* on a bus") is the same way prospects get labeled (coming out of Villanova, I pictured Brian Westbrook as a cross between Tiki Barber and Warrick Dunn).

Q: What is the one throw that scouts want to see every college quarterback make?

A: The play that still separates the college arm from the pro arm is the deep out. Defenses can't cover every spot on the field, so they often will surrender the 20-yard boundary route. It's the one area of the field they may give a quarterback regularly and dare him to throw into. NFL quarterbacks need to make that throw.

You can teach a quarterback at the NFL level to make that throw, but you'd rather see a guy come into the league with the arm strength and velocity to do it immediately.

Unfortunately, today's college game is all about quick slants and smoke screens. Sam Bradford had a career completion percentage of 68 percent at Oklahoma. Colt McCoy completed more than 70 percent of his college attempts. But they were throwing routes that were easy to complete, and that's not the game they'll play at the NFL level.

You have to throw out those stats, no matter how impressive they look on paper, and study the game tape instead. It's the only way you're going to know if a player can make the kinds of throws he'll need to make at the next level.

Phil Savage, formerly the general manager in Cleveland and someone I consider a true expert when it comes to grading personnel, appeared on the radio with Tim Ryan and me late in the 2009 season. He drew comparisons between Texas quarterback Colt McCoy and former NFL quarterback Jake Plummer. Phil said that McCoy, like Plummer, was intelligent, accurate with the ball, and mobile (though perhaps not as shifty as Jake the Snake). He compared McCoy's leadership and intangibles to Plummer's. When a coach, scout, or personnel guy hears a comparison like that, their image of McCoy becomes a little clearer.

TIME FOR THE COMBINE

Come early February, everyone can start drawing his own comparisons at the scouting combine in Indianapolis.

It's at the combine that players are often reduced to a bunch of numbers referred to as their "measurables." These numbers include everything from height and weight to the number of times a player can bench press 225 pounds. They include a prospect's time in the 40-yard dash and the short shuttle (which tests agility and lateral movement), how far he can broad jump, and how high he can jump vertically. At the combine, players will have the length of their arms measured as well as their hand size, and they'll all take the Wonderlic test. These numbers will stick to a prospect throughout the rest of the pre-draft process. Objective for the most part, they will be used relentlessly in comparing players who play the same position.

Scouts and coaches rely on measurables because they allow them to compare a prospect's physical characteristics with those of a player who's been successful in the NFL. Each evaluator has a chart defining key traits at each position, and each prospect is graded based on how his measurables stack up. If, for example, an offensive tackle is 6'5", he gets 10 out of 10 points. If he's more than 300 pounds, he gets another 10 out of 10. That player is a 20-point prospect on this particular scale. A tackle who's 6'4" and 290 might only score an 18 on this chart, which could affect his grade in the eyes of a particular team.

» THE CRUCIBLE OF THE COMBINE

It only took 4.24 seconds for the buzz to begin. That's how long it took Chris Johnson to run 40 yards at the 2008 NFL Scouting Combine—the fastest electronically timed performance in the event's history. In less than five seconds, he went from being a third-round sleeper to one of the more intriguing weapons available in the '08 Draft.

Speed alone wouldn't have turned Johnson into a 2,000-yard back by his second NFL season, of course. The 40-yard dash is just one piece of the puzzle, and the combine refers not only to a collection of players; it's really a combination of tests given to the 300 or more prospects who come to Indianapolis every February to open eyes (and doors). Beyond the position-specific drills, each player at the combine will be subjected to the following battery of tests.

On the Field
40-Yard Dash: Many prospects elect not to run in Indianapolis on what is considered a slow track, but those who do run three times, all of which are timed electronically and with hand-held stopwatches. Scouts also track a player's explosiveness by taking his times at the 10- and 20-yard intervals, which can indicate how long it takes a player to reach full speed, an important piece of data for, say, receivers.

Vertical Jump: This drill demonstrates a prospect's lower body explosiveness. A poor showing can raise red flags about a player's quickness or ability to come off the ball.

Broad Jump: The broad jump is another measure of a player's lower-body explosiveness. A sluggish or non-explosive player can get exposed when asked to perform this movement.

20-Yard Shuttle: The player starts by straddling a line in the middle of the course, then runs 5 yards in one direction, touches another line, then runs 15 yards in the opposite direction, touches another line, then finishes by sprinting through the line where he started. This demonstrates a player's ability to change directions and his short-area explosiveness.

60-Yard Shuttle: This tests endurance more than explosiveness. Players start on a line, run 5 yards, touch a line, and come back. They touch the starting line again, then run 10 yards and come back, then run 15 yards and return. It exposes the same things as the short shuttle, but it's really a measure of conditioning, especially for bigger guys.

Three-Cone Drill: The course is set up in the shape of an "L," with three cones set 5 yards apart. The player begins in his three-point stance and runs to the first cone and then back to the start. Then he runs around the second cone on his way to the third cone. He circles that cone and around the middle cone again on his way back to his starting point. Scouts and coaches are looking to weed out players who look stiff or straight-lined when they run.

Flexibility Drills: These are designed to check an individual's flexibility in such critical areas as the hamstring and groin. Tightness or stiffness could be warning signs of a player who might have injury problems at the next level.

Bench Press: This measures how many times a player can bench press 225 pounds. It's more instructive for the big-man positions (receivers aren't even asked to bench at the combine anymore), where upper body strength is so important. A good showing won't raise many eyebrows; a bad one will.

Off the Field

Height and Weight: Something as basic as a player's size can still be a mystery at the end of his college career. When players get weighed and measured in Indianapolis, their stats can be quite different from what's listed in their schools' media guides.

Wonderlic: A standardized IQ test that asks 50 questions in 12 minutes. Really smart players will get between 25 and 35 answers right. I'm not a big believer in the applicability of the Wonderlic, especially at certain positions, but it can be an indicator of potential problem areas.

Psychological Tests: Many organizations now have team psychologists on staff; the Giants, for example, put prospects through a 500-question exam (it's considerably longer than most, and some players never finish it). But the Giants value the insight it provides into a player's personality, competitiveness, and desire, and the results directly affect their draft decisions.

Team Interviews: The head coach, general manager, and personnel director will meet with a player in a controlled environment for about 15 minutes. It's an opportunity for a basic Q&A session, which most players rehearse for in advance. Still, it can be the first opportunity for coaches and staff to meet with a player face to face.

Physical Exam: The exams administered at the combine are likely the most extensive a player will undergo in his entire life. Team doctors will conduct every conceivable test, from blood work to a complete cardiovascular work-up. And, of course, they will examine the status of any injury a player may have suffered in college.

But not all numbers are equal, of course.

Hand size matters more when evaluating receivers and defensive linemen than when evaluating other positions. Arm length is a key factor for offensive linemen. If a scout finds a 6'0" cornerback who can run a 4.3 in the 40 and the short shuttle in under 4.0, he won't care if the player scores in the single digits on the Wonderlic.

NFL HEIGHT/WEIGHT/SPEED CHART

	NFL AVERAGE			NFL MINIMUM		
POS	**HT**	**WT**	**40**	**HT**	**WT**	**40**
QB	6'4"	220	4.94	6'0"	195	5.00
FB	6'0"	235	4.65	5'10"	230	4.80
RB	5'10"	210	4.55	5'8"	195	4.75
WR	6'0"	180	4.52	5'8 4/8"	170	4.65
TE	6'6"	245	4.80	6'2"	240	5.00
OT	6'5"	305	5.10	6'3 4/8"	280	5.30
OG	6'4"	300	5.15	6'2"	280	5.40
OC	6'3"	290	5.10	6'1 4/8"	280	5.30
DE	6'4"	275	4.80	6'2"	255	5.00
DT	6'3 4/8"	295	5.00	6'0 4/8"	275	5.20
MLB	6'1 4/8"	240	4.75	5'11 4/8"	235	4.80
OLB	6'2 4/8"	240	4.70	6'6"	230	4.85
CB	5'10 4/8"	190	4.50	5'8"	170	4.60
S	6'0"	200	4.55	5'10"	190	4.65

Everyone comes back from the combine with a ton of information. They've watched prospects in drills, conducted interviews with hundreds of players, and seen them all put through various tests of athleticism. Such a mass of information can be paralyzing, so sorting it all into a functional system is as important a part of the process as gathering it is.

Decision makers have to recognize that some scouts are great at gathering information but not as great at delivering it. Their scouting reports might be convincing, but they aren't good at selling their players when they're sitting in a meeting with the rest of the front office.

Some people prefer to receive their information in certain ways. For example, Mike Shanahan likes to watch highlight tapes. He watches cut-ups of 100 plays from a certain player on tape, and then makes his decisions with them in mind. That can be a dangerous way of operating if you don't have the eye and experience of Shanahan.

And, of course, there's a ton of personal information that scouts accumulate for each prospect. Some of the information speaks to a player's intangibles—qualities that are immeasurable, like leadership or poise. The rest comes from a background check that will paint a more three-dimensional picture of a prospect's character.

For instance, let's say a scout likes a player and he has all the requisite measurables, but he played at Tulane. It may be helpful to know why he went there coming out of high school instead of a powerhouse like Alabama or LSU. Maybe he was a late-bloomer. Maybe his body didn't develop until he was 20 years old. Whatever information a scout can gather may prove useful down the road.

When I was with the Jets and we had the No. 1 pick in the 1996 NFL Draft, Keyshawn Johnson was one of our leading candidates. We talked to people all the way back to his junior high school guidance counselor to get a clearer picture of a prospect we were going to invest a lot of time, money, and resources in. At USC, Keyshawn excelled at every measurable except for speed. He ran a 4.6 in the 40, which was slower than most teams would want from a No. 1 receiver. But we did some research and found that Jerry Rice ran a 4.6, so we felt comfortable overlooking that yellow flag because of Keyshawn's height, weight, hand size, arm length, and production at the college level. We also had to figure out why he had attended multiple colleges and a few high schools (as it turned out, he was looking for a team that had a quarterback who could throw—he knew he needed to play with one if he had any hope of getting to the NFL). When a team gives a first-round grade to a player, it better be prepared to go as deep into his background as necessary to eliminate any concerns it has about picking him.

After the 2008 season, Brad Childress knew he needed a playmaker receiver, preferably someone versatile who could play in the slot, run the Wildcat, and maybe return kicks. The choice came down to Jeremy Maclin and Percy Harvin. So Brad went down to Florida and spent the day with Urban Meyer to talk about Harvin, whose behavior had raised a few red flags. Then he drove with the kid to his home, where he met Harvin's wheelchair-bound grandmother. Childress wanted to know how Harvin might respond to discipline. Grandma told him, "You gotta handle him." After hearing what he needed to hear from the people who had been handling Harvin his

Q: When fans are watching a quarterback in college, what should they look for to project his potential at the NFL level?

A: Pocket presence. The NFL game is about buying time in the pocket. The average college quarterback makes his first read, and maybe his second, then he takes off (if he hasn't gotten sacked already). Once the quarterback leaves the pocket, he's reduced the amount of field he has to work with. Plus, the receivers' routes become null and void. If a defender is covering a receiver in the middle of a post-corner route and he sees the quarterback scramble the other way, why would he bother covering the corner on the far side of the field? A quarterback who can stay in the pocket and give his receiver time to build his route might be able to handle the pressure he'll face in the pros.

whole life, Childress was sold. The Vikings took Harvin with the 22nd pick in the first round, and he was an immediate difference maker for Minnesota.

After the combine comes the worldwide tour of pro days, when players work out on their own campuses. Again, they are put through all the requisite position drills and run all the tests that define a player's measurables—the short shuttle, the bench press, the 40-yard dash, and so on. If there's no one with a first- or second-round grade working out at a particular pro day, teams might only send a scout. But to some coaches, pro days are critical. Paul Alexander, the offensive line coach of the Bengals, will show up at a pro day at South Dakota State because he saw a tape of the left tackle and observed some traits that he wanted to see in person. When coaches do attend pro days, they're very interested in giving a guy instruction and seeing how fast he can learn it, take it out onto the field, and perform.

At the pro day, teams will videotape their interviews with a player. It may be the third time they've taped an interview with him—first at the Senior Bowl, then at the combine, and now at his pro day. Teams sort through all the canned answers that players have prepared for these interviews, looking for any tiny bit of information that can be used in his overall evaluation. Tim Ryan and I interview a lot of draft-eligible prospects on our radio show, and coaches around the league love it because they know we're asking the questions they want answers to. Because we know the process, we don't let guys get away with canned answers. (For those of you who listen to our show, that's where our standard line—"Not on this show, Mister"—came from.) We ask football questions, and players know their interviews with us are going to be recorded and sent to clubs around the league. I know a lot of coaches are sitting in their cars listening to our interviews to see if anything gets revealed that they couldn't elicit themselves.

After about five weeks of pro days, coaches and scouts are brought back to the team headquarters. At this point, players can't be worked out again, but a team can bring up to 25 players to its facility for one last visit and for team doctors to examine him one final time. He'll meet with coaches, the owner, and possibly the team psychologist.

There's a bit of gamesmanship involved at this point. Teams bring in not only players they will consider drafting; they also bring in players they want other teams to *think* they are considering drafting. This is where much of the buzz that contributes to the dramatics that surround the draft is created.

At last, the preparations enter their final week. The process that began with initial evaluations the previous spring; continued through the start of NFL training camp and then the college preseason; gained steam with early season evaluations and late-season scouting trips; and culminated with college bowls and all-star games, film study, the combine, pro days, and perhaps a final team visit is finally approaching the finish line. All the information that can be gathered has been gathered. Now it's time for teams to make some pivotal decisions.

It's time for the draft board to get finalized.

Every team has a different way of doing this, but each one will have a system of grading players that will allow the coach and GM to rank the prospects in order. These draft boards drive draft-day decisions, so tremendous attention is paid to every detail that could make a difference.

Teams will come up with a final numerical grade for every prospect and then rank them accordingly. Prospects are graded in a number of categories, from all the physical measurables to a film grade of their college production. Theoretically, the scale runs from 0 to 10, with increments down to the hundredth to help separate players.

A 10 would be a guaranteed superstar, a slam dunk Hall of Famer. How rare are these guys? Well, I've never seen one. But that's the hypothetical top of the chart.

A 9 would predict a surefire impact player, someone who will make a lot of Pro Bowls and lead your team to a championship. This is also where you'll find some of the unique and special athletes like Bo Jackson.

Anyone in the 8 range would be a no-brainer pick in the first round, someone with all the measurables and predictors in place. There are no emotional issues to be concerned about, and the college production is convincing.

The toughest part comes when a team needs to consider mitigating factors in order to break ties.

Let's say a team is looking at a quarterback who, after all the mathematical work is calculated, grades out at 6.0. It also has a prospect at guard who scored a 6.0. Numerically, the grades are the same. But there is a line on the draft board that specifies "areas of need," and more and more personnel guys around the league are admitting that need drives decisions more than ever before.

Longtime front office man Bill Kuharich warns against this line of thought. He urges decision makers to remove emotions from the equation, and to avoid adjusting the board for need. That way, a team won't wind up with a bunch of players who fill their positions but aren't good enough to help it win. Green Bay didn't need a quarterback when it drafted Aaron Rodgers in the first round back in 2005. Packers fans and local media didn't understand the move—by the time Rodgers led Green Bay to a Super Bowl win six seasons later, everybody had seen the light.

Still, for GMs with impatient owners and shortsighted coaches on the hot seat, need can skew the grades. Imagine a team has two veteran guards, but its quarterback is 36 years old—that could be enough in some people's minds to rank the 6.0 quarterback ahead of the 6.0 guard. Or maybe the team hadn't anticipated a need at a particular position but then lost someone to free agency in March. That need

Q: What should influence a team's decisions more on draft day—need or value?

A: When teams finalize their draft boards, they slot every player at every position into the round where their grades suggest they should be drafted. All the running backs they'd consider taking in the first round are bunched together on the board, slotted above all the backs with second-round grades, who are above all the guys with third-round grades, and so on down through the seventh round. There's even a spot on the board for backs whose grades tag them as undrafted free agents. This is called "stacking the board," and it keeps teams focused on finding value rather than reaching to fill a need.

Let's say it's the middle of the fourth round. Names are flying off the board every couple of minutes. High-stakes decisions are being made in a high-speed, high-intensity environment. A team has a need at, say, quarterback, and there are quarterbacks with fourth-round grades available. It sets the team up to make a classic need-based pick.

But before making that selection, the decision makers in the war room need to examine their board and see if there are any players of higher value they'd be passing up to take that quarterback. There may be a defensive end still available who earned a second-round grade. As much as they'd like to fill the need at quarterback, taking the player with the greater value is the smarter pick.

It can be hard to think through a choice like that when the clock is ticking, but that's exactly why teams spend so much time stacking their draft boards in the non-pressurized days before the draft.

now changes how it will look at players with similar grades that play different positions.

Then there are the subjective factors based on someone's personal experience and knowing what it takes to win in the NFL. I had the pleasure of working for the late Dick Steinberg with the Jets. At one point in the 1990s, Dick had more players active in the league than anybody else. He understood what it took to be an NFL player and found more guys who had it than most people.

Another guy who understood how to qualify information was Dick Haley, who had a huge part in building the Steelers. He understood the small college player as well as anybody. When we were considering taking Aaron Glenn, some coaches on the staff didn't want him because he was only 5'8¼". But Dick understood the importance of Glenn's 42-inch vertical leap and the timing he'd demonstrated, and Dick knew Aaron could handle a 6'4" wide receiver. Dick's sensibility won out, we took Glenn, and he played in the NFL for 15 years.

Eventually the board is finalized. There may be a few last-second modifications or manipulations (I've heard a lot of stories of GMs who snuck into the war room to change the board the night before the draft). But come draft day, the board is locked and it's time to start picking players.

Just as there are many ways to gather and sort information, there are multiple philosophies about running the war room—the office where the decisions get made and called in to a team representative at the draft, waiting by his team's helmet phone. Dick Steinberg's doors were wide open. He'd be up at the front of the room, about six inches away from the draft board, watching the names coming off as the draft unfolded. Sometimes, he'd invite me up to sit with him and talk about players. In 1994, I lobbied for taking Boston College quarterback Glenn Foley in the seventh round, telling Dick that he had a draftable grade; that eight teams were targeting him in this round; and that if we took him right away, we wouldn't have to worry about losing him. In the end, Dick drafted Foley.

Bill Parcells, on the other hand, wanted no information leaked from his war room. Right before the draft, everyone went to the bathroom. Then we came back and he locked us all in; no info was leaving that room.

Ultimately, the draft is a crapshoot. As Kuharich says, there are no virgins in the draft; everybody's been right and everybody's been wrong. You can only hope your team is right more often than wrong—especially with those early picks, because those are expensive mistakes to make.

LET'S MAKE A DEAL

One of the things that really makes draft day so much fun is the element of trading.

The willingness to trade NFL players on draft day has picked up in recent history, especially during the three-day format unveiled in 2010. The night between the first and second rounds proved a lively opportunity to talk trade. In part, that's because the continued growth of the salary cap gives teams more space to absorb bad contracts. In the past, some players had contracts that were too difficult to move; specifically, their signing bonuses were prorated over the life of their contracts and would stay on a team's books and count against its cap space even after it traded him.

Over time, teams began getting more creative with contracts, awarding more in roster bonuses (which are due in each year of the contract and travel with a player if he moves to another team) and less in signing bonuses (which stay behind as dead money).

The movement of coaches and GMs around the league also contributes to an environment more suited to talking trade. There was a time when the GM and president of a team were never fired. Coaches would come and go, but front office guys stayed put. Today, guys make multiple stops in their career. Bill Devaney is a perfect example—he started with the Redskins as an intern; in the old days, he would've eventually replaced Bobby Beathard and stayed there until he retired. But in the modern game, Devaney went from Washington to San Diego to out of football and in the media to back into football with Atlanta and then St. Louis. Along the way, he developed relationships with a lot of people in a lot of places. When a guy can pick up the phone and talk with people he knows well all over the league, the dynamic exists for conversations to turn to trade talk.

For years and years after I left the Jets, I would still talk with Bruce Allen, then the Tampa Bay general manager, about tradeable players on his roster. We talked a lot before the 2009 draft about Jay Cutler's unhappiness with his situation in Denver, even though neither of us held any front office capacity at the time. We put ourselves through the drill—if that was one of us, sitting in Denver having to deal with an unhappy quarterback that was demanding a trade, what would we do?

It takes two to trade, of course, and there are more willing partners than ever before. Trade talks go on all the time, but they really start to heat up when it comes to the draft.

It's important to know that there is no chance of pulling off a trade on draft day if you wait until draft day to start the conversation. Everything has to be orchestrated in advance for the trade to work.

I used to keep a book of potential trade partners, with initial conversations taking place on the sideline at the Senior Bowl. That's basically Phase 1—the feeling-out process. I'd talk to a colleague from another team and ask about guys on his roster who might become available. At that point, it's way too early to talk about specific deals. Why? Because it's going to come out. Unless you're dealing with someone you really know and trust—for me, that was guys like Bruce Allen and Bill Kuharich and Bill Devaney—potential trade talks are

» VALUE ADDED

The Trade Value Chart is not used to close a deal. It's used to get a conversation started.

Prior to the 2010 NFL Draft, the Eagles made it known they'd be willing to trade Donovan McNabb for a top-42 pick. Any interested team would then look at the Trade Value Chart and see that the 42nd pick is worth 480 points, then use that as a base for shaping their offer.

If Tampa Bay, for example, had been interested in acquiring McNabb, it could have simply offered the Eagles the 42nd overall pick. San Francisco, theoretically, could have offered a different package. For starters, they could have asked for McNabb in exchange for swapping the teams' first-round picks (the 49ers had the 13th pick, worth 1,150 points; the Eagles had the 24th pick, worth 740). The difference between those picks is only 410 points, so the 49ers might have had to throw in their 3rd-round pick (No. 113, worth 68 points). That package would have been worth almost exactly the value of the 42nd pick.

What Philadelphia ultimately acquired was Washington's 2nd-round pick in 2010 (No. 37 overall, worth 530 points) and either a 3rd- or 4th-round pick in 2011 (which would be worth in the neighborhood of 115 points). It may have sounded to Philly fans like the team gave away their starting quarterback, but they brought back value in the ballpark of 645 points—roughly the 29th overall pick, which was more than their stated asking price.

The bottom line is the chart does not provide teams with an exact formula, but it is a valuable tool for moving talks along from the speculative to the specific.

going to leak. Then the player is going to find out, and before you know it your idle talk has ignited a Cutler situation. A simple inquiry could have resulted in having a hostile guy on my hands.

That said, you can certainly plant non-specific seeds during this phase: "If you have a defensive end who becomes available, I may be in the market for one" or "You look like you may be in the market for a corner, and we may have one to give."

RD 1		RD 2		RD 3		RD 4		RD 5		RD 6		RD 7	
1	3,000	33	580	65	265	97	112	129	43	161	27	193	14.2
2	2,600	34	560	66	260	98	108	130	42	162	26.6	194	13.8
3	2,200	35	550	67	255	99	104	131	41	163	26.2	195	13.4
4	1,800	36	540	68	250	100	100	132	40	164	25.8	196	13
5	1,700	37	530	69	245	101	96	133	39.5	165	25.4	197	12.6
6	1,600	38	520	70	240	102	92	134	39	166	25	198	12.2
7	1,500	39	510	71	235	103	88	135	38.5	167	24.6	199	11.8
8	1,400	40	500	72	230	104	86	136	38	168	24.2	200	11.4
9	1,350	41	490	73	225	105	84	137	37.5	169	23.8	201	11
10	1,300	42	480	74	220	106	82	138	37	170	23.4	202	10.6
11	1,250	43	470	75	215	107	80	139	36.5	171	23	203	10.2
12	1,200	44	460	76	210	108	78	140	36	172	22.6	204	9.8
13	1,150	45	450	77	205	109	76	141	35.5	173	22.2	205	9.4
14	1,100	46	440	78	200	110	74	142	35	174	21.8	206	9
15	1,050	47	430	79	195	111	72	143	34.5	175	21.4	207	8.6
16	1,000	48	420	80	190	112	70	144	34	176	21	208	8.2
17	950	49	410	81	185	113	68	145	33.5	177	20.6	209	7.8
18	900	50	400	82	180	114	66	146	33	178	20.2	210	7.4
19	875	51	390	83	175	115	64	147	32.6	179	19.8	211	7
20	850	52	380	84	170	116	62	148	32.2	180	19.4	212	6.6
21	800	53	370	85	165	117	60	149	31.8	181	19	213	6.2
22	780	54	360	86	160	118	58	150	31.4	182	18.6	214	5.8
23	760	55	350	87	155	119	56	151	31	183	18.2	215	5.4
24	740	56	340	88	150	120	54	152	30.6	184	17.8	216	5
25	720	57	330	89	145	121	52	153	30.2	185	17.4	217	4.6
26	700	58	320	90	140	122	50	154	29.8	186	17	218	4.2
27	680	59	310	91	136	123	49	155	29.4	187	16.6	219	3.8
28	660	60	300	92	132	124	48	156	29	188	16.2	220	3.4
29	640	61	292	93	128	125	47	157	28.6	189	15.8	221	3
30	620	62	284	94	124	126	46	158	28.2	190	15.4	222	2.6
31	600	63	276	95	120	127	45	159	27.8	191	15	223	2.3
32	590	64	270	96	116	128	44	160	27.4	192	14.6	224	2

More conversations happen around the combine. Free agency starts on March 1, and teams start to have a better picture of what their needs are. Now the conversations begin to get more serious. A GM might tell someone, "There's a guy we're looking to draft, but I'm not sure he's going to be there when we're on the board," and then talk about what it would take to switch spots if his player was still available. The guy he's talking to might start to set parameters—"We want this year's second and next year's fourth"—and then they essentially have a deal in place.

That GM is likely to have the same conversation with two or three teams at different spots in the draft, just to give himself as many options as possible.

The tricky part, of course, is settling on the terms of the deal. That's where the Trade Value Chart comes in. The Trade Value Chart was invented by Jimmy Johnson when he was with the Dallas Cowboys so that he could quantify what would be considered a fair trade. Every spot in the draft is assigned a numerical value, and two teams need to just about break even in terms of the points exchanged to make the trade a good one.

Let's say I have the 14th pick in the first round; that's worth 1,100 points on the Trade Value Chart. You have the 10th pick (1,300). There's a 200-point gap in the perceived value of our two picks, so in order for me to trade up and swap picks with you, I'd have to give you another 200 points—which is the value of a mid-third-round pick.

The Chart has lost some of its relevance recently because of the escalating cost of first-round salaries. The 3,000 points assigned to the first overall pick isn't accurate anymore; it's so expensive to sign the No. 1 pick, a lot of teams would never even consider trading up into that spot.

Still, the Chart is a good starting point for conversations. A team knows that to jump up from 14 to 10, it'll probably cost an extra third-round pick. But if that team doesn't have a pick in the third round, it could bundle a fifth and a sixth or maybe a second in the following year's draft, or perhaps throw a player into the mix. The flip side of that trade is the team that's moving down better have a number of players it wants that's equal to the number of spots it's dropping. In other words, if a GM is considering dropping from 10 down to 14, there have to be five players he'd be happy with at 14. If there are only four, he has to either hope at least one of them slips to his new draft slot or he should cancel the deal.

Trades have to be fair in order to work—that means it has to be a good deal for both teams or a bad deal for both teams. The key is to keep the conversation going, to be willing to listen, and to have a sense of humor. Of course, there's nothing wrong with a little maneuvering and manipulation.

Back in 1993, the Jets had the third pick in the draft and the Cardinals had the fourth. After a series of maneuvers, the Cardinals were convinced we were going to take Garrison Hearst. We visited the kid many times in an effort to publicly signal we were interested in Hearst. I also took calls from teams below us in the draft, showing that we were open to trading the pick.

The night before the draft, the Cards called and said they'd like to switch spots with us. Knowing how much they wanted Hearst, we were able to switch places with them and get running back Johnny Johnson, too. They took Hearst, and one pick later we took Marvin Jones—the guy we really wanted all along.

The Cards had two possible reasons for doing business with us—either they believed we really were going to take Hearst or they believed we would deal the pick to someone else who would take him.

In cases like that, a team can use the media to its advantage. There are a few front office guys who call my show anonymously to talk up a trade possibility they have no intention of pulling the trigger on. It's all part of the art of the deal.

Agents can also be a useful tool in getting a deal done. For example, I once had to move an offensive tackle that our coach with the Jets, Rich Kotite, didn't want. The player's agent had contacts and strong relationships around the league, so I told him that if he could get me a specified compensation from someone he knew, I'd trade his guy to someplace he'd like to play. Sure enough, the agent called me back and said, "Jimmy Johnson wants him in Miami." The player wanted to be in Florida, where there's no state income tax, so the agent essentially brokered the deal. I got rid of a player I needed to move, the Dolphins got a guy they wanted, and the agent made his client happy.

(Of course, when I called Jimmy to make the deal for a fifth-round pick, he said, "No, I said it would be a sixth." I said, "I'm hanging up now." Jimmy laughed and said, "No, you're right. I said a fifth." Even when a deal is done, you can't blame a guy for trying to get a little more for a little less.)

The key to making successful deals is to avoid negotiating in the heat of the moment, but draft day is full of adrenaline, anxiety, pressure, and egos. The NFL is full of panic traders, guys who feel compelled to pull the trigger on something. Jerry Jones has been known to overpay on draft day for something he sets his mind on. Trading away next year's picks for something you want today is a credit card mentality. A GM needs to stay disciplined as the draft unfolds.

When you're able to ignore the pressure, draft day dealing can be easy. Look at the draft Charley Casserly ran for Washington back in 1999. The Redskins came into the draft with the No. 5 overall pick. Casserly pulled off an unprecedented deal—swapping his pick for every one of the New Orleans Saints' draft picks. In exchange for No. 5, Casserly brought back a first (No. 12), a third, a fourth, a fifth, a sixth, and a seventh, *plus* a first and a third in the 2000 draft.

But Casserly wasn't quite done. He took the first- and third-round picks he'd acquired, plus his own fourth and a fifth and a third from the following year, and sent the package to Chicago to move back up to No. 7, where he selected Champ Bailey, the best defensive player in the draft. In two draft-day deals, he got the guy he wanted, picked up a couple of extra picks for that year's draft, and also secured a first-round pick for the following year. (That first-round pick turned out to be the No. 2 overall pick, which Casserly used on LaVar Arrington.)

Now, do you think he'd have been able to pull that off if he hadn't been working those deals for weeks or months beforehand?

Of course not. That's why teams go into the draft having talked through and mapped out a variety of possible trade scenarios.

The next time you want to know why your team's GM isn't indulging your impulse for a quick-fix deal, remember the time-tested wise adage: if a general manager thinks like a fan, talks like a fan, and acts like a fan, he's going to be sitting with one in the stands soon enough.

BUILD YOUR OWN WAR ROOM

Forty million people play fantasy football every year. No small percentage of them do it to simulate the experience of being a general manager.

But if you *really* want to approximate the challenge of making personnel decisions for an NFL team, try walking a draft day in a GM's shoes. To do that, you need a draft board.

Obviously you don't have a director of college scouting and his staff scouring the country to gather information for you. You have to find it yourself, but there's actually a lot of material available to get you started.

I always advise fantasy players to seek their information from football sources they trust, not fantasy-specific outlets. You want to make sure your fantasy decisions are rooted in football reality. The same goes for gathering material about draft prospects.

Start with the guys you trust. For example, Mike Mayock is someone who does the same film work a college scouting director does and knows what he's looking for. Tap into the research they've done by looking at their lists of prospects position by position, and use those as a jumping-off point.

Then, start your own evaluation process where the NFL coaches start—by watching game video. You have to see things for yourself before you can have an informed opinion of a player. In the buildup to the 2011 NFL Draft, I had tons of calls to my radio show from guys saying, "I like Nick Fairley." I'd press them to say what *specifically* they liked about him, and most admitted they hadn't really studied him at all. Many had not even seen him play. They formed their opinions exclusively on what they'd been reading and hearing.

You'd be surprised how much video is out there on the Internet. Websites like YouTube can be an invaluable resource. Six weeks before the 2011 draft, a quick Google search for "Will Rackley video" would have returned a 12-play highlight package of the offensive lineman from Lehigh. On the same site, you would have then found highlight packages featuring 27 other prospects, including Mike Pouncey, Danny Watkins, and other top guys at the position.

Now, you shouldn't expect to find pristine HD footage of every prospect you want to evaluate. You're going to have to wade through a lot of homemade music montages and grainy videos. There will be a lot of fast-edit highlights that aren't going to give you a lot to work with.

But even if you find a handful of plays from every prospect, you'll see enough to get a sense of certain strengths and, more often, certain questions about a particular player. The key, of course, is knowing how to watch film with a talent evaluator's eye.

Let's use Fairley as an example. Start by looking not at the result of the play—likely a sack or a tackle for a loss, if it's on a highlight reel—but at the start of it. Take note of who he's lined up against. Get the opponent's number, look at that team's roster, and see whether the tackle Fairley's about to destroy is a freshman backup or an All-SEC senior. That will give you a little context for the play you're about to watch.

Look for other things that may have provided Fairley the kind of advantage he's not likely to see in the NFL. How many times did he wind up being blocked by a running back because the protection slid the wrong way? How many times did he come totally free? You can throw out those plays in your evaluation because that's not happening in pro football. Was he on a team that led by two touchdowns at the half in every game? That means he played his whole season in a one-dimensional situation. Those are all factors you should consider in your evaluation.

Now, let's consider quarterbacks. You probably could have found 100 plays of Cam Newton online from his days at Auburn. When evaluating him, count how many times he looked for his second or third receiver. If he sets his feet, looks at his first guy, then tucks it and runs for 25 yards, that would be a bad play. Did he go through his progression, check through all three receivers, and *then* take off for a 25-yard gain? That's a different story. Reading across the field to his third receiver is a plus, no matter what he gained once he tucked it and ran.

Essentially you're looking to see how well he's done the things that will be asked of him at the next level. Chart 20 of his escapes—was every one of them to the right side? NFL defenses will notice that and take it away from him immediately. But if five of those escapes went to the right, six went inside, and nine went to the left, now we're talking about a player who is going to cause problems for even the best defenses.

When you're watching a quarterback, chart the field zones he throws into. If you see him complete two shallow crosses, an X screen, a skinny post down the left side, and two pro outs, that should get your attention.

The question about Blaine Gabbert after his senior season at Missouri was whether he could complete passes outside the numbers. You may read about that concern in articles online or in the newspaper, but you can investigate that issue yourself by watching him make that throw. If you see him struggling to complete a ball between the numbers and the boundary, you'll be able to predict precisely what he'll struggle with during his rookie season. NFL defenses won't cover that part of the field if they don't have to. Instead, they'll put two extra guys inside and cover the zone he's more likely to throw into.

You can spend 25 minutes gathering information that will help you evaluate a player when you find a piece of video worth watching. You'll be building your own database, which you will use when compiling your own mock draft. Then, you can start to flesh out your scouting reports with other information. Inevitably, you'll come across statistics. They don't necessarily lie, but they don't tell the full story either.

Take the case of Mark Ingram, the Alabama back who rushed for 1,658 yards and 17 touchdowns in winning the Heisman Trophy as a junior. In his senior season, he rushed for about half that total on 113 fewer carries. What can you conclude from those black-and-white stats?

Not much. But a closer look will tell you more. He averaged 5.5 yards per carry—certainly a respectable number. But he gained 151 yards against Duke, which was 113th in rush defense out of 120 teams. Take away that game, and Ingram averaged 4.9 yards per carry. Still good, but enough to give you pause.

Next, look at Alabama's overall running game. Trent Richardson and Eddie Lacy each rushed for more than 400 yards, and both averaged more than 6.0 yards per carry. That tells you Alabama's offensive line dominated its opponents. Now, you can go back and watch video on Ingram in a different light. Was he running through holes he'll never see in the NFL? Or was he making guys miss and earning all of those yards on his own?

Gathering and analyzing all the information you can about a player will help you see how much separation there is between Ingram and, say, another back projected to go in the fifth round.

You can also get a ton of information out of the combine, but you have to know how to use it. Know which drills mean something to the position (like the short shuttle for inside linebackers) and which traits are most relevant to certain positions (arm length for left tackles).

Eventually, you'll have enough information to rank the top players at each position. Yes, there are still considerations—if your team runs a 3-4 defense, should it be looking for someone like Marcell Dareus (6'3", 319 pounds) or Nick Fairley (6'4", 291)? But you are just about ready to stack your draft board and create your own mock draft.

First, you must recognize there are certain positions that are more deserving of first-round consideration than others. Quarterback, pass rusher (a DE in a 4-3 scheme, an OLB in a 3-4), left tackle, cover corner, and maybe an X receiver are priorities. Your team's top need might be at center, but that doesn't mean you should take one in the first round. Unless there's an absolute standout at another position— even running back—you should focus your first-round picks on one of those elite positions.

Next, you have to evaluate the depth of a particular draft class at those elite positions. In preparing for the 2011 draft, you might have concluded there were as many as eight pass rushers with first-round grades, while there were only one or two deserving quarterbacks. When you can go eight deep at an elite position, teams know they don't have to trade up to get one. But if you needed a wide receiver, you would have to think about moving up to get Georgia's A.J. Green or Alabama's Julio Jones.

All you need now is an understanding of what the top two or three areas of need are for every team in the league. That is what drives every draft. Be prepared for those needs to change as soon as free agency begins as teams sign players to fill certain needs and lose players to create others.

Again, it's probably a good idea to turn to trusted sources of football information. Do not, by any means, put any stock in mock drafts released before the combine. People like to start talking about the draft as soon as the NFL season ends, but there's simply not enough information at that time for any mock draft to have much relevance. Teams use the combine and pro days to learn about players, and they haven't stacked their draft boards yet. Those early mock drafts are fun, but they're for entertainment purposes only.

When you're ready to sit down for your mock draft, don't do what most people do and just guess how the first round will turn out. Those people are just playing bingo.

Do a three-round mock draft. That's when it really gets fun and challenges your preparation. And if possible, don't do it by yourself. Tim Ryan and I do one on our radio show every year—he takes three picks, then I take three picks, and we alternate through three rounds. I know a group of fans that gets 32 guys on a conference call, each guy takes a team, and they go through three rounds.

Remember—you wanted to get a sense of what it's like to be a GM. Well, try filling specific needs while sticking to your draft board and looking for value as players are being picked by your competition.

Imagine you were running the Buffalo Bills' war room headed into the 2011 draft. You determined your top need was quarterback, your second need was a pass rusher, and your third need was a left tackle. The Bills entered the draft with the third pick in the first round, the second pick in the second round, and the third pick in the third round.

How might you approach the draft?

Let's say your research and evaluation process concluded that neither Newton nor Gabbert was the answer and neither were worthy of the third pick. There were eight pass rushers and five offensive tackles who you speculated could go in the first round.

So, you might go with the top tackle on your board and hope one of those eight pass rushers falls to you with the 34th pick. And if none of those pass rushers were to fall, you settle for the third- or fourth-best quarterback in the draft. That strategy could fill two of your top three holes with players who had first-round grades. You might have a tougher time finding an answer to your quarterback needs in the third round, but you would hope guys like Nevada's Colin Kaepernick or TCU's Andy Dalton could be available.

Once you've finished your three-round mock draft, your job is not done. Save all your work, and then take it out and review it next year. See how you did, where you took the bait, and where you reached.

Keep evaluating your process and your picks. NFL teams need to do that, too. Twenty-one of them passed on Aaron Rodgers in the first round of the 2005 NFL Draft. Fifteen of the players taken before Rodgers weren't even on the rosters of the team that selected them when Rodgers was leading Green Bay to the Super Bowl. What did the Packers see that everyone else missed? It's not like they needed a quarterback. What convinced them to spend a first-round pick on a guy who wasn't an immediate need?

What would you have done?

CHAPTER 15

PAIN MANAGEMENT

» NFL Teams Must Find a Way to Gain a Medical Competitive Advantage

They lost their top running back in the first game of the season. They lost their top returning tackler, their right tackle, and their starting safety in Week 4. The next week, they lost their tight end.

Before the 2010 regular season was over, the Green Bay Packers had placed 15 players on injured reserve. Six of them had been Week 1 starters. That doesn't include the two concussions suffered by Aaron Rodgers, which caused him to miss a game and a half down the season's homestretch.

About the only thing the Packers didn't lose was the Super Bowl—and they lost three key players to injury in that game.

The road to winning a championship is tough enough without having to manage season-ending injuries to so many important players. It takes a whole lot more than a few lucky breaks to survive and advance all the way to a title the way the Packers did. No, they withstood the largest spate of injuries in the league because they were built to keep rolling through the toll of a rough regular season.

It's a simple but vital formula: roster depth combined with good coaching.

Mike McCarthy and defensive coordinator Dom Capers made a point of coaching everyone to do everything. The starter got his practice reps, but his backup also got a couple of reps during the week, and that guy's backup got a rep or two as well. And they all got another turn at walkthrough. Green Bay kept picking up players, preparing them, and plugging them in.

How else can you explain Erik Walden, a free agent the Packers signed in late October, stepping in for Frank Zombo in Week 17 and making 12 tackles and getting two sacks in a win over Chicago that earned Green Bay the NFC's final playoff spot? He hadn't had a sack in his career before that must-win game.

The Packers' plan clearly accounted for the inevitability that NFL players are going to be lost to injury. That reality is not news. But Green Bay proved the importance of not getting hurt by injuries. The teams that are best able to identify, treat, and withstand injuries have the opportunity to obtain a rare but substantial edge: the medical competitive advantage.

PERFORM ANNUAL CHECKUPS

A team's medical staff wields significant influence on football decisions being made by coaches and general managers throughout the year. They provide input about the riskiness of draft prospects and whether guys on the roster can practice during the week or play on Sundays. Because of the integral nature of their role, the medical staff needs to be evaluated every year, just like every player and coach does.

You simply can't afford to make medical mistakes.

I was with the Jets in 1993 when Ronnie Lott signed as a free agent. I always wondered what might have been had the Jets taken him with the third pick in the 1981 NFL Draft. The team doctors at the time had concerns about his knee, projected that he'd have a short career, and decided he was not worth risking such a high pick. They tabbed him a "medical reject." Today, of course, Ronnie has been tabbed a "Hall of Famer."

There are examples of guys all over the league whose worrisome medical histories had no effect on their performance in the NFL. But there are ways to quantify whether your medical staff is providing advice that is leading to the right decisions.

Teams need to evaluate their own doctors.

Each team should examine the careers of every player its medical staff red-flagged before the draft. How many of those guys wound up having successful careers in the NFL? Is a team's medical staff regularly rejecting prospects with certain injuries, only to watch them end up playing elsewhere? How will teams feel about passing on Da'Quan Bowers in the 2011 NFL Draft? His knees were such a troubling question mark that every team in the league passed on the defensive end from Clemson until Tampa Bay took him with the 51st pick.

Are the doctors being too aggressive, encouraging decisions that incur too much risk? Are they too conservative? Remember, the Dolphins' doctors convinced Nick Saban not to sign a certain free-agent quarterback in March 2006 because of injury concerns. Four years, 18,000 yards, and no shoulder problems later, Drew Brees was the Super Bowl MVP for the Saints.

Not long ago, teams would cut a player the minute they heard "ACL." The way that injury is repaired and rehabilitated has come a long way. Teams went from never drafting a guy with an ACL injury to expecting he'd be back to full speed two years after surgery. Today, a player with an ACL injury could be back six months later. More than ever, teams need progressive doctors on their staff, guys who stay on top of the medical progress constantly being made.

Then, of course, there's the practical piece of those medical trends. To that end, every NFL team employs a diverse and extensive medical practice to cover pretty much every conceivable health-related concern.

The head of the medical staff is the official team doctor. These doctors have the ear of the coach and GM, but their job performance needs to be analyzed just as critically. Is he trying to please the head coach? Is he a fan of the team? Does he have his own agenda? As an orthopedic surgeon for the team, he might examine 20 knees a year. Is he thinking about his future career, seeing 200 patients a year who want to tell their friends they were treated by an NFL team's doctor?

Under the team doctor, the team retains a couple of orthopedic specialists (the team doctor often is one, and definitely should be). One of them needs to be a knee and shoulder specialist, and the other needs to treat head, neck, and back injuries.

Then there's the general practitioner. Players are under a team's care 24/7, and there are 60 of them. These guys get sick, they need prescriptions, and they're not walking into some emergency room for treatment. Everything needs to be treated in-house; there's plenty of stuff that you don't want fans reading about on the Internet.

There's also the team dentist, who plays a pretty active role in a sport where guys are getting teeth knocked out of their heads. Try to imagine being a quarterback with a tooth abscess the morning of a game.

Then comes the team trainer, who in many places reports not to the team doctor but directly to the head coach. Beyond all that ankle taping, the trainer has a critical job—giving the green light for a player to practice. The green light for playing in games probably falls under the doctor's domain. But when a player is dealing with an injury during the week, the coach goes to the trainer and asks, "Can this guy go tomorrow?" The trainer's answer will have a direct impact on the coach's game plan and his plan to install it at practice. Which is why the trainer's job is such a complicated one.

The trainer has to discern whether a player is being honest with him about an injury. To do that effectively, he must have the trust of the players and an understanding of their individual personalities.

Trainers also need to be monitoring the supplements the players are taking. There is no excuse for a player failing a drug test over supplements. If a player really cares about doing the right thing instead of creating an advantage at any cost, he will bring in what he's planning to take, hand it to the trainer, and say, "I'm taking this tomorrow unless you tell me I can't." Then the trainer either signs off or doesn't. Within the great organizations, the players and trainers have that kind of relationship.

One of the key members of the training staff is the strength coach, who often doubles as the rehab guy. When a player goes down with a high ankle sprain and the team doctor declares him out for three weeks, it's the strength coach who oversees the prescribed therapy.

Trainers and strength coaches, along with their assistants, also have to be sensitive to how players deal with injuries psychologically.

Imagine that two players suffer the same ACL injury and undergo the same procedure to repair it. Player A is aggressive in the weight room. He's been through six-month rehab stints in the past, and 30 seconds after he's out of the hospital bed, he's ready to go.

Then there's Player B, who's never been hurt before. The prospect of rehabilitation is devastating to him, and he can't get beyond his personal pity party. Even as his rehab returns his knee to full strength, he still can't shake his depression. He's physically capable of doing everything he'd done before, but he doesn't think he's fast anymore. He's not ready for that first contact.

It's up to the strength coach to identify when fear is an obstacle to the rehab process. Players aren't going to come in and say, "Hey, I'm scared to death about playing again." A trainer and strength coach who recognize this call in the team psychologist—and all teams retain one—and give their team a potential medical competitive advantage over a team that would otherwise write off that player as a "head case."

CONCUSSION CONCERNS

Throughout the 2010 NFL season, the lightning rod of all injury-related debate was concussions.

An NFL study at midseason found that concussions were being reported at a rate more than 20 percent higher than in 2009 and more than 33 percent higher than in 2008. There's an important distinction to be made here. The study showed the instances of concussions being *reported*. That's not the same thing as concussions sustained.

The NFL faces a bunch of issues when it comes to the treatment and prevention of concussions, not the least of which is a generation gap. A lot of the older players in the league—and we're not talking just about guys who retired recently but veteran players still in the league—played through concussions. So did their coaches. There is the tendency for some of them to look at the younger players suffering from concussions and lingering symptoms and ask, "Are you kidding me?"

If we're going to take a hard look at addressing concussions, we have to recognize one fundamental fact: playing football is not a job to be taken lightly.

I can't imagine there are any kids playing high school football today who haven't heard a million stories about concussions from their coaches or their parents or on TV. They are growing up in an era when concussions are part of the conversation and a very real concern.

It's a problem that the league is committed to solving. Ronnie Lott, one of the game's all-time hardest hitters, is co-chairing a new NFL Player Safety Advisory Panel, along with John Madden. Ronnie believes that it starts with young players learning proper and safer ways to tackle.

Yes, technique can go a long way toward keeping players safe from concussions. But there's another aspect that must be addressed.

We must find a way to protect players from themselves.

It starts in high school, where a lot of kids suffer concussions that go unreported and unrecorded. Then they get to college, where they begin to think that maybe they have a chance to become professional football players. All of a sudden, a freshman is covering a kickoff and suffers a concussion. But he doesn't report it. He gets off the field and hopes he can just get home, sit in a dark room, and tell his coach he has a stomach bug and has to miss practice.

Young players do not want to get to the point where they get shut down for the season or get labeled as a guy who gets concussed. They think there's too much at stake.

That behavior is only compounded at the NFL level. Players are not going to be forthright when it might jeopardize their careers and their paychecks, regardless of what it means to their long-term health. Sure, a secure veteran player who already has the big contract and banked the bonus money probably will be more honest to the team doctors about his medical situation. But the second-year guy still playing on his rookie deal, the backup tight end who is covering kicks and worrying about getting waived, is not going to speak up to his coaches.

Don't ever discount the self-perception of invincibility that is required to play football at any level. If you don't feel invincible, how in the world are you going to go out there to return a punt? Once you start intellectualizing it, thinking that there are 11 guys coming down to blow you up, a rational person would probably say, "No thanks. I'll pass."

These guys don't pass. In that way, football players are like bank robbers. No one goes out to rob a bank thinking, *I'm going to get caught today.* They don't willingly ignore the risk; they just don't even consider it.

That's why the first step in protecting football players from themselves is to not trust any of them to be honest about injuries. If you really want to know who has a concussion, you can't ask the players. Don't blame them for withholding the information. Instead, tell them, "We understand why you wouldn't tell us. But we can't let you do that anymore."

It falls to the league to determine whether a player has sustained a concussion. I've talked to many concussion scientists who tell me they can develop a baseline examination that can be administered in

10 minutes. When a test like that becomes available, I would make it mandatory for every player, every week. I don't care who you are—if you step onto the field on Sunday, you stop by the trainers' room on Monday for your baseline evaluation.

Once a player is identified with a concussion, they're off the field and the staff measures them every day. Until they are cleared by the doctors, they don't get to play. Concussions don't affect everyone the same way. Some players can come back five days later, others need three weeks. But if they're evaluated until they're cleared, it could minimize the risk of a guy coming back too soon and suffering a recurrence.

NFL commissioner Roger Goodell has made keeping players safe a priority. He's had an open-door policy on the issue, and many players have engaged him in this conversation. The league is always looking at ways to modify the game to make it safer that don't radically change the game of football.

Of course, player safety can't be guaranteed by a rule book. You can send out a memo to people saying that it's illegal to drive more than 10 mph in the parking lot, but that doesn't mean everyone's going to start driving 8 mph.

You can legislate protection of the quarterback, but that won't protect him. The league can't presume that the quarterback is safe because of something written up in a competition committee meeting. I've yet to meet a defensive player who is thinking about the rule book when he's about to take a whack at the quarterback. As Ray Lewis once told me, "I understand where they're going with these rules. But I got a job to do."

You can't fine or suspend dangerous plays out of the game, either. But the league understands it has to be proactive in investigating other ways to make the game safe.

For example, there has been considerable talk about making mouthpieces mandatory. Mouthpieces can help absorb the shock of a blow to the head, and many experts believe that could help in the prevention and severity of concussions. Players may balk at this regulation as an inconvenience. But if it will reduce the number of concussions, it's a step that should be taken.

I've also talked to Commissioner Goodell about a study conducted by a group of concussion experts recommending the elimination of the three-point stance. An offensive lineman down in a three-point stance can't do anything at the snap of the ball but lead with his helmet. He's exploding headfirst into the guy in front of him 65 times every game. The study suggests that the cumulative effect of those blows puts a player at a greater risk of concussions than some of the knockout shots we see in the open field.

And it's time that we recognize that there are fundamental elements of the way today's game is played that contribute to making players vulnerable to concussions.

Take the zone blitz, for example. The zone blitz is designed to trick the offensive line into blocking the wrong defenders. The scheme winds up creating a free blitzer, someone the protection scheme did not account for, and the risk of injury to the quarterback increases dramatically.

Consequently, head coaches and offensive coordinators have to better understand the risk and reward of play calling. Obviously, the best way to protect the quarterback is to have a smart guy playing the position who gets rid of the ball on time. Too often, though, teams are forced to send out a quarterback who doesn't yet have full command of his offense. When a quarterback has to do things he isn't comfortable doing, when he's struggling to read defenses and understand what he's seeing, and he's out on the field against an aggressive blitzing defense, he is at greater risk of getting hurt.

That may lead to coaches having to limit their playbooks. I know you need every available option to keep the defense guessing. I know you need to win the game, and that taking risks is required to win games. But if the risk gets a quarterback knocked out of the game, did the offense take more risk than it should have?

There are other systemic factors that contribute to more players suffering head injuries. The Cover 2 defense, for example, creates a huge opportunity for the kind of helmet-to-helmet hits that often result in concussions.

In man coverage, a defender chases his guy around the field and tries to tackle him. There is little space between the defender and the target, and without space, there's no velocity in the hit.

But in a Cover 2 defense, the defensive back can sit back and read the crossing pattern the receiver is running toward him. This gives a defender the chance to time his hit perfectly for the moment a receiver is most vulnerable: when he's focused on the catch, not the contact.

Remember, the defender's job is to prevent the ball from being caught. And if the catch is made, it's his job to force the ball loose.

You can't blame the defender for doing his job—provided he's not hitting an unprotected player in an illegal or reckless fashion. Nor am I suggesting that you outlaw the zone defense.

It is incumbent upon the offensive coaches to make certain their receivers know how to avoid running themselves into danger. It starts with reading coverages. If a receiver is running a shallow cross against man coverage, he can keep running away from the defender. But if he's running a shallow cross against a Cover 2, he needs to know not to carry his route into the danger zone, where there's a cornerback waiting to blow him up. He must be coached to "sit down"—to find a spot in the zone, stop, and then turn back to the quarterback.

Does that minimize the potential gain on that particular play? Probably. But a coach needs his players for 16 games or more. The long term can't always be sacrificed for the short term. A coach must make sure his receiver knows how to recognize and beat a zone and protect himself in the process. If not, he needs to find a different player or change what he's doing offensively.

THE DANGER ZONE: THE SHALLOW CROSS VS. COVER 2

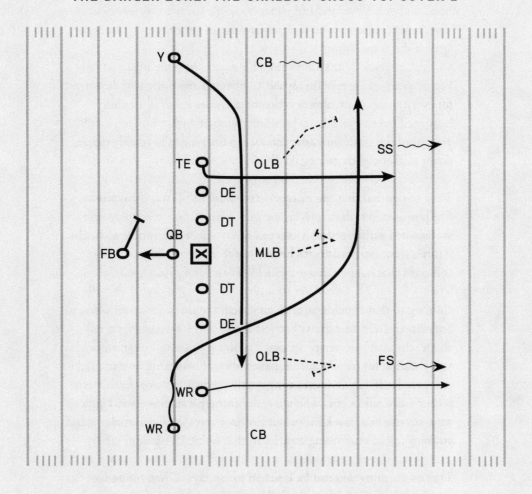

The Y receiver, lined up on the strong side, runs a shallow cross. If he doesn't "sit down," the receiver will be looking over his shoulder for the ball, leaving himself vulnerable to a dangerous shot from the cornerback.

Ultimately, the coaches who understand where injuries happen on the field are the ones best able to prepare their players to avoid them.

They're also the ones who find subtle ways to get even a slight edge against the competition.

For 30 years, every team in the NFL activated eight offensive linemen for every game. Now, almost everyone activates seven. That shift happened because coaches who were paying attention realized that 99 percent of the time, they only used seven linemen. They rarely dipped down to that eighth guy.

They recognized that there's relative medical stability at the offensive line position. Yes, those players see major contact on every play, and as discussed earlier, research suggests they may be susceptible to head injuries from repeated contact. But they're not involved in the big collisions that happen down the field. Their injury risks are different.

Coming to that conclusion enabled coaches to dress one fewer offensive lineman and add an extra safety. Jeff Fisher and I have had long talks about why that fifth safety became a position of need. Fisher, who was a safety during his playing career, talked about how teams have reacted to the spread offenses and vertical tight end threats they now face. Teams go out and draft safeties who are really cornerbacks, undersized guys who can run and cover. But when you face an offense that runs the ball, you're going to start seeing injuries to that quick 195-pound safety.

That's something you can look for on game days. When the active roster is released, see if your coach is going with seven offensive linemen and five safeties. If he is, you can feel comfortable he is someone who studies and considers the way injuries affect the game.

CHAPTER 16

STATE-OF-THE-ART FOOTBALL
» A Glimpse into the Game's Future

There was a time in the NFL when coaches couldn't challenge a call on the field. Not because no rule existed or because instant replay didn't exist. Television *itself* didn't exist.

Times change, and football—both the sport and the structure of the NFL—has always found ways to adapt and grow. In so many ways, football may be the sport best-suited for the technological advances and the global attitudes of the 21st century.

The more we are willing to utilize the best technology available, the better off the game will be. Here's a look at some of the ways I think tomorrow's NFL may be different from today's.

NO HUDDLE FOR ALL

There's already growing sentiment in NFL circles that it's time to get rid of the huddle. Coaches won't abandon it outright, but I think its use will be reduced over time. Perhaps by 2020, we'll see teams only huddling 10 times per half, and eventually, it'll be eliminated altogether.

Think about how much better the game would flow without huddles. There'd be much more live action, and much less stoppage of play. That could be a big consideration as the NFL markets itself to international fans who appreciate the continuous play of soccer. Without huddles, there would be fewer minute-long gaps in the action for people still learning about football to find themselves feeling bored (which is one of the biggest problems baseball faces as it tries to attract members of the iPod generation).

A no-huddle offense also presents more matchup problems for the defense, which leads to more big plays and scoring opportunities. When Boomer Esiason started running a no-huddle offense in Cincinnati, it didn't take him long to appreciate the matchup advantages it created. The Bengals played a West Coast offense, and when they came out in 12 personnel, Boomer found that defenses treated one of the tight ends as a receiver and countered with nickel personnel. On the next play, the Bengals went without a huddle to keep the defense from substituting and virtually assured themselves a favorable matchup if they ran the ball.

Quarterbacks in high school and college today are running spread offenses without the huddle. They just call one of their four or five plays at the line. The day is coming when all players will have audio in their helmets the way quarterbacks and middle linebackers do now. Every player on the field will be able to hear directly from their position coach or coordinator before every play.

DRESSED FOR SUCCESS

Too many players in today's game are shedding protective padding, opting for speed over safety.

There's been a lot of talk about improving the effectiveness of helmets in an effort to cut down on concussions, but I also see tremendous opportunities for advancement in all the equipment players wear. Someday soon, you'll see football players in lightweight body armor that looks like something Batman would wear. All the shoulder pads, rib pads, hip pads, and thigh pads would be part of a one-piece suit that wouldn't be heavy or cumbersome, and players won't have to make a dangerous choice that could lead to a career- or life-threatening injury.

SURFACE MATTERS

During the 2009 season, the NFL took some long-overdue steps toward addressing the issue of concussions. But an interesting technology exists that could add another preventative component to complement the improvements being made to equipment, rules, and policies.

Former Dallas fullback Daryl "Moose" Johnston came on my radio show to talk about a company he's involved with that believes it can make the field itself safer to play on. Too many head injuries are caused not by helmet-to-helmet contact but by a player's head hitting the ground during a tackle. When today's synthetic fields get worn down, the rubber infill gets compacted, which makes the playing surface harder and more dangerous.

Moose told us about equipment that can blow out the infill, then repair it or replace it—pretty much like having the cushions on your couch restuffed. Ultimately, we'd wind up with fields that are softer and safer.

IN PLANE SIGHT

Want to end once and for all the debate over whether the ball broke the plane of the end zone? Put a microchip in the ball that signals a computer up in the officials' booth when or whether it crosses the plane. A chip like that could also help officials spot the ball accurately after every play—bad spots wouldn't have to cost a team a first down anymore. It's hard to believe we still have guys walking around out there with two sticks and a chain. When you weekend warriors out there run an 8k on the weekend, they give you a chip for your shoe that tells you exactly when you cross the finish line; shouldn't we demand the same technology from the NFL?

FOR YOUR VIEWING PLEASURE

There are many simple things that broadcasters could do to better inform their audience. For example, networks already superimpose graphics to show fans where the line of scrimmage and first-down markers are. Why not add another thinner line 5 yards downfield so they can see exactly when contact with a receiver becomes illegal?

The biggest opportunity exists in letting fans watch coaches' tape—the "All-22" views that shows you every player on the field at once. Broadcasters talk about it on the telecast, and everyone around the league watches the game that way. The only ones left out are the fans.

The people running the NFL understand that there are no real secrets in football. Broadcasting coaches' tapes isn't going to reveal any information that will cause a competitive disadvantage for a team. There's absolutely no downside in allowing fans access to something that would increase their appetite for and understanding of the game. Kids who grow up playing *Madden* are used to an overhead view of the field; why force them to watch the game from the same perspective their parents did decades ago?

Just think of the revenue stream it would provide the NFL. If the league sold a subscription service making coaches' tapes available to fans online—maybe even with someone narrating what they're seeing, like a director's commentary on a DVD—they'd probably make enough money to fund the medical benefits for all retired players.

The league and the networks do understand the importance of using the newest technology to enhance the fan experience. When the NFL Network launched the Red Zone in 2009, it enabled fans to stay on top of the action from every game, all day long.

The real challenge is making the technology that's available to the fans at home available to the fans in the stands. People around the league, right up to NFL commissioner Roger Goodell, like to say that there's no substitute for the excitement of being in an NFL stadium on game day. But think about how you experience a game at home. You get to watch games in high definition, get instant replays (even cue up your own replays if you're using a DVR), and switch to the Red Zone to see every touchdown from every game. You can have your computer in front of you and track your fantasy team. And when one game ends, you just flip the channel and you're ready for the next one.

NFL owners need to enhance the stadium experience—they need to sell seats or risk television blackouts—and technology is going to make that possible. Soon enough, you'll see TV screens at every seat in the stadium (especially in the expensive sections). They'll come with the ability to switch camera angles, so fans can watch the game any way they want.

Eventually, there will be cameras in the locker room, so the fans can hear what's going on behind closed doors. There will be interactive polls, giving fans the ability to vote on whether they want their team to pass or run on the next play. Imagine the stadium JumboTron flashing a graphic that says 92 percent of the fans in attendance want the coach to go for it on fourth down.

Coaches are going to fight it, but owners know that fans want that interactive experience, and the more enjoyable the experience, the more fans will be willing to pay for it.

MAKING VIRTUAL A REALITY

One of these days, the most important person in a team's facility is going to be the video coordinator.

A lot of other sports are already making some amazing advances in the area of video training. I don't think it will be long before we see quarterbacks going into a simulator and practicing against their virtual opponents. They could take their drop while reading actual defensive coverages, then make their throws to virtual receivers. It'll be like playing Pebble Beach from the comfort of your own home.

With virtual technology, teams could begin training their players in almost real-world conditions without any risk of injury. Suddenly, a team's off-season training program has incredible value. Think of how many more practice reps a quarterback would get on his own, and how much more advanced he'd be when it comes time to step on the practice field. If a guy has taken 1,000 reps against a certain coverage in his mind, his decision-making skills have been sharpened considerably. Then he can spend more time working on the physical mechanics of the throw, since developing timing and accuracy with actual receivers will always be essential.

That's not the only way technology will change the way players prepare.

In the early 2000s, Green Bay assistant coach Ed Donatell and I started looking at ways to animate the Packers' playbook. He moved on and we never finished that project, but the day is coming when every team's playbook will be recreated as an EA Sports–style video game. When players take their playbooks home, they'll interact with it instead of reading it. They'll be able to see themselves in every play, and perhaps even enjoy the learning process.

Innovations like these can become indispensable teaching tools for coaches looking to connect with a generation of players who grew up playing *Madden* and other video games. Imagine if at the end of every page in a video playbook there was a quiz. Players would be asked questions about their responsibilities in a certain play—even something as basic as where they should line up—and check off the answers, which would then be forwarded to their coach's computer so that he could follow their learning progress.

How much more effective would coaches be if they knew going into meetings or practice what each player already knew? Let's say a team is at training camp, and the coach's installation schedule calls for teaching the 3-4 Base defense on Monday, a 3-4 Weak defense on Tuesday, and 3-4 Strong defense on Wednesday. The first practices are a building block to the subsequent ones, so if a player doesn't learn the basics, he's going to be lost by Wednesday. This new system would allow a player to go home, study the 3-4 Strong the night before it's installed, take the quiz, and alert the coach in advance to any lingering confusion over what's already been taught and practiced.

And what if a coach could download practice tape every day and e-mail it to every player, complete with audio commentary of anything that needs to be pointed out or corrected? Coaches sit in their offices and review practice tape anyway; they're either talking out loud to themselves or thinking about something they'll need to deliver in person the next day. Why wait? Why not watch the practice, provide player-specific feedback, and then make it available for players to review at home?

You can already get a college degree online; why shouldn't players be able to get a football degree online, too?

EXPANSION PLANS

I'm not talking about adding any new teams here; I think that would be a mistake. There aren't enough really good players—and certainly not enough quarterbacks—to expand beyond 32 teams.

But there are ways to grow the game, and the next frontier is the international stage.

In the summer of 2009, the owners voted down a motion to have London host a Super Bowl in the future. I don't think the league expected the motion to pass—it was a far less popular option than bringing the Super Bowl to New York, where the first Sunday in February tends to be around 26 degrees with 25-mph wind gusts—but I do think they wanted to see what the reaction would be to a greater international presence.

Like any business, in the NFL, the bottom line is the bottom line. The NFL owners see the revenue stream, they see how much money the NBA and Major League Baseball make internationally, and they're not going to ignore it. In fact, they believe they can make even more.

Since 2007, there has been one game per year played in London, and those games have been played before sold-out crowds. The 2010

» UPON FURTHER REVIEW

Two rules changes were introduced at the NFL owners meetings in March 2010. One of them—a change in the playoff overtime procedure—got a lot more attention than the other—a repositioning of the umpire. As it turned out, the one that generated less interest initially became a much bigger deal once the games were underway.

A similar thing happened one year later. Most of the reaction in the wake of the 2011 owners meeting focused on the kickoffs being moved to the 35-yard line. There's no doubt that is a game changer, as we discussed in Chapter 11. But once again, the rule that flew under the radar deserved a lot more attention than it got.

Starting with the 2011 season, all scoring plays will be under review. Not *reviewable*, as was widely reported. They will *all* be reviewed. Every touchdown, field goal, extra point, and conversion. It's not discretionary. Every single scoring play will be reviewed.

This step takes the NFL closer to the officiating system that is employed in the collegiate ranks. The league had already turned over the officiating in the last two minutes of each half to the guys upstairs in the press box. The new rule removes coaches and on-field officials from the process and puts the final decision automatically in the hands of those officials in the booth.

It creates an opportunity for the league to go out and hire 16 full-time officials, one for each game that can be played on a given weekend. I would look for senior officials, the more experienced the better, who have sharp eyes and good judgment but simply can't run around on the field anymore. These full-time officials would spend the week working at 280 Park Avenue, learning how to make the right call by utilizing all the angles used by television cameras. They'd practice as-live scenarios, familiarizing themselves with available technology and speeding up their response time.

This change was implemented because 25 percent of all coaches' challenges involved scoring plays. Now, challenges on scoring plays are no longer necessary. Every play will be scrutinized and, essentially, approved by a lead official. And that means fewer mistakes will be made on scoring plays. Coaches will appreciate not having to waste a precious challenge, and fans will be happy that the right call is being made. Now *that's* innovative.

game between Denver and San Francisco drew 84,000 fans, so clearly there's a developing fan base in Europe. On the chats I do for NFL. com, I'd say almost 40 percent of the questions come from outside the United States—and I'm not talking about Americans living abroad. These are international fans who use the chat as a way to learn more about the game they're being introduced to.

Someday, there will be an NFL team based in London. There may even be two teams in European cities, so that a team from the U.S. could go over for two weeks, play two road games, and come home. There are owners in this league who have told me they'd rather control a team based in London than the one they already own.

There's already been talk about a team like Jacksonville being relocated, but I'm not sure that's the next step. I think the move to having teams overseas begins with the expansion of the regular season. To me, adding two games to the current 16-game schedule—the concept most often tossed around during the CBA negotiations that led up to the lockout—is not the answer. I prefer 17 games, and here's why.

If we had a 17-game schedule, every team would have eight home games and eight traditional road games. But then every team could also play one game outside the U.S. each year. There could be a European game every weekend—a rotation between London, Dublin, Berlin, Paris, Amsterdam, and Rome. American fans won't object; it'll be one more chance to watch their team every season (not to mention an intriguing option for a family vacation). And no team would have to forfeit an actual home game, as Buffalo has had to do when the Bills play the occasional game in Toronto.

Instead, each team would play one neutral-site game every year, and the NFL can see which international markets will hold up. Would Mexico City sell out eight games a year? Would Toronto become a more viable option?

We could also have a game every weekend in Los Angeles and address the problem of America's second-largest market being without an NFL team.

Of course, any expansion of the schedule would have to be accompanied by an expansion of the rosters. Frankly, that's a necessity even without expansion. By Week 16 in the 2009 season, the number of backup quarterbacks forced into action was almost comical.

Instead of a 53-man roster, I think we should be looking at a 55-man roster, with 50 players active on game day rather than 45. The owners are paying these guys anyway. Why shouldn't the third quarterback be allowed to play anytime during the game instead of having to wait until the fourth quarter?

Think about what it would mean for improving the quality of play on special teams alone. Right now, the players available to special teams coaches are limited. Veterans and key starters are off-limits because teams can't afford to risk them getting hurt on special teams. So the units are stocked with offensive rookies who never played special teams in college (unless they were return men), never covered a kick or a punt before, and never had to tackle anyone. They start to learn their roles, but by mid-October, starters are getting injured and they have to step into the starting lineup. They're no longer available to special teams, so the coach is constantly rebuilding his unit. It's also the first place hit by the salary cap, as teams are forced to cut a modestly priced, experienced veteran to make room for a couple of cheaper rookies.

If we expanded the rosters even slightly, a special teams coach could have a core of guys on his units, and the overall caliber of play would be improved.

While we're at it, how about expanding the rosters on December 1? Baseball expands its rosters for the final month of the season. Why shouldn't an NFL roster expand to 60 players—with 55 active— heading into the season's home stretch? Teams could activate their taxi squad players without having to put someone on injured reserve to do so. They could also sign players out of Canada or the UFL, since their seasons are over before December 1.

Bigger isn't necessarily better. But with some common sense and careful planning, the NFL can make the sports fan's favorite sport even better.

OVER AND OUT

Garrett Hartley's 40-yard field goal did more than just send the New Orleans Saints to Super Bowl XLIV. His game-winning kick on the first possession of overtime in the 2009 NFC Championship Game brought to life one of the league's longtime nightmares—a team was eliminated (on the brink of the Super Bowl) without ever getting a chance to touch the ball in overtime.

Football, a game of skill, was reduced to a game of chance known as the coin toss. I understand why the league felt it needed to change its overtime rules—which it did two months after the Saints' Super Bowl victory. But I still would prefer to see overtime handled differently, both in the regular season and the playoffs.

Why not just continue the game where it was at the end of the fourth quarter? Just as the second and fourth quarters pick up the action where the first and third quarters ended, respectively, overtime would be a continuation of the game already underway, not the start of a new period with different rules and strategies.

Essentially, overtime would be a sudden-death fifth quarter. It would eliminate the kickoff and the kickoff return, which is the most dangerous play in football. More importantly, it would maintain the integrity of the game. No longer would a team simply run out the last minutes of regulation, choosing to take a knee and start from scratch. Instead, a team would be rewarded for the work it was doing at the end of the fourth quarter by just continuing the field-position battle that was already underway. I say just flip the field and keep playing.

CHAPTER 17

TALK THE TALK
» *Show Off Your New Football Vocabulary*

I t's one thing to be able to recognize all the things you're seeing out there on the football field. To talk about them in the language of a true football insider is another thing altogether.

I love it when we get calls to the radio show and someone starts talking to me about a "Pirate stunt" or a linebacker using leverage. Those fans are not trying to show off; they're just sounding the part.

I know a lot of NFL guys don't want the fans to talk this way because it removes the wall between them, but I think having the means to talk football with a certain amount of authority and authenticity gives a fan a key to the kingdom that he's never had before.

Here are a bunch of football terms used by the people in and around the game. Some of them are technical jargon, some are more slang. Now that you've been introduced to the concepts, why not learn to speak the language, too?

* * *

ANCHOR: The ability to hold one's ground and not be moved.

BACK SHOULDER FADE: A pass thrown behind the wide receiver when the cornerback is lined up on his upfield shoulder.

BACKED-OFF MAN COVERAGE: Man-to-man pass coverage in which the defensive back lines up several yards off the line of scrimmage. It's the opposite of press coverage.

BAIT: When a defense shows the quarterback something before the snap in an effort to influence where he'll go with the ball.

BALL ATHLETE/BALL SKILLS: Refers to how well a player reacts to the ball when it's in the air. It's a reference to a player's natural instinct for the ball.

BANDIT: A combination safety-linebacker.

BIG BUTT: Exactly what it sounds like—it's considered a positive trait, especially for linemen.

BIG ON BIG: Situations in which one large player is matched up against another.

BIRD DOG: A quarterback's tendency to keep his eyes glued to an intended receiver throughout his pattern, rather than looking away from him and toward different receivers. Bird dogging tends to tip off the defensive players about where the pass will be thrown.

BLIND SIDE: The side of the backfield opposite the quarterback's throwing arm, where he has less-than-optimal vision when setting to throw.

BLOCK-DOWN TACKLE: When the defender takes down the ball carrier with a shoulder block as opposed to using proper technique.

BODY CATCH: When a receiver cradles the ball against his body rather than snatching it cleanly out of the air with his hands.

BODY LEAN: A player with good body lean runs with his body leaning upfield so that he falls forward when tackled.

BREAK DOWN: To get into the proper position to make a tackle or block.

BRINGING HIS FEET ALONG WITH HIM: When a player keeps his feet properly balanced underneath him while blocking.

BULL RUSH: A straight-ahead power pass rush.

BURST: The ability to change speed to close or reduce space to an offensive player.

CARRIES HIS PADS WELL: Refers to a player who doesn't let his pads interfere with his speed, agility, or ability to make plays.

CENTER FIELDER: A safety who is given the freedom to roam the field, or someone who is adept at doing so.

CHIP: When a running back blocks the outside half of a pass rusher's body with his elbow and forearm—forcing him back inside to the lineman or tight end—and then releases into a pass route.

CHOPS STRIDE: When a receiver cuts down on his stride before making a break on a pattern.

CLIMBING THE LADDER: Jumping high for a pass.

C.O.D.: Change of direction.

COMBINATION BLOCK: When two offensive players carry out a block on one defender.

CONTACT BALANCE: A player with good contact balance often maintains his footing after engaging an opponent.

CUT/CUT BLOCK: A block below the knees; defensive players who frequently "get cut" are, in other words, having difficulty avoiding cut blocks.

CUTS THROUGH TRASH: When a player moves well around pileups to make plays.

DIME: Situational pass defense featuring six defensive backs. An extra DB is referred to as the nickel back, so two extra DBs are two nickels, otherwise known as a dime.

DISENGAGE: The ability of a defender to get off a block.

DOESN'T PLAY TO HIS LISTED SPEED: A player who doesn't play as fast as his times in the 40-yard dash would suggest.

DOUBLE CATCHES: When a receiver bobbles the ball and then catches it rather than snatching it cleanly.

DOWN BLOCK: A block thrown from the outside across a defender's feet to cut off his pursuit angle, as opposed to a straight-ahead block.

DROP OUTSIDE LINEBACKER: An outside linebacker who drops into coverage to defend against a pass.

DUAL READ: When a blocker (usually a running back) is responsible for the inside and outside linebackers if both blitz.

EDGE PASS RUSHER: An outside pass rusher.

EIGHT IN THE BOX: When a defensive back joins the front seven in defending the run (see Force Contain Player).

FIRE ZONE: When a linebacker or a defensive back blitzes while a defensive lineman drops into zone coverage.

FLASHES: Shows ability sporadically.

FLATTENS OUT: When the pass rusher turns in on the quarterback.

FLUID IN THE HIPS: When a player has the ability to quickly change directions.

FOOTBALL TRIANGLE NUMBERS: Size, speed, and strength.

FORCE CONTAIN PLAYER: There are three ways to get an eighth defender in the box: bring a safety down between the inside and outside linebackers (Buzz); drop the safety down into the box outside the outside linebacker (Sky); or bring the cornerback outside the outside backer (Cloud). The designations refer to the player who becomes the outside defender against a run: Buzz is the backer, Sky is the safety, and Cloud is the corner.

FRINGE PLAYER: In defensive terminology, it refers to a player who is always on the fringe of the action but never in the midst of the heavy hitting. From a roster standpoint, it refers to a player who will have a difficult time making the team.

GETS WALKED BACK: Refers to an offensive player being pushed back by a defender.

GUNNER: The farthest outside position on special teams, and typically the first man down to cover a kick.

HAND PUNCH: The way an offensive lineman punches with his hands when blocking an opponent.

HANGS IN PLANT: Refers to a defensive back who hesitates in planting his feet and driving on the ball.

HIGH CUT: A player with long legs and a short upper body.

HIGH PIN TECHNIQUE: A blocking technique in which an offensive lineman tries to pin his man in an upright position.

HIP SNAP: The way a player comes off the snap of the ball.

I & I: Instincts and Intelligence.

IN SPACE/IN AIR: An open area of the field, usually on the defensive side of the ball.

INSIDE TRIANGLE: In a 3-4, this refers to the nose tackle and two inside linebackers. In a 4-3, it refers to the Mike linebacker and two defensive tackles.

JUKE: An elusive move to avoid a tackler.

KEEPS HIS FEET CLEAN: Refers to a defender's ability to keep blockers away from his feet and from getting tangled up in a mass of bodies.

KEY AND DIAGNOSE: Read the keys of a developing play and diagnose what is about to happen.

KNEE BENDER: A player who bends at his knees rather than his waist; usually considered a positive.

LEVERAGE: When a linebacker takes on the lead blocker with his inside pad, funneling the ball carrier inside toward a free defender, or with his outside pad, funneling the ball outside toward a free defender.

LIGHT IN THE PEGS: Skinny legs.

LONG ACCELERATION/LONG GEAR: A player's ability to run faster the farther he goes, as opposed to a player who can only run fast for a short distance.

LONG STRIDER: A player who takes long steps instead of quick ones, and tends to move slower in and out of his breaks.

LOOSE HIPS: A player with good flexibility in his lower half.

LOW BLOCK SHIELD: The ability of a defensive player to keep blockers away from his knees.

MAN-OFF COVERAGE: Man-to-man press coverage when a defender is backed off the line of scrimmage, as opposed to tight bump-and-run coverage.

MIRROR: To shadow or stay in front of.

MOTOR: Refers to a player's degree of intensity on the field.

NICKEL: Situational pass defense featuring five defensive backs.

NUBS: Type of shoe that usually improves a player's speed for timing purposes.

OFF AND SOFT: When cornerbacks in coverage line up at least 7 yards deep on the receiver.

OFFSET BACK: When a running back is lined up behind an offensive tackle.

PAD LEVEL: The height and angle of a player's pads during the course of action.

PICK: The ability to identify holes as a runner.

PINS: Legs.

PIRATE STUNT: Involves three defensive linemen—two crashing down inside and the nose tackle looping outside.

PLAYING SPEED: The speed with which a player runs in pads, as opposed to his time in the 40-yard dash.

PLAYS DOWN: A guy who lines up in a three- or four-point stance rather than a stand-up position.

PLAYS HIGH/PLAYS TALL: Refers to a guy who plays too upright, which allows an opponent to get underneath him. This usually refers to a lineman.

PLAYS OVER HIS FEET/PLAYS OVER HIS PADS: A player with a good base or with his weight balanced, so as not to overextend.

PLAYS WITH HEAVY HANDS/PLAYS WITH LIGHT HANDS: A lineman with a forceful hand punch that will jar an opponent, or one who lacks that abililty.

PLAYS WITH HIS PADS TOO HIGH: A player who moves too upright, which causes him to lose leverage.

POWER TRAIN: Lower and central body as it relates to playing strength.

PRESS COVERAGE: When a defensive back lines up on the line of scrimmage and inside the receiver; also called bump-and-run coverage.

PRESS ON BLOCKERS: Refers to defensive linemen pressing on offensive linemen to keep them away from their bodies.

PROGRESSION READS: The systems used by most teams wherein the quarterback, in deciding which receiver to throw to, reads defensive keys in a specific sequence, such as beginning downfield and then progressing back toward the line of scrimmage or vice versa.

PROJECT: A player who may be selected to play a position other than the one he played in college.

QUICK HIPPED: A player with the ability to turn his hips quickly.

QUICK-TWITCH PLAYER: A quick reactor.

R & R: The ability to read and react.

RADAR DEFENSE: When nine or more defenders are standing and walking around before the snap.

RAG-DOLLED: To get tossed around.

REDUCE: When a defensive lineman on the split end side of a formation moves down the alignment one player and lines up across from a guard instead of a tackle.

ROAD GRADER: A very wide-bodied and powerful blocker.

RUNDOWN PLAYER: A player who possesses the speed necessary to catch a player from behind.

RUNS BEHIND PADS: A player who runs with good form, maintaining a good base and good balance without overextending.

RUNS NORTH-SOUTH: Runs toward the goal line rather than laterally.

RUN-THROUGH LINEBACKER: A linebacker who tends to run through gaps as opposed to taking on blockers.

RUN THROUGH THE BALL: Catching the ball without breaking stride.

SECOND LEVEL: Down the field.

SEE THROUGH BLOCKS: The ability of a defensive lineman to see beyond a block and react to what's coming.

SELL OUT: To sacrifice one's body.

SEPARATE/SEPARATION: Ability of a receiver to put distance between himself and the defender on a pass pattern.

SHADE: When a defensive lineman lines up on the shoulder of an offensive lineman rather than head on. A three-technique, for example, is a shaded defensive tackle, lined up on the shoulder or the guard instead of helmet to helmet.

SHAKE AND BAKE: Quick, elusive moves.

SMALL-AREA PLAYER: A player who is effective only when responsible for a limited area of the field.

SNATCH BLITZ: When a blitzer has the back or tight end in coverage and bull rushes the player at the line.

SPLIT GUARD/SPLIT TACKLE: A player who lines up on the wide side of the field. In college football, the ball is spotted on hash marks closer to the sidelines than in the NFL, which makes for a greater disparity in the distance from the spot of the ball to each of the sidelines.

SPLIT HIGH: Someone with long legs and a shorter upper body.

SPLITS: The space between the in-line blockers on the line of scrimmage.

STACK: A defensive alignment in which one or more of the linebackers plays directly in back of the defensive linemen.

STACK THE POINT: To hold the point of attack and not get pushed back.

STRAIGHT-LINE PLAYER: Someone who is effective running in a straight line but has trouble making cuts.

STRONG SIDE: The side of the offensive line where the tight end is lined up, making for more in-line blockers than on the opposite (weak) side.

SUGAR: Disguising a defense in an attempt to confuse the quarterback in his pre-snap read.

SWINGMAN: Someone who can play more than one position.

TAKE ON AND SHED: A defensive player's ability to take on a blocker and defeat him, as opposed to running around him.

TOP-END SPEED: Long-distance speed (anything beyond 20 yards).

TRANSITION: Usually refers to the point at which a defensive back comes out of his backpedal and switches to a sprint to cover a receiver going deep. The more smoothly a DB can do this, the more likely he will maintain tight coverage.

TRAP BLOCK: When a guard or tackle uses a short pull technique and blocks a defensive lineman who has crossed the line of scrimmage.

TWO-DEEP ZONE: A type of zone coverage in which each safety is responsible for half of the deep portion of the field. This type of coverage requires a safety to have the range to cover receivers going to the deep outside of the secondary.

TWO-GAP: A defensive lineman's ability to cover two gaps in the offensive line.

TWO-WAY GO: When a pass rusher is given the freedom to rush inside or outside against a designated blocker. It is rarely used by defenses facing a mobile quarterback.

UNCOVERED/VS. AIR: When a player has no opponent lined up directly across from him.

UNDER DEFENSE: A version of the 4-3 defense where the defensive tackle lines up on the offensive guard to the split end side.

WAIST BENDER: A player who bends at the waist rather than at the knees; usually considered a negative.

WALK OFF ON COVERAGE: When a player moves outside his normal position to cover another player; for example, a linebacker will sometimes walk off on coverage to cover a running back split wide.

WALL OFF: To use one's body as a shield rather than drive blocking through an opponent, so that the defense can't get through to the ball carrier.

WEAK SIDE: The side of the offensive line without a tight end, which contains fewer in-line blockers than the opposite (strong) side.

WINDOW: The space between two pass defenders that the quarterback wants to throw into or through.

WORK THE EDGES: When a defensive lineman works the fringes on a pass rush instead of attacking straight ahead.

APPENDIX

BECOME A TRUE STUDENT OF THE GAME
» *Play-by-Play Charts, Play Diagrams, and More*

Imagine you're sitting in the stands at a baseball game, it's the seventh inning, and Albert Pujols is coming to the plate. Across the aisle, there's a fan keeping score in his game program, so you ask him what Pujols did in his first three at-bats. The guy checks his scorecard, sees "4-3," "9," and "1B" with an arrow pointing up and to the right, and reminds you that Pujols is 1-for-3 and, more importantly, that he's hit the ball to the right side all three times he's been up. Those simple numbers on a grid give you a window into the world of baseball strategy—you can see how the pitcher, the catcher, and the manager have decided to pitch to the sport's most dangerous hitter, and how Pujols has adjusted. Now, you have information in hand that empowers you to anticipate how they'll attack him during this at-bat.

Football fans no longer need to watch their games in the dark. The pages that follow provide you a series of charts—the same charts I used when I was up in the press box for the Jets, and the same ones I use now when I'm breaking down games—that enable you to track a football game the way coaches do. You will be charting the same information that dictates decisions being made in that very game and also shapes strategy for upcoming game plans.

We have included everything you will need to track the action for a single game at any level, from an NFL game down to your local high school team. Before you fill out these charts, we recommend you make a couple of copies so you'll have blank ones to use for next week's game and beyond. Blank templates are also available at www.patkirwan.com.

Keep in mind that charting a live game can be cumbersome at first. Most football fans aren't used to jotting down notes after every play, so expect that it will take a little time before you develop a comfortable rhythm. These charts are all user-friendly, and you may find it easier at first to practice filling them out while watching a game you've recorded or are viewing on NFL Rewind.

When you're done charting a game, keep all your charts in a file. Eventually, you'll have a library of information available to you that will allow you to get ready for next week's opponent the same way your team does. Talk about a fan taking it to the next level.

Here's how you should use the charts that follow:

The **Play-by-Play** chart (p. 262–265)—also known as a Takeoff Chart—is for tracking your team's offense. You start by filling out the **SERIES #** and **PLAY #**. The first play of the game would be Series 1, Play 1. If your team goes three-and-out, the first play of the next series would be Series 2, Play 4. In other words, it's the start of the second series but the fourth overall play your team has run (not counting special teams). After each series, draw a line to separate one series from the next.

Next, track the Down & Distance and Field Position. If it's 2nd-and-7 on Miami's 45-yard line, write 2-7 in the **D&D** column and M45 in the **POS.** column. Be sure to note when a first down occurs on change of possession (P1-10) as opposed to an earned first down (E1-10). Coaches differentiate between them when gathering information, and so should you.

The next columns are for **PERSONNEL** (as we discussed in Chapter 1), **MOTION** (make note of any receiver or back who went in motion before the snap), and **FORMATION**. As you begin to learn the plays being called, you can fill in the **PLAY** column (feel free to leave it blank until you're more comfortable recognizing what's happening on the field).

The next column is **GAIN**, where you track the result of the play (for example, +3 or -1). If the play was a pass, designate the receiver in the **REC.** column (write the jersey number of the player who caught the pass).

The next two columns track elements of the defense the play was run against. If a play was run against a 3-4 front under a Cover 2 zone, write "3-4" in the **FRONT** column and "C2" under **COVER**.

The last column—**SPECIAL**—is reserved for jotting down any observation you happen to make. Maybe someone was injured on a play. Maybe you noticed a receiver who was wide open but didn't get the ball. Or maybe you noticed that through five plays, your team has thrown the ball four times and run it just once (4P-1R).

You'll note there are four of these charts, as you'll need room for as many as 80 offensive plays in a regulation game. Be sure to circle which quarter you're charting at the top of the page; it'll make it easier to keep everything straight later.

The **Situation Chart** (p. 266–269)—also known as the Down and Distance Chart—is a shorthand version of the Play-by-Play chart. At the end of a series or a quarter or a half, you take the information from your Play-by-Play chart and transfer it here, where it's easier to digest.

You can fill in the Situation Chart in one of two ways, whichever is easiest for you.

Under each Down & Distance category (again, note the distinction between first downs at the start of a possession and earned first downs over the course of a drive), you can either tally the number of **RUN** vs. **PASS** plays—enabling you to easily see what your team's tendencies are in a variety of situations—or you can write the actual gain or loss for each play. This way, you can review the chart and see that, for example, on third downs between 3 and 6 yards, your team ran the ball three times (+3, +4, -2) and threw the ball twice (INC, +19).

Next comes the **Advanced Situation Chart** (p. 268–271)—an Advanced Down and Distance Chart—which serves the same purpose as the Situation Chart, only with more detailed information. Again, take the data compiled in your Play-by-Play chart and transfer it to the proper boxes. You'll write the specific Down & Distance (in your 2nd 7-11 box, you'd have a chronological list that includes 2-7, 2-7, 2-9, 2-8, etc.), the Position on the field, the Play called, the Front and Coverage it was run against, and the Result.

Until now, you've only tracked your team's offense. The next chart (p. 274–277) enables you to chart the **Fronts & Coverages** your defense is in, sorted by various D&D situations. In the appropriate box, mark 3-4, C2, or 4-3 Man, depending on what the defense is running. This will help clarify your team's tendencies for you.

The next two charts are straightforward. First, there's the **Two-Point-Conversion Chart**. When you see coaches check their charts when deciding whether to kick the extra point or go for two, well, this is that chart. The **Time Management** chart takes the guesswork out of play-calling in the final four minutes of each half. If your team has the ball in the closing minutes, take note of how many timeouts it has left and how much time is left on the clock. Then consult this chart to find out how many plays your team has to run to run out the clock. If there's time left at the end, you'll know your coach mismanaged the clock.

The next chart—the **Prospect Scouting Template** (p. 280–281)— is for scouting players in preparation for the NFL Draft. During the buildup to the draft, a ton of information on hundreds of prospects becomes available. Fans who are serious about gathering information should be compiling the critical data the same way GMs do, and the same way I do in preparing for three days of live radio covering the draft for Sirius NFL Radio.

Most of the categories here are self-explanatory, but make sure you use the same information NFL decision makers use: the measurables from the NFL Combine. Don't take a prospect's height or weight—and *never* their time in the 40-yard dash—from their college media guides.

Without fail, those are exaggerated, outdated, or simply inaccurate. There are two categories here that I created specifically for prospects in the defensive front seven. In Chapter 8, I introduced the Explosion Number (Bench Press Reps of 225 pounds + Vertical Leap + Standing Broad Jump) and the Production Ratio (Sacks + Tackles For Loss/ Games Played). You'll need the official Combine numbers for the first formula, and you'll need to research a player's career stats online for the second. There are also columns where you can note any red flags, strengths, and weaknesses.

The final pages in this Appendix will give you the opportunity to diagram your own plays and take your own notes. A ton of callers to my radio show ask me to go through the literal Xs and Os of a particular play they saw, and they chart it while we discuss it. The template starts the way every single play in the NFL starts—with five offensive linemen. You are then free to fill in everyone around them on both sides of the ball.

PLAY-BY-PLAY

QUARTER: 1 2 3 4

SERIES #	PLAY #	D&D	POS.	PERSONNEL	MOTION	FORMATION	PLAY	GAIN	REC.	FRONT	COVER	SPECIAL

PLAY-BY-PLAY   QUARTER: 1 2 3 4

SERIES #	PLAY #	D&D	POS.	PERSONNEL	MOTION	FORMATION	PLAY	GAIN	REC.	FRONT	COVER	SPECIAL

PLAY-BY-PLAY QUARTER: 1 2 3 4

SERIES #	PLAY #	D&D	POS.	PERSONNEL	MOTION	FORMATION	PLAY	GAIN	REC.	FRONT	COVER	SPECIAL

PLAY-BY-PLAY   **QUARTER: 1 2 3 4**

SERIES #	PLAY #	D&D	POS.	PERSONNEL	MOTION	FORMATION	PLAY	GAIN	REC.	FRONT	COVER	SPECIAL

SITUATION CHART

HALF: 1 2

P 1ST AND 10			
RUN	DEF	PASS	DEF

E 1ST AND 10			
RUN	DEF	PASS	DEF

SITUATION CHART

HALF: 1   2

2ND AND 7 +				3RD AND 7 +			
RUN	DEF	PASS	DEF	RUN	DEF	PASS	DEF

2ND AND 3 TO 6 YDS				3RD AND 3 TO 6 YDS			
RUN	DEF	PASS	DEF	RUN	DEF	PASS	DEF

2ND AND 1 TO 2 YDS				3RD AND 1 TO 2 YDS			
RUN	DEF	PASS	DEF	RUN	DEF	PASS	DEF

SITUATION CHART

HALF: 1 2

P 1ST AND 10			
RUN	DEF	PASS	DEF

E 1ST AND 10			
RUN	DEF	PASS	DEF

SITUATION CHART

HALF: 1   2

2ND AND 7 +				3RD AND 7 +			
RUN	DEF	PASS	DEF	RUN	DEF	PASS	DEF

2ND AND 3 TO 6 YDS				3RD AND 3 TO 6 YDS			
RUN	DEF	PASS	DEF	RUN	DEF	PASS	DEF

2ND AND 1 TO 2 YDS				3RD AND 1 TO 2 YDS			
RUN	DEF	PASS	DEF	RUN	DEF	PASS	DEF

ADVANCED SITUATION CHART

HALF: 1 2

P 1-10

D/D	POS.	PLAY	FRONT	COV.	R.

Run_____ Pass_____

E 1-10

D/D	POS.	PLAY	FRONT	COV.	R.

Run_____ Pass_____

2ND AND 7 +

D/D	POS.	PLAY	FRONT	COV.	R.

Run_____ Pass_____

2ND AND 3-6

D/D	POS.	PLAY	FRONT	COV.	R.

Run_____ Pass_____

ADVANCED SITUATION CHART

HALF: 1   2

2ND AND 1-2

D/D	POS.	PLAY	FRONT	COV.	R.

Run   Pass

3RD AND 7 +

D/D	POS.	PLAY	FRONT	COV.	R.

Run   Pass

3RD AND 3-6

D/D	POS.	PLAY	FRONT	COV.	R.

Run_____   Pass_____

3RD AND 1-2

D/D	POS.	PLAY	FRONT	COV.	R.

Run_____   Pass_____

ADVANCED SITUATION CHART

HALF: 1   2

P 1-10

D/D	POS.	PLAY	FRONT	COV.	R.

Run_____   Pass_____

E 1-10

D/D	POS.	PLAY	FRONT	COV.	R.

Run_____   Pass_____

2ND AND 7 +

D/D	POS.	PLAY	FRONT	COV.	R.

Run_____   Pass_____

2ND AND 3-6

D/D	POS.	PLAY	FRONT	COV.	R.

Run_____   Pass_____

ADVANCED SITUATION CHART

HALF: 1   2

2ND AND 1-2

D/D	POS.	PLAY	FRONT	COV.	R.

Run   Pass

3RD AND 7 +

D/D	POS.	PLAY	FRONT	COV.	R.

Run   Pass

3RD AND 3-6

D/D	POS.	PLAY	FRONT	COV.	R.

Run_____   Pass_____

3RD AND 1-2

D/D	POS.	PLAY	FRONT	COV.	R.

Run_____   Pass_____

FRONTS & COVERAGES

HALF: 1 2

D / D CATEGORIES

P 1st-10	E 1st-10	2nd 7 +	2nd 3-6
(Man) (Zone) (Blitz)	(Man) (Zone) (Blitz)	(Man) (Zone) (Blitz)	(Man) (Zone) (Blitz)
TOTAL:	TOTAL:	TOTAL:	TOTAL:

2nd 1-2	3rd 7 +	3rd 3-6	3rd 1-2
(Man) (Zone) (Blitz)	(Man) (Zone) (Blitz)	(Man) (Zone) (Blitz)	(Man) (Zone) (Blitz)
TOTAL:	TOTAL:	TOTAL:	TOTAL:

FRONTS & COVERAGES

HALF: 1   2

RED ZONE

1st Down	2nd Down	3rd Down	4th Down
TOTAL:	TOTAL:	TOTAL:	TOTAL:

2 MINUTE & 2 MINUTE RED ZONE

2 MINUTE	2 MINUTE / RED ZONE

FRONTS & COVERAGES

HALF: 1 2

D / D CATEGORIES

P 1st-10	E 1st-10	2nd 7 +	2nd 3-6
(Man)	(Man)	(Man)	(Man)
(Zone)	(Zone)	(Zone)	(Zone)
(Blitz)	(Blitz)	(Blitz)	(Blitz)
TOTAL:	TOTAL:	TOTAL:	TOTAL:

2nd 1-2	3rd 7 +	3rd 3-6	3rd 1-2
(Man)	(Man)	(Man)	(Man)
(Zone)	(Zone)	(Zone)	(Zone)
(Blitz)	(Blitz)	(Blitz)	(Blitz)
TOTAL:	TOTAL:	TOTAL:	TOTAL:

FRONTS & COVERAGES

HALF: 1   2

RED ZONE

1st Down	2nd Down	3rd Down	4th Down
TOTAL:	TOTAL:	TOTAL:	TOTAL:

2 MINUTE & 2 MINUTE RED ZONE

2 MINUTE	2 MINUTE / RED ZONE

TWO-POINT CONVERSION CHART

LEAD BY		TRAIL BY	
1 point	Go for 2	1 point	Go for 2
2 points	Go for 1	2 points	Go for 2
3 points	Go for 1	3 points	Go for 1
4 points	Go for 2	4 points	Decision
5 points	Go for 2	5 points	Go for 2
6 points	Go for 1	6 points	Go for 1
7 points	Go for 1	7 points	Go for 1
8 points	Go for 1	8 points	Go for 1
9 points	Go for 1	9 points	Go for 2
10 points	Go for 1	10 points	Go for 1
11 points	Go for 1	11 points	Go for 2
12 points	Go for 2	12 points	Go for 2
13 points	Go for 1	13 points	Go for 1
14 points	Go for 1	14 points	Go for 1
15 points	Go for 2	15 points	Go for 1
16 points	Go for 1	16 points	Go for 2
17 points	Go for 1	17 points	Go for 1
18 points	Go for 1	18 points	Go for 1
19 points	Go for 2	19 points	Go for 2
20 points	Go for 1	20 points	Go for 1

TIME MANAGEMENT CHART*
ALL SEQUENCES START ON FIRST DOWN

Time Remaining	3 timeouts	2 timeouts	1 timeout	0 timeouts
4:00	Run Nine QB Snaps	Run Eight QB Snaps	Run Seven QB Snaps	Run Six QB Snaps
3:00	Run Six QB Snaps (may punt and leave 6 sec, 0 timeouts	Run Six QB Snaps	Run Six QB Snaps	Run Five QB Snaps
2:00	Run Six QB Snaps	Run Five QB Snaps	Run Four QB Snaps	
* This assumes opponent uses timeouts early in 4 min.				

PROSPECT SCOUTING TEMPLATE

PLAYER	SCHOOL	POS.	HT	WT	ARM LENGTH	BENCH REPS	40-YARD DASH	VERTICAL JUMP

BROAD JUMP	EXPLOSION NUMBER	SHORT SHUTTLE	3-CONE DRILL	PRODUCTION RATIO	RED FLAGS	STRENGTHS	WEAKNESSES

PLAY DIAGRAMS

PLAY DIAGRAMS

NOTES

NOTES

NOTES

=ACKNOWLEDGMENTS=

We would like to thank everyone whose energy, expertise, and enthusiasm contributed to the process of turning a fun idea into this book.

Specifically, we want to thank Paul Alexander, Pete Carroll, Bill Cowher, Bill Kuharich, Mickey Kwiatkowski, Tim Ryan, Bob Wylie, and Gary Zauner for generously sharing their time and insights. Also, we are grateful for the guidance and direction we received from Triumph Books, particularly Tom Bast, Mitch Rogatz, Paul Petrowsky, and our unflappable, eternally patient editor, Adam Motin (we wish for him a strong season for his beloved Bears). Big thanks as well to Craig Ellenport of NFL.com, Sean Butler and Ken Ilchuk, and especially to Bill Maier for his ambitious vision and tireless commitment to this project.

Of course, we are indebted to the support of our respective families.

Pat would like to thank Janet, Elizabeth, Sean, Anne, Billy, Jim, Kevin, and Derek Johnson. David would like to thank Elizabeth, Maia, Dylan, Barry, Susan, Carol Ann, and George. We could not have done this without your encouragement and indulgence.

=ABOUT THE AUTHORS=

Pat Kirwan, one of the nation's most well-respected and popular NFL analysts, is the co-host of *Movin' the Chains* on Sirius NFL Radio and a featured columnist on NFL.com. Since 2003 he has been an editorial contributor to the *NFL Today* on CBS and makes frequent appearances on TV and radio programs across the country, including ESPN, the NFL Network, and Sporting News Radio. Prior to joining CNN/SI in 1998, Pat spent 25 years working in football, coaching at the high school and college levels before joining the New York Jets' staff as a defensive assistant coach. He eventually moved into the front office, becoming the team's Director of Player Administration. The father of three grown children, Pat lives in the New York area with his wife Janet.

David Seigerman is a veteran sports journalist whose writing career began in newspapers (*Newsday, Jackson Sun*) and moved on to magazines (*College Sports Magazine*). In 1996 he moved from print to broadcast media, becoming a field producer for CNN/SI and eventually the managing editor at College Sports Television. Since 2003, he has been a freelance writer and producer, and co-wrote and co-produced the feature-length documentary, *The Warrior Ethos: The Experience and Tradition of Boxing at West Point*. He lives in Larchmont, New York, with his wife Elizabeth and their two children.